Who Owns Culture?

Rutgers Series on the Public Life of the Arts

A series edited by
Ruth Ann Stewart
Margaret J. Wyszomirski
Joni M. Cherbo

Joni M. Cherbo and Margaret J. Wyszomirski, eds.,
The Public Life of the Arts in America

Jan Cohen-Cruz, *Local Acts: Community-Based Performance
in the United States*

Lawrence Rothfield, ed., *Unsettling "Sensation":
Arts-Policy Lessons from the Brooklyn Museum of Art Controversy*

Susan Scafidi, *Who Owns Culture? Appropriation and
Authenticity in American Law*

Who Owns Culture?

APPROPRIATION AND AUTHENTICITY IN AMERICAN LAW

SUSAN SCAFIDI

RUTGERS UNIVERSITY PRESS
New Brunswick, New Jersey, and London

LIBRARY OF CONGRESS CATALOGING-IN-PUBLICATION DATA

Scafidi, Susan, 1968–
    Who owns culture? : appropriation and authenticity in American law /
Susan Scafidi.
      p. cm. — (Rutgers series on the public life of the arts)
    Includes bibliographical references and index.
    ISBN 0-8135-3605-7 (hardcover : alk. paper) — ISBN 0-8135-3606-5
(pbk. : alk. paper)
    1. Intellectual property—United States. 2. Material culture—United
States. 3. Folklore—United States. 4. Culture and law. 5. Indigenous
peoples—Legal status, laws, etc.—United States. I. Title. II. Series.
    KF2979.S28 2005
    346.7304′8—dc22   2004021381

A British Cataloging-in-Publication record is available
for this book from the British Library.

Manufactured in the United States of America

For Jeff

Contents

Preface and Acknowledgments

IN WRITING *Who Owns Culture?*, I have found that questioning the ownership and authenticity of "cultural products"—whether cuisine, dress, music, dance, folklore, handicrafts, images, healing arts, rituals, performances, natural resources, or language—seems guaranteed to produce the sort of mild indignation often caused by the discussion of politics over a holiday dinner. One outraged soul will demand immediate justification: "Hold on! Why exactly doesn't the legal system protect our community against cultural appropriation? We've given a lot to this country, and we deserve to benefit from our contributions." At the other end of the table, someone is certain to interrupt: "Wait a second—it's the mix of cultures that makes America great! Are you telling me I can't borrow from other groups?" (In this vein, one of my more fashion-conscious students was overheard telling classmates in a horrified whisper, "I've read one of Professor Scafidi's articles. I don't think she believes in accessorizing!") From the family intellectual provocateur may come a semi-historical factoid such as, "You know, Marco Polo really brought spaghetti from China," a remark likely to spark debate over which aunt or uncle makes the best old-style tomato sauce to accompany the pasta—cooked al dente, of course. The practical peacemaker at the dinner table, level-headed and eager to move on to dessert, will remind everyone that culture is fluid and evolving, and, in any case, it would be quite difficult to establish restrictive forms of ownership or to police cultural borrowing of everyday art forms. And so back to the particular fish or fowl, sweets or savories, and especially family recipes that mark a particular cultural occasion. Whether they are called objects of cultural elaboration, traditional knowledge, folklore, cultural heritage, or intangible cultural property, it is far easier to consume cultural products than to analyze them.

To address the threshold challenge of nomenclature, I have chosen the term "cultural products," which emphasizes the ongoing nature of the products' creation and the often controversial but significant role of the market in their life cycles. International interest in this category of cultural goods, in particular the United Nations Educational, Scientific, and Cultural Organization (UNESCO) Convention for the Safeguarding of the Intangible Cultural Heritage, adopted on October 17, 2003, has emphasized documentation, education, and preservation.[1] If this convention is ratified, it will become the first binding multinational instrument for the protection of intangible expressions of culture. While the values associated with protection are of tremendous importance, especially given the current state of international and domestic law, the benefits of interaction and exchange in the service of cultural understanding are similarly compelling. Although the United States should strongly consider joining the UNESCO convention, mechanisms such as national inventories speak to the warehousing rather than the evolution of living culture. Ratification of the convention or a similar initiative is more likely if it appears sympathetic to concerns regarding trade and commercial interaction, while avoiding misappropriation or exploitation. In exploring possibilities for the balanced protection of cultural products, American law should be tailored to facilitate the initiative of old and new source communities—whether directed toward commodification or preservation of their cultural products—and their participation in the life of the nation as self-defining cultural groups.

The concept of "culture" itself, particularly as an object of ownership or as a locus of authenticity, offers an additional challenge. According to one literary theorist, "'Culture' is said to be one of the two or three most complex words in the English language. . . ."[2] Among academic disciplines, the concept of culture is originally the anthropologists' turf and even there is subject to widespread agnosticism.[3] Such persistent ambiguity is not necessarily a barrier to lawyers, judges, or even legal academics, however, as the law itself evolves along with understanding of its terms of art, as in the case of reasonableness, privacy, and even justice itself.[4] Although a definitive ruling must await another day, a working legal definition of culture might begin in the Habermasian "lifeworld" of everyday actions and beliefs.[5] Self-defined subsets of individuals who share particular beliefs, practices, experiences, or forms of expression thus form cultural groups.

Despite these complexities, *Who Owns Culture?* attempts to open a wider public, interdisciplinary conversation about the importance of cultural products in American life, as well as their nearly invisible status within our legal system. Now, more than ever, we are eager to bind ourselves into one nation—but, at the same time, to preserve our separate traditions and cultures. The early twenty-first century may be an *e pluribus unum* moment, and we may all love New York, but few of us wish to bring the homogenizing melting pot to a rapid boil. We instead celebrate our diversity (and demonstrate our individual savoir-faire) through consumer culture, as we eat, dress, dance, and speak in the idiom of our neighbors. Indeed, the tension-filled history of American immigration and even internal migration indicates that the cultural products of others are often easier to accept and assimilate than the individuals (or huddled masses) themselves.

When it comes to disagreement about the ownership and authenticity of cultural products, however, or about their appropriate context and uses, there are few rules or even guideposts to ensure quality, prevent faux pas, or give credit where it is due. Although public awareness of the value of creative enterprise rose dramatically with the Internet Revolution, the legal protections of copyright, patent, and trademark do not ordinarily extend to cultural creations. In fact, group authorship creates legal unease, and communal or traditional artistry often goes unrecognized.

This lack of protection for cultural products does not automatically suggest that more laws are the answer, however. As both a legal historian and a professor of intellectual property, I share the concern of many of my colleagues that, in some areas, intellectual property protection has over the years expanded to a degree that threatens to impoverish the public domain and strangle creative enterprise.[6] This is not to suggest that intellectual property protection is unnecessary; even Hobbes warned that in the state of nature "there is no place for

Industry; because the fruit thereof is uncertain: and consequently no Culture of the Earth . . . no Arts; no Letters; no Society . . . ."[7] Nevertheless, community-based artworks, and the informal networks that produce them, receive no such expansive protection. It would be unfortunate if, in the rush to denounce congressional extension of copyright term limits or the judicial expansion of patentable subject matter, we were to overlook the lack of protection for cultural products—without even asking ourselves why. The choice to forego legal protection is as socially significant as the choice to expand protection, and the unregulated freedom to engage in cultural appropriation may be as powerful a stimulus to creativity as the promise of protected economic rewards.

When we consider the protection of cultural products, moreover, we must concurrently remain aware of the effect of such protection on the source communities themselves. International discussion regarding indigenous heritage underscores the importance of this inquiry.[8] Culture is naturally fluid and evolving, and well-intentioned legal protections may provoke ossification of a culture and its artifacts. In addition, a source community may include dissenting voices, and a grant of legal protection to those who speak on behalf of the community may silence those voices—always an issue when rights are vested in a group rather than an individual. Any determination regarding the ownership and protection of cultural products must thus proceed with caution, taking into account both cultural and economic effects on the source community, as well as the interests of the nation and world community as a whole.

National pride, communal identity, law, tradition, value, consumerism, appreciation, and habit all play a role in the production and adaptation of cultural products in the ongoing search for an authentic America.[9] At the end of the day, however, the central question, "Who owns culture?", can be answered only by its creators—all of us.

In this spirit, I would like to thank my co-creators—family, friends, students, colleagues, and supporting organizations—and their many cultures, without whom this work could not have been written. All errors and omissions remain, of course, my own.

From its outset, this project has received extraordinary support, starting with a generous research award from the Center for Arts and Culture in Washington, D.C. At the Yale Law School, Dean Harold Koh, Dean Anthony T. Kronman, Deputy Dean Kate Stith, Associate Dean Barbara J. Safriet, the Honorable Guido Calabresi, Professors George L. Priest, John G. Simon, and Judith Resnik, and many other members of the faculty and administration offered a warm welcome back. At Columbia Law School, Professor and Vice Dean Katherine Franke and Professor Kendall Thomas graciously extended the hospitality of the Center for the Study of Law and Culture, and Professor Franke later gave generously of her time and insight in reading the manuscript. The editors of the *Boston University Law Review* not only published the article that presaged this book but also allowed it to be reprinted in its revised and expanded form.[10] Dr. Bruce Muck and Jon-Bernard Schwartz provided expert research assistance; James Pan and his staff performed technological wizardry; and Nancy Eagan deftly managed long-distance administrative support. The director of Rutgers University Press, Marlie Wasserman, was the first to imagine the book and has waited patiently for it to become a reality.

Colleagues across the country and around the world from many disciplines, and especially the growing community of intellectual property scholars, have offered valuable advice and criticism. Among them are Michael A. Adler, Keith Aoki, Ann Bartow, Robert Brauneis, Mary Ann Case, Margaret Chon, Edward F. Countryman, Graeme B. Dinwoodie, Patty Gerstenblith, Shubha Ghosh, Wendy Gordon, Hugh Hansen, Sarah Harding, Cynthia Ho, Sonia Katyal, Roberta R. Kwall, Carol Rose, Madhavi Sunder, Keith Terry, David J. Weber, Peter K. Yu, and many others to whom I am grateful. In addition, I would like to thank the organizers of and participants in the Second Annual Intellectual Property Scholars' Conference, co-sponsored by Benjamin N. Cardozo Law School, the University of California at Berkeley Boalt Hall School of Law, and the DePaul University College of Law; the Commodification Futures conference co-sponsored by the University of Denver, American University, and the University of North Carolina; the Traditional Knowledge, Intellectual Property, and Indigenous Culture symposium at Benjamin N. Cardozo Law School; the Tenth Annual Fordham Conference on International Intellectual

Property Law and Policy; and the Program on Nonprofit Organizations at Yale University.

This work also owes much to teachers, mentors, and advocates. I have received both academic guidance and inspiration from the Honorable Dorothy W. Nelson; Professor Charles E. Curran; the late Roland E. Murphy, O. Carm.; Rosalind S. Fink; and an extraordinary network of women and men who embody the highest standards of our profession. Professors Kathleen Neils Conzen, R. H. Helmholz, and William J. Novak have offered direction and insight on this and other projects. In addition, like many scholars, I have found my students to be among my greatest teachers—thank you for bringing your experiences and ideals to class and beyond.

Few authors would complete their intellectual odysseys without the sure knowledge of extended family and close friends. Heartfelt thanks to all the members of my own source community, especially A. F. and Wilma Scafidi, Mark Scafidi, and Cosper Scafidi. Finally, without the encouragement and confidence of the Honorable Morris S. Arnold and, above all, my esteemed colleague and spouse, Jeff Trexler, this book would not have been written.

Who Owns Culture?

Introduction

COMMUNITY-GENERATED art forms have tremendous economic and social value—yet most source communities have little control over them. Euro-American authors adopt the voice of a geisha or shaman, white suburban youths perform rap music, and New York fashion designers ransack the world's closets for inspiration. While claims of authenticity or quality may prompt some consumers to seek "cultural products" at their source, the communities of origin are generally unable to exclude copyists through legal action. Like other works of unincorporated group authorship, cultural products lack protection under our system of intellectual property law. But is this legal vacuum an injustice, the lifeblood of American culture, a historical oversight, a result of administrative incapacity, or all of the above?

Who Owns Culture? examines the issue of group authorship and intellectual property, with particular attention to cultural appropriation in American life. What prompts us to offer legal protection to works of literature but not to folklore? Why can a country-music writer demand royalties from performers she has never met, while an Appalachian folk musician cannot? These questions reveal not only the hierarchy of American cultural values but also the entrenched preferences at the heart of intellectual property law.

The early chapters of *Who Owns Culture?* address the basic concepts of cultural commodification, property ownership, and the parameters of a new category of "cultural products." Chapter One describes the commercialization of culture and the role of cultural products in American life, introducing the tension between appropriation and protection, public property and private ownership—topics that form a central theme of the book. While any discussion of commodification invokes the specter of Karl Marx and exploited workers, the perspective on commodification of culture in this work is a multivalent one. The commodification of cultural products may indeed be an exploitive or colonialist misappropriation, but cultural appropriation may also be beneficial to both the source community and the nation as a whole. The task of the legal system should not be to protect a unitary vision of culture but to establish a means of creative self-determination among source communities.

Since asking "Who owns culture?" requires a common definition of ownership, Chapter Two offers a brief definition of property as understood in American law. This discussion covers ownership of both tangible and intangible property and notes that cultural products lack the legal protection offered to other forms of property. It also reviews the justifications for legal protection of intellectual property, identifying a distinction between standard economic ownership and the often legally invisible affiliative claims of ownership that may be expressed by a creator.

Chapter Three describes cultural products as "accidental" property, in that they originate in community practices outside the realm of commercial endeavors. The form of cultural products results in part from communal agency and in part from the influences of necessity, communal expression, and function.

Chapter Four describes categories of cultural products and the ways in which source communities transform and elaborate their meanings. To further highlight the relationship between cultural products and property ownership, this chapter provides comparisons with intellectual property and with traditional cultural property, also known as antiquities, cultural patrimony, or cultural heritage. While cultural products and cultural property both capture the spirit of a community, traditional cultural property is likely to consist of unique rather than reproducible items.

The chapters that follow discuss the contested control or ownership of cultural products and the effects of their appropriation outside the source community. Chapter Five discusses the relationship between ownership and authenticity, returning to the concept of affiliative ownership introduced earlier. While a source community may be unable to prevent nonconforming use or outsider appropriation, it can at least claim that its own version of a cultural product is original and therefore superior. Such claims, however, raise complex issues of cultural evolution, community membership, and even freedom of expression. The search for subjective authenticity is nevertheless a crucial element in the formation and maintenance of communal identity.

Chapter Six explores the internal tensions that arise when members of a source community disagree about a particular expression of their collaborative creation. Moving to the issue of outsider appropriation, Chapter Seven describes the factors that prompt cultural borrowing and also discusses source-community reactions. Chapters Eight and Nine address the potential effects of cultural appropriation on source communities and on the products themselves, looking initially at the destructive effects of misappropriation and then at the beneficial results of permissive appropriation.

In Chapter Ten, the focus moves from the appropriation of cultural products that originate within a particular source community to the reverse appropriation of commercialized intellectual properties—including literary characters, brand names, and television series—that are adopted by a defined group and subsequently take on a life of their own. This chapter also raises the question of whether the members of a particular community who become celebrities or public figures are themselves transformed into cultural products. In terms of cultural ownership, what does it mean to "belong to" a source community?

The final chapters return to the question of why cultural products are legally invisible and why their appropriation is largely unregulated, despite the significance of cultural products to both America as a whole and individual source communities. Chapter Eleven offers possible civic reasons for the legal vacuum, with particular attention to the role of cultural appropriation in binding together a multicultural nation. This review of the potential benefits of cultural exchange, while not ignoring its dangers, sets the stage for the focus of equitable cultural-product protection to move from pervasive economic control to affiliative ownership.

Finally, Chapter Twelve invokes principles of ownership and intellectual property to suggest a balance of interests between source communities and the majority public. Central to this resolution are community activism and the possibility of instituting different levels of protection for community-generated art forms, depending on their significance within the source communities and the degree to which those groups have engaged in voluntary commercialization. The grid presented in this chapter suggests one schema for categorizing cultural products as a basis for facilitating both source-community affiliation and modulated public access. The chapter concludes by offering a vision of cultural appropriation that protects not only community authenticities but the ongoing performance of an authentic America.

As part of the Public Life of the Arts series, *Who Owns Culture?* attempts to redefine community-group authorship for the modern era by examining cultural production and appropriation in America. This issue is not unique to the United States; indeed, international developments regarding the protection of traditional cultures, such as the UNESCO Convention for the Safeguarding of the Intangible Cultural Heritage, may exercise significant influence on the future of American law. Reform, like charity, should nonetheless begin at home.

This book aims to spark a broad interdisciplinary discussion of cultural production, a previously marginal area within the law, by bringing together scholarship from the fields of law, cultural history, sociology, anthropology, art, literature, and religious and ethnic studies. Ultimately, the goal of *Who Owns Culture?* is to suggest a legal paradigm that strikes an equitable balance between source-community rights and the public interest in cultural products. Both our diverse nation and our postmodern consciousness have taught us to value others' cultural products. The law should reinforce this lesson not by allowing unlimited appropriation of these art forms but instead by striking a protective balance central to the past and future of American culture.

CHAPTER 1

The Commodification
of Culture

[S]he was surrounded by her garments as by the
delicate and spiritualized machinery of a whole
civilization.

—Marcel Proust

AMERICA IS A nation of nations. Our imagined
community rests not only on a unifying mythology of freedom and
independence but also on intertwined tales of regional and ethno-
cultural character.[1] We are Italian-American mafiosi and African-
American gangsta rappers, WASP country clubbers and Jewish
intellectuals, gay decorators and Latin lovers, rednecks and computer
geeks. These labels reek of stereotype and foment prejudice, yet they
remain the signposts of multicultural America—often (although not
always) with the advice and consent of the labeled.[2]

The origins of the ethnic, regional, social, and cultural groups that
make up the American landscape are as diverse as the groups themselves. Some are the product of waves of immigration, as economic
opportunity, war, natural disaster, the quest for religious freedom, and
the rise and fall of immigration quotas prompted the relocation of
groups large enough to form new communities on U.S. shores. Other
groups, like African-American slaves and their descendants, Native
Americans forced onto reservations, and gay and lesbian activists
fighting for civil rights, take shape through domestic adversity. Still
other communities, like the Daughters of the Confederacy or Maine
lobstermen, coalesce through shared regional and historical ties; more
recently, the poverty and violence of urban areas have produced a

distinctive culture of their own. Personal hardship, such as losing a loved one in the 9/11 terrorist attacks or living with a physical disability, can also bring individuals together as a recognizable group. Even shared avocations may produce distinctive cultural groups, such as science fiction enthusiasts, opera buffs, and sports-team fans.

While some cultural groups remain largely invisible to outsiders, others occupy significant territory in the majority consciousness. An announcement of Bavarian heritage or of support for a local badminton team is likely to draw a blank stare or, at best, a polite nod. By contrast, mentioning a childhood in Pennsylvania Dutch country or wearing a Yankees baseball cap leads to immediate recognition—in the latter case, not always positive.

Many characteristics affect public recognition or ignorance of particular cultural groups. These include the size of the group, its geographic concentration or distribution, its historical significance, the physical appearance or behavioral characteristics of group members, the group's collective interaction with the majority public, and its economic or political influence. The public identity of a cultural group and its variation over time are determined by a complex range of circumstances and interactions.

CULTURAL APPRECIATION

One of the most significant differences between recognizable and invisible cultural groups, and the most relevant factor for purposes of this study, is the degree to which a particular group has been commodified. As a nation of consumers, we define many of our experiences and associations through acquisition. When we travel, we purchase miniature replicas of Mount Rushmore or the Statue of Liberty; when we graduate, we collect diplomas; when we enjoy a concert or a sports event, we buy the T-shirt. Similarly, when we encounter other cultural groups, we are most likely to pay attention to those that offer us the potential to acquire distinctive merchandise, experiences, or souvenirs. If these cultural products are not readily available, we collectively lose interest and move on to the next opportunity for interaction.

Consumers respond to cultural products in the marketplace and elsewhere much the way that decorator crabs gather seaweed and adorn their shells. In an educational exhibit at the Monterey Bay Aquarium, the marine biologists placed decorator crabs in separate tanks with different materials—not only the seaweed ordinarily found growing on the ocean floor but also brightly colored yarn available at local craft shops. Skilled in the art of camouflage, the crabs living with the yarn affixed bits of the foreign material to their shells in lieu of seaweed. When we decorate our homes, dinner tables, and persons with others' cultural products, we exhibit behavior similar to that of the decorator crabs, albeit with more complex motives.[3] Distinguished anthropologist Clifford Geertz notes that human intellectual capacities evolved in the presence of culture and require the presence of significant symbols in order to function; he concludes, "We are, in sum, incomplete or unfinished animals who complete or finish ourselves through culture."[4]

Similarly, when bohemians in 1920s Manhattan visited Italian restaurants in Greenwich Village or when modern gastronomes comb Chinatown for the perfect dim sum, the goal is not only to procure lunch but to add cosmopolitan luster to the identity of the diner.[5] In his critique of the role of taste in enforcing social-class distinctions, French sociologist Pierre Bourdieu refers to this selective version of cultural appreciation as the acquisition of "cultural capital."[6] When the transaction is voluntary, it may benefit both the source community and the general public.

In order for an ethnic, regional, social, or cultural group to register upon the American mental landscape, then, the nation as a whole first extracts what might be termed an identity tax. This tax is payable to the public domain in the form of distinctive cultural products, including cuisine, dress, music, dance, folklore, handicrafts, healing arts, language, and images. Chinese medicine, Ethiopian restaurants, Australian Aboriginal instruments used in the theme of the *Survivor* reality television series, and Andean street musicians all contribute to the national culture. In many cases, consumption of these cultural products is the first—or indeed only—contact that many Americans have with cultural groups other than their own. Were it not for their cultural products, many groups would remain largely invisible.

When cultural products enter the marketplace or otherwise become accessible to outsiders, society at large claims the right to sample them and in return recognizes a group identity constructed from a simplified set of defining characteristics. This identity is necessarily limited—an entire culture cannot be read in the gold embroidery of an Indian woman's sari or illuminated by the flames from a dish of American-style Greek *saganaki*. Cultural products do, however, provide a starting point for recognition of the source community as well as a means of allowing outsiders a degree of participation in and appreciation of that community.

Although the commercial availability of cultural products is one means of cultural exchange, payment of the identity tax can also involve the informal or even inadvertent contribution of images, aromas, superstitions, melodies, or spoken phrases. The locus of this exchange might be the street festivals and family-owned restaurants of immigrant America, the society columns and shelter magazines of urban society, or the home pages and bulletin boards of cyberspace. Wherever cultural groups or their everyday art forms come into contact with the general public, they enrich the public domain of American culture and work to establish their own communal identities within it.

The perceived advantage to American consumers of an ever-expanding range of cultural products is fairly straightforward. Nativist sentiments or certain strains of extreme social conservatism aside, we are cultural gourmands. The more parades, radio stations, publications, and decorative housewares are available, the greater our pleasure in the diversity of choice. This sentiment has echoes in classical antiquity: Herodotus praised ancient Greek society for its cultural acquisitiveness, noting that Greek and Libyan armies copied elements of one another's armor and that the Greeks borrowed many of their gods from Egypt. Even manners and morals could be borrowed, according to one scholar who notes that "nearly all the people on Herodotus's map shop around for the *nomoi* they find most useful or pleasurable."[7] Similarly, the European Renaissance owed much to open trade routes with the Islamic world and Asia. From the point of view of the American majority public today, the appreciation of others' cultural products—

although not necessarily the presence of the others themselves—is a fringe benefit of globalization, integration, and the commodification of culture.

CULTURAL APPROPRIATION

Far from an uncontested process, however, the movement of cultural products from subculture to public domain provokes both majority-minority struggles and fraternal conflict. Outsiders attracted by particular art forms are seldom content to limit themselves to recognition and appreciation of the source community or even to limited consumption at the invitation of the community. Instead, members of the public copy and transform cultural products to suit their own tastes, express their own creative individuality, or simply make a profit. This "taking—from a culture that is not one's own—of intellectual property, cultural expressions or artifacts, history, and ways of knowledge" is often termed "cultural appropriation."[8]

Some cultural products can be freely shared with the public; others are devalued when appropriated by the majority culture: consider the distinction between popularizing a Caribbean dance rhythm and secretly recording and distributing a Native American sacred chant. German philosopher Jürgen Habermas addresses the problem of cultural commodification and the distorting effects of commerce on tradition and culture, stating, "The media of money and power can regulate the interchange relations between system and lifeworld only to the extent that the products of the lifeworld have been abstracted, in a manner suitable to the medium in question, into input factors for the corresponding subsystem, which can relate to its environment only via its own medium."[9] The abstraction of a dance rhythm from its cultural lifeworld, whether via a market system or an intellectual property system that permits unfettered copying, may not severely harm either the source community or the cultural product itself. By contrast, the appropriation of a secret or sacred cultural product is much more likely to cause damage.

Even when voluntary, contributions to popular culture are subject to gross distortion: can Mexican national cuisine be faithfully represented by Taco Bell? The large-scale culture industry is perennially under attack for its tendency to simplify and standardize, to the detriment of "authentic" culture or artistry. German scholars Max Horkheimer and Theodor Adorno, writing from Los Angeles during World War II, noted, "Pseudo individuality is rife: from the standardized jazz improvisation to the exceptional film star whose hair curls over her eye to demonstrate originality."[10] For Horkheimer and Adorno, cultural conformity raised the specter of fascism. In the realm of cultural appropriation, replacement of homemade tortillas or the small neighborhood *taquería* with a mass-market product or chain store may create a barrier to cultural identity and national diversity.

Within a cultural group, members may debate the authenticity of particular cultural products, a difficulty exacerbated by their constantly evolving nature. Which version of a recipe or folktale is the "real" one? In some cases, there may be a reasonably clear ur-product, like Neapolitan pizza, and competing regional versions, like those made with a thin crust in New York, in a deep-dish style in Chicago, and with unusual gourmet toppings in California. In other cases, the origin of a cultural product may lie in an obscure past, or splinter groups may exert competing claims to the true tradition. When claims of originality or authenticity move beyond good-natured rivalry, which may actually spur creativity, they can hamper the ability of certain members of a cultural group to participate in the creation of cultural products or distort the identity of the group as a whole.

Perhaps the most contentious internal issue of all is how to regulate the general public's access to the cultural goods of a particular community—and who should benefit economically from their distribution. Since cultural groups are often loosely organized networks with shifting membership or degrees of affiliation, they tend to lack a single authoritative voice that might channel cultural appreciation or prevent cultural appropriation. The power to control economic exploitation of cultural products is similarly decentralized; while source communities may lament the loss of profits to outsiders or the uneven sharing of economic benefits within the community, they cannot remedy the situation.

The commodification of culture, and especially the role of cultural products, is a mixed blessing for the general public and for source communities. If the identity tax were not involuntary and automatic, cultural groups might choose to forego the benefits of potential public recognition in favor of protection against appropriation. Alternatively, they might exercise greater influence over the copying and reinterpretation of their cultural products, offering the public a guarantee of quality, historical knowledge, and the elusive promise of authenticity. At present, however, cultural products that catch the public eye circulate in a largely unregulated sphere of mixed appreciation and appropriation.

LEGAL CULTURE

Despite the significance of artistic and social conflicts over the nature of cultural products in American life, these disputes occur in a legal vacuum. Other forms of creative production receive extensive, even excessive, protection against copying under our system of intellectual property law. Cultural products, however, are indefinite works of unincorporated group authorship, and they present a particular challenge.

Intellectual property law is a relatively young discipline with a distinguished family tree. From its Romantic ancestry, intellectual property derives an emphasis on individual genius. From its Enlightenment parentage, it inherits a tremendous confidence in the ability of the rational mind to create, to solve, to progress, to assign value. So great is this confidence in the power of intellectual creation that intellectual property law challenges the market itself, granting limited monopolies and blocking access to otherwise public goods in order to ensure continued "Progress of Science and useful Arts," in the constitutional phrase.[11] With the late twentieth-century rise of the Information Age and the recognition of ideas as wealth-generating capital, intellectual property protection has risen dramatically in importance. Its limitations, consequently, are becoming apparent.

One of the limitations of our current scheme of intellectual property protection, besides the often-cited narrow scope and great expense, is the treatment of group authorship. From high tech to low tech, from the Linux operating system to Native American folklore, our system struggles to assign intellectual property rights to authors who fail to evoke the Romantic image of the solitary artist scribbling away in an unheated garret or the unkempt scientist waking from a fitful nap on a cot in the laboratory with a sudden flash of insight. Even a patent "owned" by a multinational conglomerate must list its humble human inventor. Lawmakers have been subjected to extensive criticism and even legal challenge for their expansions of intellectual property protection in other areas, yet our system continues to neglect the intellectual property rights of a group, especially one without a preestablished corporate identity.

This legal neglect of cultural products may be ascribed to the history of intellectual property law, the complex nature of cultural products and the concomitant difficulty of providing a legal framework, or simply cultural bias. Before proposing an extensive system of protection for cultural products, however, we should consider the possibility that the relative absence of law—like law itself—may spark creativity or even preserve national character. As we strive to maintain the rich texture and common goals of our heterogeneous polity, we must attempt to balance the tension between the public domain and private property, cultural appreciation and cultural appropriation.

CHAPTER 2

Ownership of Intangible Property

In the world of Robinson Crusoe property rights play no role.

—Harold Demsetz

AN UNDERSTANDING OF the concept of property ownership is second nature to any child who has ever shared a sandbox. *My* corner, *my* bucket, and *my* sandcastle define the terms of engagement, and any interloper who disregards these claims is likely to provoke open warfare. These apparently simple assertions of ownership—over a sandy bit of permanent real estate, a personal object that can be taken home at the end of the day, and an embodied architectural design, respectively—nevertheless represent a complex system of property law. The categories of real property, personal property, and the relative newcomer intellectual property are the pillars of this social system, which is outlined in more detail in the Appendix.

Among the forms of property, intellectual property provides the best analogy to cultural products. Both categories embody intangible ideas, and both are vulnerable to theft by copying, whether that unauthorized reproduction is known as intellectual property infringement or cultural appropriation. A review of intellectual property and its unique characteristics will thus assist in formulating a theory of cultural ownership and protection.

At the outset, it is important to understand why intellectual property requires greater protection than its counterparts in order to remain subject to private ownership. Then, given intellectual property's lack of natural defenses, societies must consider why they should dedicate resources to the protection of it. Why spend money and establish laws to protect authors and inventors? Historically, one justification is utilitarian. Legal protections allow authors and inventors to capture the economic value of their creations, thus giving them incentives to continue to create, an endeavor that is perceived as an overall benefit to society and humanity. The other traditional justification is ethical. If an author or inventor creates something, shouldn't she be able to keep it? This justification might suggest either standard economic ownership or an affiliative ownership, which focuses on the right to claim authorship and exercise certain forms of control over the creation. Because the law has long conceived of creation as an individual phenomenon, the application of protection is more complex when there is more than one author or inventor of record—and virtually nonexistent when creation flows from a community rather than discrete individuals. The following pages offer a general outline of these legal themes, setting the stage for an examination of cultural products and the potential role of intellectual property law in their protection.

DEFINING INTELLECTUAL PROPERTY

When protected by law, the intangible aspects of creations of the human mind constitute intellectual property. Aesthetic, technological, symbolic, or informational, intellectual property is separable from the tangible objects in which the creation is manifest.[1] A book, for example, may embody the narrative developed by its author, the name and symbol of its publishing house printed on the spine and title page, and an innovative technique or adhesive for fastening its pages to the binding. When buying an individual volume, however, a purchaser does not also obtain the author's copyright, the publisher's trademark, or the inventor's bookbinding patent. Despite the intangible character of intellectual property, its ownership adheres to the same principles as other forms of property, subject to statutory and judicial limitations.[2]

The Heightened Role of Law

While much tangible property can receive recognition and protection through private means, intellectual property depends heavily on statutory safeguards.[3] A house is easily recognizable as property, and its owner can surround it with a fence or guard it with an alarm system. An invention, by contrast, can slip from its owner's exclusive possession as easily as textile-manufacturing technology emigrated from England to America in the late eighteenth and early nineteenth centuries, traveling in the memories of such aspiring industrialists as Samuel Slater and Francis Cabot Lowell.[4]

Legal realist Felix Cohen once described property as "[t]hat . . . to which the following label can be attached: To the world: Keep off unless you have my permission, which I may grant or withhold. Signed: Private citizen. Endorsed: The state."[5] This state endorsement and the legal forces backing it are far more active in the creation and maintenance of intellectual property than in the protection of real or personal property. An owner seeking some return on her investment in intangible property cannot ordinarily, except in the case of the embodiment of some trade secrets, physically surround it with a barrier. Instead, she must rely on the law to create boundaries in the public mind. As Michael Heller notes, "Because people cannot physically hold intangible property, they may have relatively unformed intuitions about viable boundaries" and must instead look to legal rules for guidance.[6]

Because intellectual property approaches the definition of a public or noncompetitive good, which additional persons may enjoy simultaneously at no additional cost, the law reminds the public that exclusivity is one of the prerogatives of ownership.[7] The highly publicized debate over Napster and the uploading and distribution of MP3 files via the internet, for instance, was described by Chief Judge Marilyn Hall Patel as concerning "the boundary between sharing and theft, personal use and the unauthorized worldwide distribution of copyrighted music and sound recordings."[8] In college dormitories and on internet bulletin boards, in law school classrooms and the popular press, music lovers debated the location of the "boundary" described by the court and the potential consequences of moving it. One contested issue involved the cost to musicians and record companies: is music in MP3 format similar to a public good, enjoyable by many at little or no cost, or is the music industry losing millions of dollars in sales?

The ensuing discussion highlighted the deep ambiguity surrounding our societal acceptance of intangible goods as property; surely, no such division of opinion would have accompanied the announcement of a series of record-store burglaries. Concluding that Napster's service fell on the wrong side of the legal boundary, the court noted that "virtually all Napster users engage in the unauthorized downloading or uploading of copyrighted music; as much [sic] as eighty-seven percent of the files available on Napster may be copyrighted, and more than seventy percent may be owned or administered by plaintiffs."[9] Those statistics, combined with the large number of users of Napster and similar programs, illustrate the disjunction between intellectual property law and the lack of societal consensus regarding what should be respected as "property."

Intangible goods that do not receive legal protection often pass into the public domain to be enjoyed by "free riders." Consider the fans who sit on rooftops surrounding Wrigley Field in Chicago to watch the Cubs lose game after game. These fans do not lessen the enjoyment of those who purchase tickets to view the spectacle or those who subscribe to cable television services in order to watch the game. In fact, the rooftop crowds may enhance the overall experience of the baseball game by creating a festive atmosphere around the ballpark. Should the team owners seek to enjoin the unauthorized viewing or even rooftop attempts to record and broadcast the games, however, intellectual property law would be of little assistance.[10] Although the Cubs have claimed that surrounding rooftop owners have engaged in both copyright and trademark infringement by tapping into the Cubs instant-replay broadcasts and game commentary and by using Cubs and Wrigley Field logos, these charges are most likely a tactic in a dispute regarding revenue sharing and a controversial proposed expansion of Wrigley Field.[11] As Judge Ralph Winter noted in *National Basketball Association v. Motorola*, there appears to be a "general understanding" that sporting events themselves are not subject to copyright protection.[12] In the Wrigley Field example, the ballpark could theoretically add visual barriers to prevent rooftop viewing, assuming the approval of city officials, but intellectual prop-

erty law places the team's athletic performances outside the realm of "property."

Theories of Intellectual Property Protection

Societal discussion regarding the legal boundary between intellectual creations that constitute property and those that do not revolves around the broad themes of utility and ethics.[13] In the United States, the primary justification for the legal creation and protection of intellectual property is utilitarian or economic incentive-based. In this regard, the Constitution empowers Congress "[t]o promote the Progress of Science and useful Arts, by securing for limited Times to Authors and Inventors the exclusive Right to their respective Writings and Discoveries."[14]

The Founders envisioned that copyright and patent protections, unlike homologous rights to real and personal property, would incorporate temporal limitations but also be sufficient to provide incentives to the creators of intellectual property.[15] This utilitarian approach limits the bundle of rights associated with intellectual property protection in order to balance the social and economic value of innovation, or "Yankee ingenuity," with other national interests, including market competition and freedom of expression. The requirements found in successive American patent and copyright statutes embody this tension between granting ideas the status of private property and leaving ideas to enrich the public domain in both creative and economic terms. Similarly, federal trademark and trade-secret law, although derived from the Commerce Clause, illustrate a balance between public and private interests.[16]

While the Constitution's focus on particular creative individuals, "authors and inventors," is not necessary to a utilitarian model of intellectual property protection, it reflects what Martha Woodmansee and Peter Jaszi term "a quite radical reconceptualization of the creative process that culminated less than 200 years ago in the heroic self-presentation of the Romantic poets."[17] Michel Foucault challenged this restrictive view of authorship over thirty years ago, and literary and legal scholars have echoed his critique.[18] Nevertheless, despite the proliferation of corporate intellectual property and the generative techniques of the digital age, the sole creator remains the primary target of the utilitarian incentives of intellectual property law.

The ethical, or "moral rights," justification for the legal creation and protection of intellectual property, by contrast, focuses predominantly on the inherent justice of rewarding the author for her creative efforts, especially in the realm of copyright. These authorial rewards take the form of both the economic rights found in utilitarian-based systems and the inalienable moral rights of attribution or paternity, integrity, disclosure or publication, and withdrawal or retraction, which constitute a permanent affiliative ownership.[19] Expressed in terms of Lockean labor theory, the ethical justification argues that when a creator deliberately combines her mental efforts with language, images, techniques, or other ideas in the public domain, the resulting product should be identified as her intellectual property.[20] Central to this notion of personal rights is the construction of the author or creator as a solitary genius, as opposed to an earlier notion of collaborative creation. Woodmansee has traced the development of this understanding of authorship in copyright law, noting, "The notion that the writer is a special participant in the production process—the only one worthy of attention—is of recent provenience. It is a by-product of the Romantic notion that significant writers break altogether with tradition to create something utterly new, unique—in a word, 'original.'"[21]

This exclusive celebration of one individual not only obscures the role of the community and society at large in the development of intellectual property but also shifts attention away from the need for a robust public domain from which an author or inventor may draw inspiration, a strong component of utilitarian theory. Indeed, Wendy Gordon has argued that judicial invocation of Locke to justify extensive intellectual property protection at the expense of the public domain misapprehends natural-rights theory.[22] Although the focus of ethical theory on the Romantic genius of the creator is not as developed in trademark or trade-secret law as in copyright or patent law, the issues of who conceived an idea and whether it is sufficiently original or different from existing intangibles remain consistent themes.

Authors' rights have long occupied the core of the European civil law of intellectual property, but the influence of these rights on the common law has increased with the growing internationalization of intellectual property law.[23] Both the 1989 decision by the United States to join the Berne Convention for the Protection of Literary and Artistic Works and the passage of the Visual Artists' Rights Act of 1990 indicate the increased presence of moral rights protection in American law.[24] In the Agreement on Trade-Related Aspects of Intellectual Property (TRIPS), the specific exclusion of the Berne Convention provision concerning moral rights, Art. 6(bis), however, reflects continuing ambivalence toward these provisions.[25]

Despite the marked differences between the utilitarian and the ethical justifications for the legal protection of intangible creations of the human mind, the two theories set similar limits on the subject matter of intellectual property. Both common law and civil law incorporate a conception of the agents of creation, especially of authors and inventors, that reflects a post-Enlightenment, individualistic worldview. The two perspectives also share an understanding of the temporal parameters of originality or innovation: the law may protect only newborn ideas, and such protection expires when ideas have matured. These narrow definitions of agency and novelty, along with utilitarian theory's desire to expand the public domain, help define the boundaries of intellectual property—boundaries that may be excessively rigid or even theoretically unjustified.

Many other statutory requirements also contribute to setting the parameters of what constitutes intellectual property in the United States. Among these are the existence of a tangible embodiment of the idea, the utility of a patentable invention, the public use of a trademark, the commercial advantage gained through a trade secret, and the legal formalities required to obtain or protect ownership rights in the various forms of intellectual property.[26] The law's limited conceptions of creation and originality, however, are the defining elements that flow most directly from the philosophical underpinnings of intellectual property law. These elements, together with the utilitarian desire to enrich the public domain and the common law emphasis on tangible embodiment, also form the greatest barrier to protection of cultural products.

CO-OWNERSHIP OF
INTELLECTUAL PROPERTY

The legal persistence of the solitary, Romantic ideal of authorship has tended to divert attention from the collaborative development or concurrent ownership of intellectual property. As a result, applicable doctrine has been meager. While the law offers a reasonably sophisticated description of the author or inventor vis-à-vis the public, or of the intellectual property owner vis-à-vis would-be infringers, it remains silent or even dismissive regarding the internal social dynamics of collaboration or co-ownership.[27] Unlike the older field of real property law, intellectual property law cannot draw on established forms and social conventions for the sharing of property. Analogy to real property forms, moreover, often fails to address the complexities of concurrent ownership of intellectual property, which may involve collaborative creation as well as joint ownership of completed or existing intellectual property.[28] As Rochelle Cooper Dreyfuss and others have noted in calling for greater attention to the cooperative production of intellectual property, the rapid development of intellectual property as an economic engine has not resulted in a commensurate elaboration of formal legal rules or informal social norms.[29]

Existing federal intellectual property statutes offer only minimal provisions for concurrent ownership.[30] In addition, while co-owners of intellectual property can use private contracts to develop alternative ownership structures, subject to the restrictions of federal law, this approach is inefficient and unpredictable. Creating a unique ownership agreement is likely to prove more expensive and time-consuming than reliance on a realistic and reasonably detailed statutory default system. In the case of newly created intellectual property, contractual negotiations should ideally take place before the creative process begins to avoid later misunderstandings regarding rights to commercial exploitation, royalties, or rights to use the work in future projects. Because a private ownership agreement requires legal forethought and communication on the part of creators, it is more likely to be executed in an institutional setting, such as a university or business corporation, than in informal creative collaborations.

The further the reality of the creative process moves from the Romantic paradigm—progressing from the individual genius, to the corporate entity, to formal cooperation between legally sophisticated corporate entities, to the ad hoc artistic or inventive collaboration that has so far characterized the digital age—the less likely the participants are to plan and to execute successfully a private co-ownership agreement. Intellectual property law, with its myopic focus on the sole author or inventor and its failure to develop adequate structures for concurrent ownership, cannot provide sufficient protection to a wide range of creators.

BEYOND THE BOUNDARIES OF PROPERTY LAW: UNPROTECTED INTANGIBLES

Still more likely to fall outside the realm of intellectual property are the creative expressions of an unincorporated group, such as a particular race, ethnicity, religion, sexual orientation, profession, avocation, class, or even gender or age category. The intangible products of these cultural groups, whether created deliberately or as a by-product of social interaction over time, tend to fail the tests of agency and novelty common to the utilitarian and ethical theories of intellectual property protection. Consider cultural products such as cuisine, dress, music, dance, folklore, handicrafts, images, healing arts, and language. Manifestations of these forms appear in both traditional and more recently emergent culture groups: distinctive cultural dress may be an Indian woman's sari or a sadomasochist's leather harness; folklore may involve the appearance of Coyote in a Native American myth or kidney thieves in an urban legend on a website; the language may be Yiddish or American Sign Language. In none of these cases, however, is authorship sufficiently identifiable to meet the standards of intellectual property law. In none of these cases is the cultural artifact, once developed within the community of origin and declared valuable, sufficiently new to qualify for legal protection. Lacking both a Romantic author and a "Eureka!" moment, intangible cultural products are legally invisible.

Not all cultural products have equal significance for their source communities, and not all (or even many) deserve protection as intellectual property. Not only would such protection create a tremendous administrative and economic burden, but the loss of socially beneficial cultural exchange would also be tremendous. The American legal system, however, has already begun to seek a balance between cultural appreciation and cultural appropriation of Native American handicrafts, and legal scholars have considered the proposal that protection of indigenous artworks should be expanded on both a national and a global basis.[31] The blanket exclusion of other intangible cultural products from legally protected ownership in some form is also ripe for review.

CHAPTER 3

Cultural Products as Accidental Property

Ye Pow'rs wha mak mankind your care,
And dish them out their bill o'fare,
Auld Scotland wants nae skinking ware
That jaups in luggies;
But, if ye wish her gratefu' prayer,
Gie her a haggis!

—Robert Burns

AT A HOLIDAY concert performed by the Turtle Creek Chorale in Dallas, not all of the music was audible. After simultaneously singing and signing "Silent Night," the performers fell silent and repeated the piece—in sign language only. The blue lighting in the symphony hall, the graceful movement of hundreds of hands in unison, and the familiar melody echoing in the minds of the audience combined to produce a powerful synthesis of communication and choreography. For many in attendance, the dramatic use of silence by a gay men's chorale also invoked the memory of those members of the group whose voices were permanently silenced by AIDS and who are remembered annually at the concert.

Sign language is, of course, also used in everyday settings as a primary form of communication among people who are hearing impaired, their families, and their friends. Indeed, wherever there are communities of hearing-impaired people, indigenous and localized forms of sign language appear as a necessary and natural mode of communication. Not until the eighteenth century did French educators attempt to standardize sign language and use it as a tool for educating nonhearing students, and only in 1960 was American Sign Language—as opposed to signed English—first recognized by an academic linguist as a complete, independent communication system.[1]

Neurologist Oliver Sacks has noted that while most of us take speech for granted, hearing-impaired people "have a special, intense feeling for their own language: they tend to extol it in tender, reverent terms. . . . The deaf feel Sign as a most intimate, indissociable part of their being, as something they depend on, and also, frighteningly, as something that can be taken away from them at any time . . . ."[2] Outside linguistic recognition of sign language thus validated the community's cultural product and paved the way for a potentially disabling medical condition to be transformed into "Deaf identity" and "Deaf pride."[3] The use of sign language by the Turtle Creek Chorale, not merely as a service to hearing-impaired patrons but also as an artistic component of the performance, demonstrates the maturation of its public identity as a cultural product as well as its indispensable status within the hearing-impaired community.

Sign language and other intangible creations of a cultural group are "accidental" property in the sense that neither commodification nor reduction to ownership serves as the primary impetus for their development. Unlike commodities as understood by Karl Marx, cultural products originate and exist outside the marketplace, at least for a time. They are not intended as performances for outsiders, nor are they destined for sale to tourists. Instead, authentic cultural products are intrinsic to quotidian activities and celebratory occasions within the source community. As such, they instantiate the internal dynamics, shared experiences, and value systems that bind the community together. Only through the passage of time, attempts at organization or standardization, or interaction with the majority public do cultural products take on the characteristics of property.

"Accidental" Creation

When injured veterans returned home from service in World War II, a significant number of these previously active men found themselves confined to wheelchairs. In an effort to pass the time, direct their energies, and recover their previous *joie de vivre,* the patients in

Veterans Administration hospitals turned to sports—and wheelchair basketball was born. The sport quickly spread to civilians, and paraplegic athletes and those with spinal-cord injuries were joined by players with other types of disability.[4] Today, the National Wheelchair Basketball Association (NWBA) includes over 180 amateur teams, including men's, women's, intercollegiate, and youth organizations. International competition under the auspices of the International Wheelchair Basketball Federation is also fierce.[5] Presumably none of the men and women athletes in wheelchairs who have contributed to the success of their sport would have chosen their disabilities, yet their serendipitous creation of wheelchair basketball has produced a distinctive form of cultural product.

The 2002–2003 bylaws of the NWBA indicate that the organization recognizes the amateur sport as more than just a game; rather, it is a communal creation that links disabled people and contributes to their group identity within society. First among its listed purposes is "[t]o act as an agency for the promotion and continued growth of wheelchair basketball for the good it has done the participants and disabled people everywhere, and the role it has played in educating the public as to the nature of disabilities, and in removing the apathy surrounding the physically disabled."[6] The association also attempts to guard against malfeasance from both within and outside the sport, including "any malpractices of non-accredited individuals who may attach themselves to wheelchair basketball."[7] Wheelchair basketball may be an accidental product created out of adversity rather than by design, but its source community nevertheless understands its importance and works to protect it against adulteration.

Creation as Necessity

Practical philosophers from Plato to Benjamin Franklin have recognized that necessity is the mother of invention, and this is true not only in the realm of physical limitation but also in times of economic necessity or scarcity. Whatever Robert Burns' poetic vision of the Scottish national dish, it was surely hunger or frugality rather than aesthetic vision that inspired the first haggis. Indeed, the appeal of haggis outside the source community is such that it is unlikely ever to be a significant target of cultural appropriation. Culinary economy in other contexts, however, has produced comfortable, humble fare that is later elevated to gourmet status. Southern Italians and American Southerners both view cornmeal mush as a familiar staple, whether it appears as fine-ground yellow polenta or coarse-ground white grits. In neither case is the dish particularly elegant, though, and the one-time association of corn with animal feed does little to elevate its image. The ubiquity of polenta at chic American trattorias in the early 1990s thus raised a few knowledgeable eyebrows at the prices charged for "peasant food," while the popularity of gourmet cheese grits served with grilled shrimp and asparagus prompted a new respect for regional cuisine. While these dishes may periodically put on airs for company, they still anchor family meals in their original, unassuming forms.

Patchwork quilts, by contrast, began as a creative way for women to utilize scraps of fabric or worn-out garments to make necessary bedding, although today their labor-intensive nature seems at odds with our throwaway society and free access to Target and Wal-Mart. In earlier generations, quilt making provided not only a means of recy-cling but also an opportunity for social contact. Women with their small children could gather around a quilting frame, discuss com-munity matters, tell old stories, and stitch their shared experiences directly into the quilts.

Patterns varied from community to community, as available mate-rials differed and cultural values dictated certain limitations. Tradi-tional Amish quilts, for example, were unlikely to include patterned fabric, which many communities considered too worldly, and some avoided the use of bright yellow or white. The frequent use of black backgrounds, however, was a distinctive note in keeping with the Amish emphasis on simplicity, humility, and the avoidance of external decoration—and perhaps also the availability of black fabric from old clothing. Similarly, unnecessary decorative touches were shunned but might be replaced by elaborate flower, wreath, or grapevine patterns stitched to secure the cover of the quilt to its backing.[8]

Scholars have even argued that in the antebellum South, slaves used variously patterned quilts as code to facilitate their escape to freedom. When hung over a fence or in a cabin window, patterns like the North Star and Flying Geese apparently provided navigational or directional guidance, while Tumbling Boxes indicated that it was time to pack and leave.[9] If such a code existed, then the quilts embodied not only the cultural values and aspirations of the source community but also a means of achieving them.

Pockets of active quilt making still exist among women in isolated enclaves like the historically African-American town of Gee's Bend, Alabama, or Amish communities in Pennsylvania and Ohio. Many of the quilts produced today are for sale to tourists, decorators, or collectors, and these commercial products are more likely to follow established patterns and to incorporate popular colors than to be innovative or to reflect community values.[10] The purchasers, for their part, often view the quilts as folk art and are as likely to display them on a wall as on a bed.

The public interest in quilts as folk art dates to the 1960s, a period of increased interest in handicrafts. The African-American quilters of Gee's Bend benefited not only from this shift in popular taste but also from the civil rights movement. The Freedom Quilting Bee, a cooperative organized by a visiting Episcopal priest to promote economic empowerment among poor Alabama women, produced quilts for sale in New York City. These quilts were featured at Bloomingdale's, in *Vogue*, and by the society decorator Sister Parish.[11] In 1971, the Whitney Museum of American Art in New York City mounted an exhibition of quilts from different communities. This show, perhaps the first curatorial recognition of quilts as American women's artwork, subsequently toured through the United States and Europe, elevating the status of the humble patchwork quilt.[12]

The glitzy 1980s and minimalist 1990s saw a diminution in the popularity of handmade quilts, but the Freedom Quilting Bee is reorganizing for a new century, and quilting shows—including a tour of Gee's Bend handiwork that originated at the Museum of Fine Arts in Houston and included the Whitney—are among the most crowded and highly praised museum exhibitions.[13] *New York Times* art critic Michael Kimmelman, noting both the quilts' origins in poverty and their independent styles, calls the Gee's Bend quilts "some of the most miraculous works of modern art America has produced," comparing them to the work of Henri Matisse and Paul Klee. He also acknowledges the communal nature of the quilts' creation and attributes their idiosyncratic character to the town's isolation and closeness; as he observes, "Benders would see each other's work on clotheslines or in their neighbors' houses, and there were familial traits, inherited across generations, prompting a legacy of borrowing, stealing, and mutually respectful call and response."[14] Although quilting in many communities began as a necessary household chore, it became a recognizable cultural product, and it may survive in some form through its "accidental" conversion into commercial property.

Creation as Communal Expression

Like physical or economic necessity, a community's desire for internal self-expression may lead to the creation of distinctive cultural products. These collective art forms capture the mood and the emotional life of an era and of a people who may lack a more formal voice. As such, cultural products become a spontaneous embodiment of the spirit of a people or an age.

One such product appeared in the bars and brothels of Buenos Aires in the late nineteenth century, following a wave of immigration similar to that experienced by its North American counterpart, New York City. The primarily Italian and Spanish men, along with French, German, and Irish immigrants, dreamed of fortune but instead found grueling work in the slaughterhouses and factories on the fringes of the port city. At night, they drank, sang, danced, and fought alongside the local *porteños*, including the macho *compadres* who formed a link to the disappearing world of the gaucho; the young, streetwise *compadritos* with their slouch hats, neckerchiefs, high-heeled boots, and prominently displayed knives; sailors on shore leave and soldiers from the nearby barracks; and other transient or marginal characters. From this atmosphere of loneliness and longing, male competition, and alcohol-infused aggression, the tango was born.

While the precise origins of the tango are obscure, its original music and choreography borrowed from many cultures, including the Spanish-Cuban habanera, best known today from Georges Bizet's opera *Carmen,* and the European polka. These combined with Native American rhythms and earlier Spanish music to form the local Argentine *milonga,* the forerunner of the tango. *Compadritos* who danced the *milonga* also copied or parodied the movements that they observed when they visited African-Argentine dance halls, in particular the sudden, suggestive pauses and dramatic contortions associated with the *candombe,* itself a local fusion of various African traditions. The early instrumentation and lyrics of the tango were similarly borrowed and improvised, with the accordion-like German *bandoneon* soon becoming essential and the Italian-influenced local argot providing the poetry of love, loss, and tragic destiny. Even the precise etymology of the term "tango" is unclear, with both African languages and Latin (via Portuguese slave traders) cited as possible sources for the name of the newly evolved dance.

The partnered choreography of the tango reflected the circumstances and venues of its origin, primarily lower-class brothels and dance halls frequented by *compadritos* and immigrants, and it incorporated both sex and violence. At times the men danced together, pantomiming duels over an affront or a woman; at other times they danced with female partners, often for hire, in a more explicit sexual choreography. Over a short period of time, however, the tango made its way to somewhat more respectable venues, losing some of its aggressiveness but none of its lascivious reputation. Professional tango musicians and dancers emerged, organ grinders and bands added tangos to their repertoires, and composers produced tango music for publication. The formal disapproval of the upper classes remained firm, however, even as their sons slipped away to pass the evening "slumming" with other accomplished dancers.

After 1910 the tango swept through Paris and on to other cosmopolitan capitals, much to the dismay of elite Argentine expatriates embarrassed by the dance's association with barbarism and prostitution. The Argentine embassy in Paris banned the tango, and clergymen and social columnists on both sides of the Atlantic attacked its immoral influence and its proletarian, mixed-race origins. Nevertheless the popularity of the dance endured, and even Hollywood followed the trend, with Rudolph Valentino dancing a tango in his 1921 breakthrough film, *The Four Horsemen of the Apocalypse*. Not all the Argentine poets and lyricists who championed the tango accepted this international dilution of their cultural product into nothing more than an exotic dance, yet the somewhat more tamed and refined version of the tango reimported from Europe quickly became a symbol for the Argentine masses, who reacted strongly to any stylistic changes.

During the first half of the twentieth century, the tango became the universal voice of the common people, as the lyrics told stories not only of violence and tragic love affairs but also of poverty, nostalgia, immigrant life, and social injustice. The great writer Jorge Luis Borges, who later composed tango lyrics himself, expressed the belief that these verses expressed the spirit of their times better than the work of conventional poets. In response to political instability and social unrest, the Argentine government in the 1920s and 1930s banned some of these lyrics from the radio. Later, in the 1940s, efforts at purifying the language used on the radio led to a ban on the Italian-influenced dialect used in many tangos. The rise of Juan and Eva Perón to power ended this censorship, as the couple cultivated the support of the people and shared their allegiance to the tango.[15]

Although the popularity of the tango waned after the 1950s, it remains a significant Argentine cultural export. In international ballroom dancing, or dancesport, competitors perform a precise, standardized version of the tango—beautiful in itself, but also an example of the displacement and cultural atrophy parodied in the movie *Strictly Ballroom* and its versions of the *paso doble*. Among the successful international revues created by Argentines, *Tango Argentino*, *Forever Tango*, and *Tango X Two* have recounted the history of the tango and revived interest in the dance as an art form.[16] These commercial endeavors no longer embody the essence of a transformed *porteño* community, but they may preserve the spirit of the tango among the performers and reflect the pride of a cultural group in its history. The birth of the tango as a form of expression was accidental, but the preservation of its idiom as a cultural product is quite deliberate.

PERSISTENT INTANGIBLE EXPRESSION

All cultural products, like all forms of intellectual property, incorporate an intangible element that may be subject to theft by copying.

For intellectual property, the intangible element is an idea; for cultural products, the intangible element may be an expression of community beliefs, values, aesthetics, or practices. Anglo-American common law generally does not protect ideas alone but instead requires that they be reduced to some concrete form before they become property. Thus common law copyright regimes, unlike their continental European civil law counterparts, require fixation in a tangible medium of expression; patent laws require embodiment or at least a description of the invention's embodiment; and under TRIPS even trademark laws may require visual perceptibility if a national regime so prescribes.[17] This requirement is seldom a barrier to intellectual property protection, as the commercial goals of many authors and inventors would lead them to record or build tangible expressions of their ideas even if not required by law. The accidental nature of cultural products, however, causes many of them to remain intangible or subject to only limited fixation.

While some cultural products assume tangible form as a matter of course, others remain intangible unless and until they are deliberately fixed or recorded. Amish quilts, for example, incorporate intangible or conceptual patterns but are likely to be of little use unless they are pieced from scraps of fabric and stitched together. The physical or economic necessity that gives rise to cultural products in the form of handicrafts, cuisine, dress, and architecture also requires that these products be reproduced in tangible form. A family recipe in the abstract is far less satisfying than a steaming dish on the dinner table.

By contrast, it is the nature of other forms of cultural expression to remain unfixed, at least while they remain within their communities of origin. *Compadritos* and recent immigrants to Buenos Aires originally danced the tango at particular venues and at particular times of day, creating a repeated pattern of expression, but it was not important to them that they photograph, film, draw, or otherwise record the choreography of their movements. Cultural products like music, dance, folklore, language, and ritualistic healing arts (as opposed to medicinal substances and medical devices), while also necessary to their source communities, need not assume a permanent form. The World Intellectual Property Organization's (WIPO) Model Provisions for National Laws on the Protection of Expressions of Folklore

Against Illicit Exploitation and Other Prejudicial Actions lists four categories of "expressions of folklore," three of which are intangible: verbal expressions, musical expressions, and expressions by action. Tangible expressions are grouped together in a fourth category, which corresponds roughly to handicrafts and perhaps architecture.[18]

While ephemeral art forms may be recorded in various ways, the persistent intangibility of many cultural products is a matter of both practice and local choice. Intangibility in creative expression is not merely the default mechanism of societies that lack literacy, musical notation, choreographic instruction, or pattern books. Rather, intangibility has a value of its own—a value pertaining to immediacy of transmission, communal participation, and perhaps fluidity of detail. In Marshall McLuhan's oracular phrase, "The medium is the message," lies the core intuition that every mode of communication carries its own unique set of values.[19] We, esteemed reader, are members of a superliterate class in a literate society accustomed to the fixed expression of creativity, and we must remind ourselves that intangible expressions of communal creativity are important because they are not written, not in spite of this fact. This reminder is necessary even if we are concurrent participants in traditional knowledge systems, given the strong textual orientation of Western culture. Recognition of intangibility as a cultural choice also permits acknowledgment of the value of accidental property without altering it to suit existing paradigms of creativity.

To understand intangibility or the spoken word as a cultural choice rather than a default mechanism of illiterate societies, consider the example of Islam and its religious texts. Islamic society in the Middle Ages was in many ways more sophisticated than that of Western Europe, and it was responsible for (among other things) the Aristotelian revival and the transmission of knowledge from Asia to Europe. Islam was and is also indisputably a literate and text-based culture, with the Qur'an having central importance. Note that calligraphy has persisted as one of its most developed art forms, due in part to the limited prohibition on depiction of human and animal images and in part to the reverence for religious writings.[20] Indeed, Karl Lagerfeld's inadvertent embroidery of fragments of verses from the

Qur'an on a Chanel bustier modeled by Claudia Schiffer allegedly resulted in threats against both the designer and the model.[21]

Despite this respect for scripture, medieval methods of studying the Qur'an and other religious texts nevertheless reveal the persistence of a strong oral culture. God's first revelation to Muhammed opens with the command "Recite in the name of thy Lord."[22] Study of the Qur'an thus consisted of group recitation and memorization, with the text used primarily as a guide to memory rather than as a repository for memory. Similarly, reports of Muhammed's words and actions, known as the hadith, often take the form, "I heard from X, who heard from Y, that the Prophet said or did Z." The oral chain of transmission was preserved, the hadith were memorized and recited, and these reports were written only to preserve accuracy.[23]

Islamic law in the Middle Ages also demonstrated an ambivalent attitude toward written documents. The preferred form of contract was an oral agreement in the presence of witnesses, who could later be called upon to verify its terms. Written documents, by contrast, could be manipulated or falsified.[24] This persistent preference for oral over written agreements may offer one reason for the historical weakness of copyright laws in some Islamic societies.[25]

The refusal of the Ottoman Empire to accept the printing press in the fifteenth century, and its grudging acceptance three hundred years later, is described by many Western scholars as an enormous mistake that led to the modern cultural isolation of Islam.[26] Characterizing the rejection of printing as a "mistake," however, reflects the limited perspective of a highly literate society. Whether the Islamic mistrust of printing resulted from fear of desecration of the Qur'an or from the power of the calligraphers' guild, it reinforced the importance of oral culture by a complex society with both oral and literary capacity. Although Western Europe took the opposite path, with the printing of the Bible in vernacular languages ushering in the Protestant Revolution and a new emphasis on written text, the European choice was not inevitable or without negative consequences—as the subsequent fragmentation of Christianity and disagreement over the accuracy and interpretation of its religious texts suggests. The decision to embody a cultural product in tangible form, as well as the method of doing so and the relative importance attached to oral and written forms, may have a lasting effect on the product and its source community.

Turning to the study of modern indigenous cultures, there is an academic emphasis on the role of spoken language. A casual perusal of a bookstore shelf might reveal *Black Elk Speaks, Sacagawea Speaks, Medicine Woman Speaks, Buffalo Woman Comes Singing, Native American Folktales*, and *Sacred Language: The Nature of Supernatural Discourse in Lakota*, to list only a few volumes. Some of these works represent the tendency of the publishing industry to mimic successful titles, and others illustrate the postmodern fashion of labeling perspectives as "voices." Still, the continuing emphasis on speech or intangible expression written down for the benefit of the reader reflects the continuing importance of oral tradition.

When a source community does not choose to embody its cultural products in tangible form, outsiders who come into contact with this accidental property may undertake to record it themselves. This practice, against which there is little defense save secrecy, gives rise to a number of questions. Should the stories of a cultural group be fixed or written down in a form accessible to the public, or is something lost in the efforts of the Brothers Grimm and their modern counterparts? Why are the scribes recording a community's folklore so seldom insiders? Who has the right to record or fix cultural products, necessarily choosing among versions and altering the stories or histories in the process? Is a Disney version inevitable? What does fixation save, and what might it destroy?

There appear to be both benefits and drawbacks to intangible expression, limited tangible representation, or an emphasis on the oral over the written word as a cultural value or preference. The positive dividends vary by society but might include immediacy of transmission, the creation of living memory, the opportunity for fluidity and cultural evolution, and freedom from the permanent distortion that may occur through fixation. As viewed by a literate society accustomed to fixed expressions of creativity, however, one major drawback to intangible expression is legal uncertainty. If a proposed object of legal protection is indeterminate, it may be quite difficult to establish a property regime or to conclude that infringement or theft has occurred.

A system designed to protect "accidental property" against outside appropriation could choose to require that all cultural products, like intellectual property, appear in tangible form—but this requirement might itself distort or otherwise harm the everyday art forms it seeks to protect. A less invasive approach might be to protect the substance of cultural products rather than their outward forms. Cultural products are important not primarily for their individual attributes, which may evolve over time, but for their role in a source community and their significance to particular members of that community. As such, cultural products serve as the chief repository of social memory around which the community conceives or imagines itself, whether they appear in traditional forms or in the fluid medium of the internet. As anthropologist James Fentress and historian Chris Wickham have observed, "Social memory is not stable as information; it is stable, rather, at the level of shared meanings and remembered images."[27] It is the substance and stability of the source community, then, that cultural products embody—whether in tangible or intangible form.

EXCHANGE OF CULTURAL PRODUCTS

Cultural products, particularly when they appear in tangible form, may be the subject of commercial or noncommercial exchange within the community. Since this exchange occurs among group members who already share the same culture and jointly "own" its cultural products, however, it does not involve the transfer of identity, although it may reinforce beliefs, aesthetic preferences, practices, or values that the parties hold in common. The cultural goods may be treated as property, but their social function is primarily communal rather than individual.

Consider the Roman Catholic who visits a local convent to purchase a rosary for her godchild. Buyer and seller already share the same religion, and thus the market exchange of the tangible religious object does not transfer an intangible good. Moreover, while the seller may realize a profit on the transaction, noncommercial cultural forces dictate the form, function, and significance of the object. Similarly, the gift from godmother to godchild may offer cultural education or reinforcement, but the recipient already belongs to the community and thus partakes of its culture. The godchild now "owns" the rosary beads, but so does the source community.

When nonmembers come into contact with a source community, as in the earlier examples of sign language, patchwork quilts, and tango dancing, intangible cultural products and their tangible embodiments take on the external social characteristics of property. The source community may simply use or possess cultural products in the presence of outsiders, transfer cultural products to outsiders via commercial or noncommercial exchange, or try to exclude outsiders. Like other intangibles, cultural products are noncompetitive goods and may be easily appropriated by nonowners. Nonmembers who acquire or otherwise come into contact with cultural products may respond by expressing cross-cultural appreciation, attempting to join the source community, transforming the products' meaning, or displaying ignorance of their cultural significance.

As a rosary moves outside its source community, it may be admired as an object of religious art, play a role in proselytizing, be included by Madonna in a music video as a commentary on conservative religious practice, accessorize the punk or goth style of a rebellious teenager, be worn unwittingly as a necklace, or be copied by a jewelry designer.[28] These sorts of cultural appropriation are quite common in everyday life. In a similar vein, a distinguished African-American member of the U.S. Court of Appeals for the Eighth Circuit has periodically worn a yarmulke while on the bench, explaining to lawyers that the head covering was a gift from a Jewish colleague who heard him complain that the air vents in the ceiling of the courtroom gave him a chill. The judge's remarks indicate that he is aware that the yarmulke has religious significance for others, and yet he has chosen to reinterpret it from the bench as an ordinary hat.

COMMUNITY MEMBERS' participation in the creation of cultural products, together with their responses to outsider interaction with these products, is analogous to the internal social dynamic of concurrent property ownership. To an even greater extent than federally recognized intellectual property, cultural products lack a legal paradigm for shared control, a lacuna that results in potential intragroup conflicts.

Not only does the "accidental" transformation of cultural products into property discourage a common understanding of their ownership, but the amorphous nature of unincorporated group authorship also complicates private consensus. Source communities must resolve for themselves these ownership issues—and even more intractable membership issues—before considering legal protection for their creations. Legal analysis of the pertinent questions, however, may benefit both culture groups and society at large.

CHAPTER 4

Categorizing Cultural Products

It's not the architectural sense of these buildings
that captivates me but the world they translate.

—Jean Baudrillard

ALEX HALEY WRITES that when his ancestor Kunta
Kinte began to consider marriage, he hesitated at first over the form
of the ceremony. Unlike the dances, songs, prayers to Allah, and talking drums to relay the news that would have accompanied a wedding
in his home village in Africa, a slave ceremony in the antebellum
South would probably involve "'jumpin' de broomstick' before witnesses from slave row, which seemed ridiculous to Kunta for such a
solemn occasion." On his wedding day, Kunta nevertheless linked
arms with his bride and obeyed the command to "jump into de holy
lan' of matrimony," successfully clearing the broom laid on the grass in
front of the couple.[1]

According to historians, "jumping the broom" is an ancient marriage ritual among Anglo-Saxons and Celts, as well as African Americans. Slaves in America were often prohibited from marrying,
although sometimes they were permitted a brief ceremony conducted
by the slave owner or, still more rarely, a member of the clergy.
Instead, they developed alternative rituals, including the practice of
laying an everyday household broom on the ground to symbolize
hearth and home, joining hands, and jumping over it. Despite the
masters' lack of respect for slave marriages, slave culture thus demonstrated its ability "to absorb, reconfigure, and legitimize new ritual
forms, even those masters imposed out of jest or ridicule."[2]

Many of the modern descendants of these slaves choose to incorporate the ritual of jumping the broom into their wedding ceremonies or receptions, using not humble household objects but specially designed and decorated wedding brooms.[3] Some brooms feature traditional materials traceable to the era of slavery; others feature modern themes or incorporate family keepsakes. The embodiment of this cultural product has developed into a cottage industry, complete with internet marketing and feature reportage in the *Wall Street Journal*.[4]

As in the case of jumping the broom, source communities may transform ordinary objects or activities into cultural products through public ceremony or private interaction, intentional design or unstudied behaviors, or a combination of these methods. A wedding ceremony is an essentially private activity, albeit with public effect, even though it may be celebrated in a public fashion and thus witnessed by outsiders. For African Americans, jumping the broom was once a ritual performed of necessity, but it has become a thoughtful and deliberate choice for contemporary couples. Over time, these and other creations become associated with their cultures, first internally, as "the way we do things," and later externally, as "the way they do things." In these transformations of objects or practices into products imbued with cultural meaning and value, the common denominators are ongoing source-group participation and continuing source-group recognition of the developed—although not final—products. As cultural products leave their communities of origin and circulate as property, their significance within the source communities is central to their need for protection.

METHODS OF TRANSFORMATION
INTO CULTURAL PRODUCTS
Organic v. Cultivated Transformation

Most cultural products originate from unstudied behaviors and ordinary objects that, with the passage of time and the evolution of particular details, become recognizable traditions. Clothing, for example, is a simple necessity in a postlapsarian world, and there are a limited number ways to cover a human body or to protect it in the course of various activities. Fashion in the form of particular garments, uniforms, costumes, ornaments, and even colors, however, may indicate

membership in a particular cultural group or participation in its ceremonies and rituals. Wearing a kimono invokes Japanese culture in much
the way kente cloth invokes Ghanian and more generally African culture; an accountant may wear a suit and tie while a police officer wears
a blue uniform; a Muslim woman may wear hijab while a Roman
Catholic nun wears a habit; an American teenager may identify herself
with either school colors or gang colors; funeral mourning in different
societies may call for black or white; a bride may wear either white or
red on her wedding day and, once married, may don a ring on her fin-
ger or a bindhi on her forehead. Anthropologist and former geisha Liz
Crihfield Dalby observes, "Once worn, a kimono defines itself as part
of the discourse of Japanese life, unquotable out of context."[5] Items of
clothing or personal ornament thus become fashion, which in turn
becomes specific to or associated with a particular group or sub-
group—in other words, a cultural product.

Items of clothing, especially those that have developed significance within a particular culture, easily identify their wearers within
that culture.[6] Although French semiotician Roland Barthes criticizes
fashion journalism for failing to "honor the poetic project which
affords its object," he also acknowledges the communicative potential
of clothing itself, noting that it "mobilizes with great variety all the
qualities of matter: substance, form, color, tactility, movement, rigidity,
luminosity" and that "touching the body and acting as its substitute
and its mask, it is certainly the object of a very important investment."[7] Outsiders may admire or copy culturally distinctive clothing
without any awareness of its meaning, however, as they lack familiarity with the everyday behaviors or community practices that formed
the cultural products over time.

The celebration of Kwanzaa, another African-American tradition, exemplifies the putatively less common situation in which a cultural product results from formal or deliberate individual action rather
than as a gloss on longstanding group practices. Political scientist and
ethicist Maulana Karenga created Kwanzaa in 1966, at the height of
the civil rights movement, for adoption by the African-American
community. A cultural rather than religious holiday, Kwanzaa draws
on the ancient tradition of the harvest festival in order to "reaffirm

and restore . . . rootedness in African culture," to gather community members together on an annual basis, and to promote seven distinct African communitarian values among members of the African-American diaspora.[8] Copyright law protects the tangible embodiment of Karenga's creation, his book, as an original work of authorship. The underlying "idea" of Kwanzaa, however, is excluded from copyright protection. To the extent that the African-American community has adopted, celebrated, and enriched the holiday as a cultural product, it likewise receives no legal protection. Perhaps realizing that his idea was not protected, Karenga has entrusted Kwanzaa to Organization Us, the "authoritative keeper of the tradition." This organization, chaired by the holiday's founder, not only disseminates information regarding Kwanzaa through an official website but would presumably also be available to settle disputes regarding the cultural product.[9]

Private v. Public Transformation

While "jumping the broom" and Kwanzaa are private or semi-private activities, one resulting from historical necessity and the other from intellectual activism, public activities as simple as wearing clothes or as elaborate as staged dance performances may also constitute cultural products. Annual outdoor celebrations of St. Patrick's Day, Chinese New Year, Mardi Gras or Carnival, Gay Pride, Columbus Day, and other festivals, parades, and religious processions all exemplify the phenomenon of cultural expression in the form of public ceremony.

Although the precise origins of Mardi Gras in New Orleans are obscure, residents have celebrated some form of the holiday since the eighteenth century, and it has in many ways come to define the city. The festival adapts the medieval European tradition of Carnival, a time for last-chance feasting and post-Christmas celebration before Lent.[10] The medieval celebration was marked not only by material excess and masked misbehavior but also by turning the social order upside down, crowning peasants as kings for a day and mocking the foibles of the upper classes—activities that Mikhail Bakhtin has described both as an inversion of reality and as a manifestation of the carnivalesque spirit of excess and possibility.[11] Disapproving religious reformers in the fifteenth and sixteenth centuries associated Carnival itself with pre-Christian pagan rituals, although the implication of a direct link was probably inaccurate.[12] Mardi Gras, or Fat Tuesday, in the Christian calendar is the final day before the Lenten period of penitence and self-denial. New Orleans is known for neither of these things at any time of year, but its multicultural residents—and its tourist bureau—wouldn't miss the opportunity for a party.

Mardi Gras in New Orleans is a distinctly American pastiche, borrowing not only from French traditions but also from a combination of African, Spanish, and Caribbean styles. The Anglo-American fascination with Greek and Roman mythology and the influence of Native American culture have also contributed regularly to the elaboration of Mardi Gras in the form of parade floats, masqueraders, and dancers. Although the longtime reluctance of certain sponsoring krewes, or carnival societies, to admit African Americans, Jews, or Italian Americans has been the subject of rancorous civic debate, the overall spectacle includes participants from across the spectrum.[13] Each annual celebration is in its own moment a funhouse mirror of society; it deliberately distorts everyday social roles and allows revelers to test boundaries, temporarily join other groups, and emulate forbidden or marginal practices. As Samuel Kinser has described it, Mardi Gras is both ceremonious and grotesque, reflecting its organizers' understanding of the social order and allowing participants "not simply to express our repressed selves but to construct our ideals."[14] The ever-evolving culture of the city and of each of the krewes that contributes to the public festival is expressed in Mardi Gras.

Like other cultural products, public performances not based on federally recognized "works of authorship" are outside the realm of intellectual property law—despite their status as protected expressions under the First Amendment.[15] In the case of *Production Contractors, Inc. v. WGN Continental Broadcasting Co.*, a company hired to organize and promote the McDonald's Charity Christmas Parade invoked intellectual property law in an attempt to prevent live broadcast by an unauthorized television station. Despite the parade's corporate sponsorship and professional management, its participants and viewers presumably experienced it as a celebration of both civic pride and a religious holiday. The plans called for over one hundred units, including local community marching bands, decorative floats, and politicians. The court held that since the parade itself was not copyrightable, the organizer could not prevent an independent broadcast of the event, and the court also dismissed trademark and unfair-competition claims.[16]

The transformation of objects and activities into cultural products—whether unconsciously or intentionally, in private or in public—does not fit the current model of intellectual property authorship. Moreover, the appearances and expressions of cultural products are likely to change over time, requiring continual reassessment of their identity and value. Cultural products are nevertheless human creations distinguishable from quotidian activities or objects on the basis of their heightened cultural significance within the source community.

SOURCES OF DISTINCTION: SYNTHETIC V. NATURAL PRODUCT

In addition to mode of transformation, cultural products may be categorized according to their relationship to human endeavor. Some cultural products are newly created from public domain concepts by members of a source community; others exist independently and are imbued with meaning or put to use by the community. As with intellectual property, it may be argued that the scope of protection afforded a cultural product should depend in part on the contribution of its creators.

Most cultural products, whether they appear in tangible or intangible form, are initially unique to their source community. Like tango dancing or Mardi Gras in New Orleans, the new cultural products may derive from preexisting forms that have been combined and altered to express the spirit of a different people, place, and time. In other cases, like sign language, the new creations may owe little if anything to outside influence. Whether adapted or cut from whole cloth, cultural products that owe their basic forms to communal creation are unlikely to appear outside their source communities unless borrowed.

Cultural products that take shape independently of a source community and are later adopted for a particular expressive or practical use, by contrast, are likely to exist in their basic forms outside the community. Many cat lovers are quick to claim that cats were considered sacred in ancient Egypt, thus distinguishing that culture from its impliedly less enlightened contemporaries or from most modern communities. This special relationship between one culture and a particular animal does not, however, make the presence of cats elsewhere less legitimate or a sign of cultural appropriation—even when they are practically worshiped by their owners. Animals, plants, the passage of seasons, and meteorological or geological events all exist independently of human effort, yet they may take on particular significance as cultural products.

When a preexisting object or activity is both adopted as a cultural symbol and put to a unique or distinctive use, the community has a more exclusive claim to the cultural product than when these conditions are not present. International debate in this area has focused on the need for protection of what is often termed indigenous peoples' "traditional knowledge," "folklore," or more recently "intangible cultural heritage," particularly with respect to the cultivation and uses of local plants. Cultural groups may consider a particular plant sacred, cultivate it as a staple crop, or exploit its medicinal properties. The potential value of certain plants has not escaped the notice of researchers or of multinational corporations, who use "bioprospecting" in addition to synthetic processes in their attempts to develop commercial pharmaceuticals and agricultural products. In a few cases, corporations have attempted to gain exclusive control of these genetic resources by patenting them, sparking protest by the source communities.[17]

The U.S. Patent and Trademark Office (USPTO) was the site of one such protest in 1999, when a group of South American tribal religious leaders wearing shell necklaces and feathers chanted and sipped a ceremonial drink as part of their challenge to a patent on a sacred plant. Ayahuasca, or "vine of the soul," is a hallucinogenic plant sacred to a number of indigenous peoples in the Amazon basin. An American graduate student in pharmacology brought home a sample of the plant from Ecuador, founded the International Plant Medicine Corporation, and in 1986 obtained a patent on an alleged new variety of *Banisteriopsis caapi*, which he called "Da Vine." Although the patent was never exploited, the Coordinating Body of Indigenous Organizations of the Amazon Basin (COICA) was incensed to learn of the patent's existence. A lawyer for the Center for International Environmental Law, who filed a patent-reexamination request on COICA's behalf, likened the ayahuasca patent to a patent on the Christian cross or the Eucharist. While a patent granted by the USPTO is enforceable only within the United States and thus could have no effect on the indigenous peoples' use of the plant, the concept of a sacred object being transformed into private property for commercial purposes was both alien and offensive.[18] While the local peoples could not claim economic ownership of each living plant, their prior knowledge of the plant and its properties—without which it would not have interested the collector—are significant cultural products. Similar cultural clashes have arisen with respect to the corporate appropriation of neem-tree extracts, turmeric, and basmati rice, long cultivated in India, as well as the hoodia cactus from the Kalahari Desert in southern Africa.[19]

In an attempt to combat such alleged "biopiracy," the 1992 Convention on Biological Diversity (CBD) suggests guidelines that attempt to balance the interests of the developed world with those of the developing world in the conservation and use of genetic resources. These guidelines, however, focus primarily on regulation of access at the national level and on profit sharing, although the CBD does provide that member nations shall "respect, preserve and maintain knowledge, innovations and practices of indigenous and local communities embodying traditional lifestyles relevant for the conservation and sustainable use of biological diversity and promote their wider application with the approval and involvement of the holders of such knowledge, innovations and practices and encourage the equitable sharing of the benefits arising from the utilization of such knowledge, innovations and practices."[20] Given the complex range of relationships between multinational corporations and research organizations, national governments, indigenous source communities, and their cultural products—relationships that may be multiplied if a biological resource is available across geopolitical boundaries—it is difficult to ensure consistent protection for cultural groups. Even were the United States and other countries to ratify the CBD, the cultural rather than economic concerns of indigenous source communities might remain unaddressed.

The World Trade Organization (WTO), through discussions regarding the TRIPS Agreement, and the World Intellectual Property Organization (WIPO) are also considering the relationship between intellectual property protection and indigenous peoples' cultural products. These efforts may take the form of national legislation, as suggested by WIPO's Model Provisions for National Laws on the Protection of Expressions of Folklore Against Illicit Exploitation and Other Prejudicial Actions; the creation of databases of traditional knowledge that might be used to prevent patenting by outsiders; the international use of geographical indications to protect a range of cultural products; the creation of a *sui generis* international system of protection; or amendments to the TRIPS Agreement. While these efforts are in their early stages and the scope of protection is unlikely to extend beyond indigenous peoples, the 2001 Doha WTO Ministerial Declaration's call for further examination of the protection of traditional knowledge and folklore is a significant step toward increased recognition of the issue.[21] Similarly, UNESCO's inclusion of "knowledge and practices concerning nature and the universe" in its Convention for the Safeguarding of the Intangible Cultural Heritage indicates an expanded understanding of the scope of source-community activity.[22]

Whether synthetic or naturally occurring, cultural products are defined by their relationship to their source communities. This link between a group and its cultural expression requires communal effort, whether in the creation of the object or practice or in the adoption of a product for a significant purpose. It is this relationship, rather than the impermanent and evolving products themselves, that may be the primary candidate for protection.

EXCLUSIVITY AND COMMUNITY STATUS

Thus far we have categorized objects and activities according to the processes by which they are transformed into cultural products and the role of human endeavor in producing them. Perhaps the most important distinctions from the perspective of the source community, however, relate to the status and significance of the cultural products within the community. Cultural products may be considered private, secret, even sacred, or they may be everyday practices and items freely available to the outside public without restriction. An annual new year celebration according to one calendar may be marked by a religious ritual performed on behalf of an entire community by one individual, the details of which are known to only a few members of a priestly class, while the new year according to another calendar may be ushered in with fireworks and public parades. The outside discovery or appropriation of a private cultural product is likely to draw a more pronounced response from the source community than the appropriation of a public cultural product, which might even receive community approval.

Similarly, while cultural products typically begin life as accidental property outside the realm of commercial exchange, the source community may elect either to participate in or to oppose commodification of the product. While African Americans construct and sell made-to-order wedding brooms, the official Kwanzaa website carefully distinguishes between the positive value of *ujamaa*, or cooperative economics as it might be practiced by small-scale artists and vendors, and the incursions of the corporate world. According to the website, "The challenge, for the African American community as well as African communities everywhere is to resist the corporate commercialization of Kwanzaa; to reaffirm the essential meaning of Kwanzaa and refuse to cooperate with the corporate drive to dominate and redefine it and make it simply another holiday to maximize sales."[23] Similarly, the holders of traditional knowledge may choose to cooperate in licensing cultural products like medicinal herbs to pharmaceutical companies, or they may attempt to oppose the commodification of these products. Self-reflective community standards and beliefs may thus play an important role in the categorization and preservation of cultural products.

CULTURAL PRODUCTS, INTELLECTUAL PROPERTY, AND CULTURAL PROPERTY

The category of cultural products itself to some extent overlaps the established fields of both intellectual property and cultural property, but offers a different emphasis. As we have seen, intellectual property at common law is a protected category of intangible ideas embodied and reproduced in tangible form, while cultural products are the frequently unprotected expressions of shared values or experiences that are created and reproduced by a source community in either tangible or intangible form. The traditional category of cultural property also involves the embodiment of intangible cultural values, albeit in specific, unique objects. The inclusion of intangibles under the rubric of cultural property or "cultural heritage," to use the preferred term among historians, archaeologists, and anthropologists, is a more recent development.[24]

In a classic article on cultural property law, John Henry Merryman briefly defines cultural property as "objects of artistic, archaeological, ethnological, or historical interest."[25] Analyzing various definitions of culture, legal scholar Patty Gerstenblith notes that "the one constant is the physical embodiment of culture in tangible objects, which are generally classified as cultural property. Although these objects of cultural property undoubtedly symbolize different traditions, thoughts, and ideals, it is the objects themselves that remain with us through out the passage of time."[26] These understandings of traditional cultural property focus on unique objects of cultural importance and on their age, a factor that often results in the use of "antiquities" as a synonym for "cultural property." While the scope of cultural property law is expanding and the term "cultural heritage" is becoming increasingly common in legal circles as well, the use of the term "cultural property" and the distinction between traditional cultural property and frequently intangible cultural products nevertheless remain useful for rhetorical and analytical purposes.

The distinctions among intellectual property, cultural products, and traditional cultural property can be further understood with reference to architectural forms. The architectural plans for a new building are the intellectual property of their creator and are protected by copyright law. Although the architect necessarily makes reference to standard functional elements—walls, windows, a roof—the original aspects of the design as a whole belong to an individual or design team, just as an author combines existing words into a new work. Certain architectural forms associated with a particular group may also be cultural products, however. The Latin-cross design of a Western European church, with its long nave leading from the entrance to cross a shorter transept and finally reach the apse, is immediately familiar to many Christians. The design not only reproduces a primary symbol of the religion but, as with many sacred buildings, embodies the form of its rituals. In the words of Danish architect Steen Eiler Rasmussen, the central axis of a cathedral "indicates the direction of the great religious processions and of the attention of the worshipers. From pillar to pillar, from arch to arch, from vault to vault, the eye follows the great, solemn rhythm throughout the church."[27] However often it is replicated, and whatever its decorative flourishes, the design remains that of a distinctive cultural product. By contrast, a particular architectural structure of historical or artistic importance is neither simply the intellectual property of its creator nor a replicable cultural product, but cultural property. In this regard, the Greek Parthenon, as well as the great sculptures removed from its façade in the early nineteenth century, exemplifies cultural property protected under both national laws governing landmarks and international treaties.[28] Thus, intellectual property, cultural products, and traditional cultural property all incorporate valuable intangible components that represent the spirit of their creators.

When these three categories overlap, they may either coexist harmoniously or cause tension within a community. The Vietnam Veterans Memorial in Washington, D.C., designed by Maya Lin while she was still a Yale undergraduate, ignited a controversy that reflected not only Americans' ambivalence about the war itself but also our shared expectations regarding a monument or memorial.[29] Most of the monuments on the Mall are white, neoclassical, figurative, and majestic— columns, obelisks, friezes, and statues are the vocabulary that Americans had come to expect in monuments, and we replicate them in state capitols and graveyards across the land. Lin's original design was black, modern, abstract, and humble, not remotely resembling our usual cultural products. Yet her design was selected to become an object of cultural property, a unique structure representing an element of American culture and a moment in our shared history. The award-winning submission described the plan as "meant not as a monument to the individual but rather, as a memorial [to] the men and women who died during this war, as a whole. . . . We the living are brought to a concrete realization of these deaths."[30] Vietnam veterans and others noted the absence of the usual heroic elements of a memorial in Lin's design and protested vehemently, calling the proposed structure a "black gash of shame." Ultimately the dispute resulted in a political compromise that added more familiar figurative and symbolic elements, in the form of a statue of three servicemen and an American flag, to the original design.[31] As constructed, the Vietnam Veterans Memorial thus embodies the genius of a gifted architect, the American public's understanding of what constitutes a memorial, and the goal of creating a unique and meaningful national symbol.

Both intellectual property law and traditional cultural property law attempt to protect such physical embodiments of intangible goods. Intellectual property, however, protects ideas that may be appropriated and replicated in tangible form coequal with the first embodiment. Cultural products are similarly replicable, although they need not appear in tangible form. By contrast, much traditional cultural property consists of unique, one-of-a-kind objects; mere copies or counterfeits are of comparatively little value. Melina Mercouri, former Greek minister of culture, has referred to the Parthenon (Elgin) marbles as "our history" and "our soul."[32] Greece would not be satisfied if its demand for return of the marbles from Britain were answered with an artist's copy, nor is the British Museum willing to accept a substitute.[33] All three categories thus involve protection of intangible human creations that may be embodied in tangible form, although cultural products typically remain unprotected by law.

The nature of the intangible good varies among intellectual property, cultural products, and cultural property. In the case of cultural products and cultural property, the intangible good is the *Volksgeist,* or the self-imagination of a particular community. Intellectual property, by contrast, protects an innovative idea in the form of a new invention or artistic creation.

Intellectual property, cultural products, and traditional cultural property also offer different paradigms of authorship. While objects of cultural property are often created by an individual, like intellectual property, their status as cultural property derives from community recognition rather than Romantic genius. Cultural products share the element of communal recognition found in cultural property, but their original authorship is likely to have a communal or participatory structure as well.

Finally, each of the three categories displays quite different temporal requirements. As we have seen, intellectual property law protects only new ideas, and then for a limited period of time, while traditional cultural property law protects historical objects that have acquired cultural significance over time. In other words, intellectual property protects the new and innovative; cultural property protects the old and venerated. Cultural products derive from the ongoing expression and development of community symbols and practices, and thus they are neither new nor old but in a sense both. Any extension of legal protection to cultural products must take into account the singular configuration of this category of intangible property.

CHAPTER 5

Claiming Community
Ownership via Authenticity

> The figures on a [totem] pole are an outline of the
> story that goes with the pole. If it's a serious
> traditional story that is family history and belongs
> to your uncle or grandfather, for instance, you have
> to check with them to get their permission. . . .
> Nowadays many carvers use a general story, a
> public story, because the poles they're doing are
> carved for everyone.
>
> —Norman Tait, Nisga'a carver

CANAL STREET IN lower Manhattan, as the informed
tourist knows, is perhaps the nation's most concentrated retail outlet
for counterfeit merchandise and bootleg recordings. "Prada" bags,
"Fendi" wallets, "Chanel" sunglasses, "Rolex" watches, and DVD
copies of the blockbuster movie opening next week are all available
for remarkably small sums of cash. Even occasional crackdowns on the
flow of illegal merchandise, like the public destruction of confiscated
goods by a fleet of bulldozers in a Mexico City soccer stadium in
1994, do not seem to lessen the availability of inexpensive copies of
designer merchandise or other items.[1] Some of these products are
obvious fakes, with misspelled labels and distorted logos, while others
are nearly identical to the versions sold in Madison Avenue boutiques.

Why, then, are many knowledgeable consumers willing to pay
many times the street price for "real" luxury goods? The answer may
lie in the presumption of quality associated with legitimate merchandise, which is a key element of trademark law, or with a certain dis-

comfort associated with flouting the law. It may also be, however, that "authentic" goods–even when compared with virtually identical and much less expensive counterfeits–offer the purchaser a certain intangible value. The consumer who shuns Canal Street and opts to purchase the genuine article advertises her individual ability to distinguish real from mass-produced fake, her aristocratic intolerance for invisible flaws, her appreciation of fine craftsmanship, her economic position, and her membership in an elite society welcomed into the most exclusive retail venues. For the creator of the original product, an assertion of authenticity may thus compensate for an inability to secure or protect ownership of an embodied idea, creation, or design.

Because cultural products, like intellectual properties, are noncompetitive, intangible goods, it is often difficult or impossible to control their proliferation and use. In the absence of legal intervention to establish property rights, the question instead revolves around who is entitled to assign form and meaning, or at least a semiotic range, to a cultural product; who can assert a right to define the normative use of a cultural product; or who may give permission to copy a cultural product. The issue of control does not arise when source-community members have exclusive possession of their cultural products and use them in a consensual manner. Rather, conflict may appear in the case of contested or nonconforming use by source-community members or in the case of any use by nonmembers.

In the unregulated, intangible world of cultural products, unenforceable assertions of ownership can instead take the form of claims of "authenticity." Among the currently accepted definitions of "authentic" offered by the *Oxford English Dictionary* are "[r]eally proceeding from its reputed source or author," as opposed to counterfeit, and "[e]ntitled to acceptance or belief, as being in accordance with fact."[2] This objective sense of authenticity combines the ideas of original and authoritative, the result of an evolution of meaning that linked the originally disparate roots of "author" and "authentic."[3] The usefulness of this concept lies not only in its ability to link cultural products with their source communities in a form of affiliative ownership but also in establishing source communities as the definitive repository of cultural meaning with respect to those products.

The philosophical quest for authenticity in human life, as expressed by Søren Kierkegaard, offers a more subjective, self-referential understanding of the term. The authentic in this sense exists outside of general social or ethical norms and is manifested instead in the search for personal identity and meaning.[4] Martin Heidegger internalizes the understanding of authenticity, literally *eigentlichkeit,* or "own-ness," suggesting that an individual can achieve his or her "ownmost possibility" through conscious insight and resolute action.[5] Communities, too, can engage in a version of this process of reflexive authentication. Cultural products may originate as accidental property, but the collective awareness and intent of the source community transform them into objects and practices that instantiate the authenticity of the community and are themselves authentic only if they maintain a legitimate link to the community. In a discussion of aesthetics, journalist and author Virginia Postrel suggests that the concept of authenticity is most useful as a signal of subjective identity, a match between form and desire.[6] Source communities are thus called upon to take an active and ongoing role in confirming and maintaining themselves through the authenticity of their cultural products.

While a source community may be unable to prevent nonconforming use or outsider appropriation, it can at least charge that the modified or stolen cultural product is not original or genuine. Such arguments are reminiscent of advertisements from the cola wars, in which Coke claimed to be "the real thing," while Pepsi assured consumers that they had chosen "the right one, baby, uh-huh." Coca-Cola and Pepsi are both registered trademarks, but the formulas for their respective beverages are legally protected only as easily reverse-engineered trade secrets, a situation that gives rise to a need for secondary protection. The rhetoric of authenticity performs much the same social function as property ownership, placing the claimant group in a position superior to all others with respect to the item in question. Recall the example of Kwanzaa: while Karenga's creation has become a cultural product through his gift to the African-American community, Organization Us preserves the holiday's authenticity through an "official" website with multiple references to the founder.[7]

Claims of authenticity rest upon multiple criteria, the significance of which may be interpreted in various ways. The characteristics of the cultural product itself, the identity of its creator, and the relationship of the product to the source community all affect the likelihood that the general public will perceive the product as part of or belonging to a cultural group. Anthropologist Brian Spooner, in an insightful essay on authenticity and oriental carpets, emphasizes the role of the Western outsider or consumer in bestowing the mantle of authenticity on the work of others. Although objective factors like continuity of form and design may contribute to a perception of authenticity, Spooner describes the actual negotiation as taking place apart from the source community. "We talk commonly as though our idea of authenticity depended on our reconstruction of the history of the craft, which in turn depended on a combination of the material facts before us in the carpets and in scanty textual and archaeological sources. . . . [U]nderlying the discussion is an interest in the possibility that the evolving constellation of social relations in our complex society generates a need for authenticity, which leads people to cast around for cultural material on which to work out the obsession for distinction."[8]

In the context of modern American life, however, many cultural products appear to the general public not as foreign imports from distant source communities but as glimpsed, overheard, or shared elements of domestic source communities. The creators of cultural products thus have a much greater opportunity to participate in the negotiation of their authenticity than in the example Spooner offers. Given these complexities, the concept may be more appropriately one of plural "authenticities" than of one authoritative judgment.

PRODUCT AUTHENTICITY

An initial determination of authenticity may begin with close observation of the product itself. The quality, craftsmanship, materials, color, tone, gesture, pattern, or design of a cultural product all offer clues as to whether it might be considered genuine. A prospective buyer of one of the Turkmen pile carpets that Spooner discusses might lift a corner of the rug and rub it between her fingers, spread it out under the light to see its colors more clearly, turn it over to examine the weave, attempt to identify its age, consult a guide or catalogue regarding the design, and inquire among collectors about the reputation of the merchant. If she is satisfied that this carpet sufficiently resembles the Platonic form of its class, in both its method of creation and its final embodiment, then she will consider the carpet to be authentic and may begin to bargain for it.

Some cultural products, however, appear in multiple competing forms, leading to disputed claims of authenticity. Barbecue lovers from North Carolina typically bathe their pulled pork in spicy vinegar, while those from Kansas City are more likely to slather beef with a sweet tomato-based sauce. In this case, basic agreement on slow cooking in a specially prepared pit or its modern equivalent preserves the core concept of barbecue, and the use of regional appellations as necessary prevents a war between the states. Nevertheless, assertions that a particular style of barbecue sauce is the real one are best made among like-minded partisans.

Claims of product authenticity are also problematic to the extent that they cast cultural products as eternal and unchanging. If a German-American grandmother spent hours grating cabbage for sauerkraut, does it devalue the embodied product's cultural association if her granddaughter achieves the same result with a Cuisinart? Adds or omits caraway seeds? Substitutes gourmet Savoy cabbage? Or even serves a canned version? By nature, cultural products develop through community participation over time. It would be incongruous to recognize as authentic only those frozen at a particular moment. The products themselves are nevertheless a natural starting point in a determination of authenticity.

SOURCE-COMMUNITY AUTHENTICITY

An alternative understanding of authenticity focuses on the provenience of the cultural product rather than on the specific elements of the product or the process of its embodiment. This concept of certification according to source informs the laws of geographical indication that protect certain regional handicrafts in Mexico, over a hundred local cheeses in Europe, and distinctive wines and spirits throughout the world.[9] In the case of other cultural products, the members of a source community may be scattered rather than living and working together in a particular location, and thus authorship may be a more effective measure than geography. Under this scheme, if a product were attributable to a member of a source community's diaspora, it would be "authentic."

In modern society, individuals regularly belong to more than one unincorporated culture group and may move in and out of such communities over time. A gay, mixed-race, Christian Scientist fencing champion and cattle rancher may choose to identify primarily with one group or another, despite certain parameters set forth by society, and may at some point abandon a particular community and its cultural products. The communities themselves nevertheless have a continuing existence, as well as the ability to define membership.

The prototypes for community-oriented certification of authenticity are public and private efforts to protect Native American cultural products from widespread counterfeiting. The Indian Arts and Crafts Act of 1990 strengthens the power of the Indian Arts and Crafts Board, originally established in 1935, to "promote the economic welfare of Indian tribes and Indian individuals through the development of Indian arts and crafts and the expansion of the market for the products of Indian art and craftsmanship," through *inter alia* the creation and registration of trademarks. The Act also increases the civil and criminal penalties for misrepresentation of goods as Native American.[10] While the complex and troubled history of federal recognition of Native American tribes, together with the widely varying criteria for tribal citizenship, has resulted in harsh criticism of the Act's inability to protect all artists claiming Native American descent, the basic intent of the Act is sound.[11]

In the private sector, the nonprofit Indian Arts and Crafts Association, established in 1974, "works to stop fraud and abuse within the market for Indian art through education, publicity, authentication, and use of [its] logo to indicate certified ethical businesses."[12] Members of the association include not only Native American artists but also wholesale and retail art dealers, collectors, and museums willing to sign a code of ethics. Some future combination of the enforcement mechanisms available under federal law and the preservation of autonomy through private community actions may ultimately prove the best guarantee of authenticity, at least for commodified cultural products.

Native American law scholar Carole Goldberg has argued persuasively that the Native American example should not serve as a universal model because other racial and ethnic groups entered North America as individual slaves or immigrants and lack sovereign political structures; nevertheless, the efforts to protect Native American cultural products offer important lessons for other groups.[13] If source communities wish to signal the authenticity of their cultural products, they might facilitate protection by formalizing the often implicit or mutually understood criteria for membership. Aspects of this process would no doubt create conflict, as particular individuals were excluded and their abilities to self-identify with a particular group were diminished. Such disputes might even invite First Amendment analysis, as an individual's right to free expression clashed with a group's freedom of association.

In most cases, however, the problem is no more intractable than defining membership in the Daughters of the American Revolution, a small religious sect, a gay men's chorale, a Czech polka band, or the local numismatic society. Levels of membership or source-community "adoptions" are also possible, much the way the Anglo-Saxon Protestant elite appears to have recognized the talent of Jewish clothing and housewares designer Ralph Lauren as an official purveyor of Eastern establishment or country-club style. (One biography, *Genuine Authentic*, is at pains to uncover Lauren's heritage and chronicle his carefully constructed and maintained cultural identity.)[14] Privacy is not at issue, moreover, as an individual would only need to become a card-carrying member of a particular culture group if she wished to assert publicly the authenticity of her interpretation of that group's cultural products. Assertions of authenticity on the basis of source-community authorship may thus have the potential to protect both cultural products and their creators, while augmenting judgments based on the products themselves.

Authenticity of a Central Authority

Although the source community as a whole participates in the creation of a cultural product, authenticity may also be traced to a particular leading figure within the community. Without Chez Panisse owner Alice Waters, there might be no California cuisine–and no genre of menu writing that calls for a recital of each ingredient and invokes the organic farmer who raised it. Even creations that begin life eligible for protection as intellectual properties attributable to one individual may ultimately be declared cultural products and their inventor a prophet.

When a shaman, a chef, a musician, or a storyteller receives credit for inspiring, exemplifying, or preserving a cultural product, moreover, her students and practitioners of the art may consider only her interpretation of the tradition to be authentic. The centuries-old division between Sunni and Shiite Muslims, for example, originated in a dispute over the identity of the legitimate heir of Muhammad. Charismatic group leaders and even well-known community members may lend an aura of authenticity to a cultural product.

The need for a central authority to buttress claims of authenticity is particularly great when the cultural product itself is multifaceted and diffuse. Yoga, one of six systems of Indian philosophy, is an ancient Hindu tradition that informs meditative spiritual practices throughout Asia.[15] Often translated as "yoke" or "union," yoga is a collective term for a range of paths to spiritual transcendence or union with the object of contemplation.[16] The forms of physical activity associated with yoga are interpretations of hatha-yoga, the "forceful yoga" of the body. Like other forms of yoga, it teaches the practitioner to transcend the self, in this instance by developing the body and preparing it for an ecstatic state.[17] It is also an exercise fad in the United States.

The complexity of yoga practice as not only a philosophy but also a system of exercise lends itself to the establishment of schools of yoga with celebrated teachers and devoted students. Indeed, much of the early interest in yoga in America crystallized around Indian teachers like B.K.S. Iyengar, who first made the trip to the United States in the 1960s and inspired students to travel to India for further study.[18] Today, Los Angeles– and New York–based teachers have developed their own trademarked styles of practice and well-publicized followings—a *New Yorker* cartoon depicts a woman inquiring, "Which celebrities do this type of yoga?"[19] A pair of articles in the suddenly ubiquitous *Yoga Journal* reflects on the Indian and Indian-American communities' reaction to the popularity of yoga among mainstream Americans, capturing the ambivalent feelings of source-community members who grew up with yoga as a way of life or family practice rather than a constellation of celebrity teachers, practitioners, and product designers.[20] In the American popular imagination, however, authentic yoga and Indian culture itself are virtually inseparable from these larger-than-life figures. In addition to Nuala sweats, a Gucci mat, and a Marc Jacobs bag, the aspiring American yogi or yogini needs to find the right guru.[21] In the absence of such leading figures, who come to represent the source community as a whole, the determination of authenticity would be a far more complex process.

COMMODIFICATION AND THE ESTABLISHMENT OF AUTHENTICITY

Although outsiders' commodification of a cultural product without the authorization of the source community may dilute or destroy the product or its identification with the source community, limited communal commodification may instead enhance the value of the product by forestalling inferior copies and providing an authentic version. The source community may intend this production and distribution for its members only, or the product may be made available to the public. Such voluntary commercial efforts provide an opportunity for education regarding the cultural product and its normative use. In addition, they reinforce the relationship between the source community and its tangible or intangible expressions.

The birth of extreme sports, with their distinctly noncommercial, rebel aesthetic, occurred in Santa Monica, California, in the early 1970s. Modern freestyle skateboarding, as chronicled in the documentary *Dogtown and Z-Boys,* began in an inauspicious area known as Dogtown.[22] Its early practitioners were a group of young men and a few women who spent most of their time surfing or proving their worthiness to surf a small stretch of the coast blighted by the ruins of a failed theme park. When the surf was not breaking, the local kids practiced their moves on skateboards, surfing the concrete and asphalt waves of the streets of Dogtown and startling passing cars and pedestrians. Not content with conquering the streets, the skaters sought new venues—including a schoolyard that had conveniently banked asphalt walls sloping down to a flat playground surface.

In response to this newly discovered terrain, the skaters began to develop a unique style that combined surfing with skateboarding. They imitated stylish surfers and crouched low to the ground, using their outstretched hands to execute sharp turns before shooting up the embankments and gathering speed again on the way down. Aerial moves consisted of grinding pivots on the cusp of the wall, with as many as three of the four skateboard wheels leaving the ground. After a short time, the skaters sought still more challenging venues and found them in the empty swimming pools that had resulted from a long-term drought in the region. In these empty pools in the wealthy enclaves of Santa Monica, which were scouted out by guerilla skateboarders who took turns watching for the police, an aggressive new form of skating took shape.

Around this time, one of the owners of the Zephyr Productions Surf Shop, a meeting place for the Dogtown surfers, decided to help provide community for the kids he saw surfing and skating on the local streets. To this end, Jeff Ho sponsored two surf teams, one for established surfers and the other for the next generation. Ho and his partners were already iconoclasts, designing, manufacturing, and selling their own surfboards and other gear, which reflected the graffiti-covered urban aesthetic of the neighborhood and included technological innovations based on the designers' surfing prowess. When the junior surf team evolved into the Zephyr Competition Skate Team, complete with T-shirts and matching Vans shoes, the shop owners prepared to crush skateboarding stereotypes as well.

Competitions and celebrity acclaim followed as the Z-Boys, collectively and then individually, began to capitalize on their achievement. The team members sold their performances and their personalities, appearing live and on screen. The owners of the Zephyr shop entered into a partnership to produce skateboards commercially, creating some boards that ultimately found a place in the Smithsonian Institution. Craig Stecyk, an artist who decorated many of the surfboards and skateboards, became the Z-Boys' Boswell, submitting occasionally pseudonymous articles and photographs to *Skateboarder Magazine* to chronicle the rise of this new urban phenomenon, as well as the culture and the architectural landscape that had given birth to it.

As the phenomenon and the Z-Boys matured, the lure of individual sponsorship and other commercial deals grew, and the team members ultimately went their separate ways. The style and culture of skateboarding that they had established endured, however, and reports of the death of Dogtown were largely exaggerated. As Stecyk, writing as John Smythe, noted in 1979, "Can people involved with such a variety of activities be considered dead? Energy equaling life, I think not. What has happened is that Dogtown as we knew it has given way to the next phase. For instance, the name Dogtown is now 'trademarked.' The skaters, instead of walking, now drive imported cars. Some now carve for currency. Once unknown names are now famous ones. Dogtown has gone uptown; or more precisely, Uptown has gone Dogtown."[23] Rather than destroying Santa Monica–style skateboarding, the commodification of the sport with the consent of its star athletes allowed the culture to evolve and grow beyond the few square miles where it all began.

The life cycle of most fads is relatively short, and skateboarding declined in popularity after a period of time. A distinctive subculture inspired by the Z-Boys and their cultural heirs endured, however, and has conquered new terrain in the form of new maneuvers performed in dedicated skate parks, snowboarding, and even sky surfing.[24] Skaters' clothing, always less than preppie, has evolved and become baggier in response to both the sympathetic rebellion of hip-hop culture and the need for freedom of movement in executing ever more daring moves. Meanwhile, skateboards from the 1970s appear in contemporary galleries, and fashion stylists snap up vintage T-shirts and Vans, perhaps to "inspire" designers to send reworked versions of these colors and graphics down the runway.[25] While the Lost Boys have grown up, their documented performance style and their material culture remain true to their roots. Admittedly, not all tales of insider-approved commodification are equally beneficial to the source community, and the demands of commercialization may harm the cultural products or even destroy the community itself. Without the early commodification of Dogtown skateboarding, however, the authenticity of its progeny would be difficult to measure.

DANGERS OF AUTHENTICITY

Like commodification, the use of authenticity to support or replace assertions of ownership and to bind a cultural product to its source community has the potential to harm as well as to benefit the community. When members of a cultural group disagree about the authenticity of a cultural product, there may be pressure to disown the product or shun the individuals who participated in its creation as themselves inauthentic representatives of the spirit of the community or even traitors to the community.[26] When successful, such efforts by authoritative figures within the community to police its expressions can impede the natural evolution of cultural products or even the culture itself. On a more general level, feminist legal scholar Berta Hernandez-Truyol notes that not all voices within a community are equally respected, warning against the persistence of systematic discrimination against women behind the veil of cultural relativism.[27] Authenticity under certain conditions may be used to legitimate morally unacceptable perspectives and silence dissenting views, particularly when basic human rights and freedoms are implicated. Although these are extremely important concerns, they do not negate the potential usefulness of authenticity as a tool for cultural protection. Such dangers do remind us, however, that authenticity is a more valuable concept if it recognizes that a single cultural group may speak with multiple voices.

Another danger inherent in the pursuit of authenticity, and particularly in the commodification of cultural products, is the simplification of objects and performances for public consumption. Recall that authenticity is a label applied only when a cultural product comes into contact with the outside world; just as a fish is the last to recognize water, members of a source community have little need to analyze uncontested everyday objects and activities. By joining in the process of negotiation by which outsiders establish the authenticity of another's product, however, community members may be tempted to serve up their goods in modified form. As Spooner notes in his discussion of oriental carpets, "The more we reveal our need for authenticity to the Turkmen, the more they frustrate our search by adapting their wares in ways they image should please us."[28] Since cultural

products are not static, some alterations are the natural result of interaction and inspiration; others may be the result of an overzealous
attempt to standardize and fix a product's authenticity in the public
eye. In proceeding to add flexible claims of authenticity to the traditional rhetoric of ownership, then, source communities and perhaps
the legal system must proceed with caution.

Authenticity Marks and Marketing

Authenticity is a powerful marketing tool, and one that appeals to
the current generation of cynical consumers exposed since birth to the
siren song of corporate advertising. With the advent of the internet-
based virtual world, the quality of authenticity appears to be particularly
valuable or persuasive. The ability to harness claims of authenticity and
convince the mainstream community that source-community embodiments of a cultural product are superior to copies is a potential source
of both economic and social power. In addition, strong assertions of
authenticity may decrease the incentives for outside appropriation and
thus prevent the dilution of cultural products. For those products that
the source community is willing to commodify, authenticity may offer
protection nearly equivalent to intellectual property ownership.

Source communities attempting to assert the authenticity of their
cultural products may either engage in direct marketing or rely on in-
termediary outlets. Ten Thousand Villages, a nonprofit program of the
Mennonite church, invokes the value of authenticity to sell cultural
products from the developing world and help provide food, education, health care, and housing to artisans and their families. This
charity, with dozens of retail shops throughout North America, offers
literature describing featured source communities and notes, "In our
mass production world, villages are still a setting of individualized creation of authentic handicrafts. Making handicrafts is a way to pass
one's culture and skills to the next generation. But as the outside
world pushes at the village, taking its natural resources and often its
children, it becomes more and more difficult to live the village way of
life." The sales material goes on to request, "When your own cultural
celebrations (birthdays, weddings and holidays) call for gift-giving,
choose gifts from Ten Thousand Villages."[29] Sympathetic consumers

are lured by the promise of authenticity and then given the opportunity to participate in and even rescue the lifestyle of the source community through purchase of its cultural products. Even the prospective buyer's own culture receives a token of respect, as authenticity is source-specific and does not negate the importance of the outsider's own celebrations. Much the way that Starbucks promotes its Fair Trade Blend of coffee as a socially conscious alternative to our usual caffeine-laced indulgences, Ten Thousand Villages employs the promise of authenticity to sweeten the usual burden of charitable donations and uplift the materialism of gift shopping while at the same time protecting artists and their cultural creations.

Even the marketing of cultural products designed primarily for the source community itself can benefit from assertions of authenticity. For many members of the Jewish community, the consumption of kosher food products is a religious requirement rather than merely an optional expression of communal values. The authenticity of a kosher product is thus a matter of some importance, and both state laws dealing directly with kosher certification and federal trademark law have been invoked to assure consumers that the products they purchase meet their standards. The United States Patent and Trademark Office lists over two hundred live trademarks for products described as kosher, some of which are simple assertions by the manufacturer that the product is kosher and others that indicate the approval of a particular rabbi or rabbinical organization.[30] The letter "K" alone is not one of these registered marks, as in the absence of other design elements it is not sufficiently distinctive to indicate the source of the goods or their certification. A manufacturer wishing to advertise its products as kosher without an outside inspection might thus simply mark its goods with a "K." Despite this loophole, educated consumers are able to identify the mark or marks of trustworthy companies or certifying organizations and select grocery items that satisfy their own criteria for purity and authenticity. The use of kosher marks thus accommodates multiple perspectives within the community, allows members of the community to recognize authenticity on the basis of authoritative figures or organizations, and reinforces the concept of community control through authenticity.

Other source communities seeking to police the authenticity of their commodified cultural products might also seek assistance within federal trademark law. Indeed, the law might be modified to create a category of "authenticity marks," similar to the certification marks of standards organizations or the collective marks of membership associations. As the Patent and Trademark Office has already supervised the creation of a special registry for Native American symbols apart from trademarks, it might even be possible to eliminate the standard registration requirement of use in trade, provided that a suitable justification were available under the Commerce Clause.[31] This legal recognition of authenticity would offer a middle ground between source-community ownership of a full bundle of property rights and the current legal vacuum. Such marks could be registered by source-community organizations that demonstrate a valid association with the word or symbol—admittedly a contentious issue—and then affixed to commodified cultural products. The absence of an authenticity mark would alert potential consumers of cultural products to a lack of association with the presumed source community. This compromise between ownership and anarchy does not settle the conflicts associated with contested internal use or objectionable external appropriation, but it is one potential vehicle for recognizing the significance of cultural products.

AUTHENTICITY THUS JOINS ownership as a secondary tool for protecting against the appropriation of intangible goods. Where economic ownership is impractical or potentially harmful, affiliative ownership can preserve the connection between source community and cultural product, thus facilitating the performance and preservation of communal identity. Like reevaluation of the authorship paradigm or of the temporal requirements associated with intellectual property ownership, the process of defining authenticity suggests a possible route for extending legal protection to cultural products.

CHAPTER 6

Family Feuds

When I had looked around a little,
I turned toward my feet and saw two figures
    so close together
that the hair on their heads was tangled.
"Tell me, you whose chests are squeezed
    together,"
I said, "who are you?" And they bent their
    necks back,
and when they had lifted their faces to me,
their eyes, which were wet before,
dripped tears over their eyelids, and the cold
    froze
the tears between their lids and locked them
    together again.
No vice has ever bound board to board
so tightly; and so like two rams
they butted their heads together, so much
    anger overcame them.

—Dante Alighieri

FOR IRISH AMERICANS, Saint Patrick's Day is an opportunity to celebrate civic, cultural, historical, political, and social achievements with a public parade. For gay and lesbian Irish Americans, March 17 is also a day of protest. Ever since the Ancient Order of Hibernians denied a request from the Irish Lesbian and Gay Organization (ILGO) to march in New York City's 1991 parade, the debate over who is entitled to assert authentic Irish-American identity and participate in the parade has made national headlines. The 1991 compromise, in which New York Mayor David Dinkins persuaded the parade organizers to allow the gay and lesbian contingent to march without a banner as guests of another group and then marched alongside them himself, was short-lived. Along the parade route, the mayor was pelted with taunts and cans of beer, and John Cardinal O'Connor refused to descend the steps of Saint Patrick's Cathedral to greet him. After the parade, the African-American mayor commented, "It is strange that what is now my most vivid experience of mob hatred came not in the South but in New York—and was directed against me, not because I was defending the rights of African Americans but of gay and lesbian Americans."[1] Prominent Irish Americans, including columnist Anna Quindlen, excoriated the Hibernians for perpetuating the stereotype of "the small-minded Irishman" with their discriminatory stance.[2] The battle for control of the two-century-old parade nevertheless continued into the courtroom.

Meanwhile, in Boston, members of the gay community rallied to ILGO's cause, forming the Irish-American Gay, Lesbian, and Bisexual Group of Boston (GLIB) in order to march in the Saint Patrick's Day–Evacuation Day parade. The origins of this event lie not only in a religious festival commemorating the patron saint of Ireland but also in George Washington's 1776 military victory leading to the evacuation of British troops and sympathizers from the city.[3] While the New York parade might be characterized as a religious celebration, despite the finding of the New York City Commission on Human Rights that the parade is "a secular event which is a celebration of a broad range of values surrounding Irish heritage," the Boston parade includes an indisputably secular, patriotic theme.[4] The South Boston Allied War Veterans Council, which receives an annual permit to organize the parade, nonetheless denied GLIB's request to participate. According to the Council and longtime member John J. "Wacko" Hurley, their "decision to exclude groups with sexual themes merely formalized that the Parade expresses traditional religious and social values."[5]

Like its New York counterpart, GLIB sought assistance from the judicial system, invoking the Massachusetts public-accommodations law. For a time, it appeared that GLIB might succeed where ILGO had not. The trial court, unpersuaded by the probability that homosexual individuals had marched in existing parade contingents over the years, found clear violation of the public-accommodations law. In addition, after examining the Council's inconsistent and casual practices regarding admission to the parade, the trial court concluded that the parade was so broadly inclusive as to lack an expressive purpose under the First Amendment. These findings led to a permanent injunction allowing GLIB to march, which the Supreme Judicial Court of Massachusetts upheld.[6] The U.S. Supreme Court, however, had not yet spoken.

Writing for a unanimous Court, Justice David Souter took the position that parades are inherently expressive and thus entitled to broad First Amendment protection. The opinion states, "Real 'parades are public dramas of social relations, and in them performers define who can be a social actor and what subjects and ideas are available for communication and consideration. . . .' Hence, we use the word 'parade' to indicate marchers who are making some sort of collective point, not just to each other but to bystanders along the way."[7] Even the relatively vague and unarticulated expression of the Boston parade is covered by the First Amendment under the Court's ruling, which does not require that expressive acts have a "narrow, succinctly articulable message" in order to qualify for protection.[8] Because GLIB wished to express a distinct message of its own, the opinion functionally treated any attempt to force the Council to include GLIB as a parade unit as tantamount to putting words in the Council's mouth.[9] The state supreme court's application of the public-accommodations law, having thus run afoul of the First Amendment, stood little chance. If a parade organizer chooses to exclude a particular group or message, that decision receives constitutional protection, regardless of state laws to the contrary.

Whether or not this opinion represents sound First Amendment jurisprudence, its pattern of constitutional analysis is unable to encompass the complex social relations underlying contested internal control over cultural products. The legal battle over ILGO's and GLIB's participation in their respective cities' parades may have ended with the Supreme Court's decision, but the political battle did not. Protesters still line parade routes, and the decision by New York's mayor regarding whether, when, and with whom to march down

Fifth Avenue still receives public scrutiny. Parade organizers likewise attempt to use the parade to police the boundaries of community membership. As a cultural product, Saint Patrick's Day has evolved from modest religious roots in Ireland to a major display of Irish-American civic pride, yet the organizations in control of this annual event have attempted to halt its continued transformation and to limit the scope of community authorship.[10]

As in the case of Saint Patrick's Day parades, contested or nonconforming internal use of a cultural product occurs when members of the source community disagree as to a particular expression or evolution of their collaborative creation. Such differences of opinion may result in accusations that a member or segment of the community does not authentically represent its nature, has betrayed the community, or has devalued or even defiled the community's cultural products. The gay and lesbian organizations' application to join the New York and Boston parades, the curbside protests, and the existence of alternative parades all indicate a basic disagreement as to the criteria for membership in good standing in the Irish-American community and its public celebrations. As we shall see, other internal disputes revolve around the characterization of a community in the public forum, the normative use or meaning of a cultural product, and the commodification or distribution of a cultural product.

PUBLIC IMAGE OF THE
SOURCE COMMUNITY

Among the most contested cultural products within a source community are those that define the community in the national consciousness. Italian Americans over the past century have paid their identity tax in the form of cuisine, opera, and images of the Mafia. From *The Godfather* to *The Sopranos*, neckless male characters in pinstripes and pinkie rings have defined a cultural group with ponderous phrases about blood and honor. Some Italian Americans, however, contest the way in which these fictional images perpetuate a stereotype of ignorance and criminal violence.

Such community objections to film portrayals date to the early twentieth century, when the motion-picture industry engaged in rigorous self-censorship through the Production Code to avoid offending the sensibilities of both domestic and international audiences. The Code required that "no picture shall be produced that tends to indicate bigotry or hatred among people of differing races, religions, or national origins," and it further admonished that "[t]he history, institutions, prominent people and citizenry of other nations shall be represented fairly."[11] In the 1932 film *Scarface*, based on the story of Al Capone, this injunction is honored by a brief segment in which an older Italian immigrant laments the "shame" that the glorification of criminality in the media brings to the Italian-American community.[12]

Over time the Code, combined with pressure from foreign governments and American immigrant groups, virtually eliminated both foreign villains and explicit connections between organized crime and ethnicity, at least until World War II and the shift in American perceptions. Even comedic portrayals were subject to scrutiny, although some managed to slip through the cracks and offend their targets. In 1937, the Italian government (representing a distinct but related source community) went so far as to ban the Fred Astaire movies *Top Hat*, which included an Italian musician cutting somewhat less than a *bella figura*, and *The Gay Divorcee*, with its caricature of an Italian professional co-respondent. Although some in the industry felt that the insistence on positive images had gone too far, Hollywood nevertheless became more circumspect in its representation of nationality. In the 1939 film *The Roaring Twenties*, the gangster "Nick Brown" is played by the fair-complexioned Paul Kelly, does not speak with an Italian accent, and is not identified as a member of the Mafia—even though he spends much of his time on screen eating spaghetti.[13]

The decline of the Hollywood studio system in the 1950s led to the reappearance of explicitly Italian gangsters in films, and *The Godfather* in 1972 broke new ground by elaborating the ethnicity of its characters. As one scholar has noted in her examination of "Italianicity" (using Roland Barthes' term for embedded codes that speak to the cultural knowledge of the audience) in the movie and its sequels, Italian-American culture offered raw material particularly well suited to the fantasies and anxieties of its mainstream audience. The perceived deterioration of American families and the mistrust of governmental

authority instilled in viewers a desire for the intense bonds of the
Corleone family and the lionhearted strength of its patriarch and his
unambiguous code of honor. Even the largely homogenous ethnicity
depicted on screen arguably appealed to white audiences concerned
about the effects of integration and the civil rights movement.[14] Italian Americans themselves, living outside this two-dimensional landscape, had no such need to mythologize a criminal stereotype that had
led to persistent discrimination. Indeed, Mario Puzo wrote the original crime novel only after his earlier attempts at chronicling the Italian-American immigrant experience met with commercial failure,
and Francis Ford Coppola agreed to direct a movie based on the
"trash" script only to save his nearly bankrupt independent studio.[15]
Nevertheless, *The Godfather* created a myth that was embraced by
generic America.

Italian Americans remain divided regarding their public association with fictionalized mafiosi. On the one hand, family ties, loyalty,
honor, and power are desirable attributes; on the other, violence, vul-
garity, sexism, anti-intellectualism, and criminality are not. This debate
has taken on new life with the success of the HBO television series
The Sopranos. As a result, officials in both New York and New Jersey
have denied the series permission to film on public property, citing its
negative portrayal of an ethnic group.[16] In addition, when New York
mayor Michael Bloomberg invited two members of the cast to march
with him in the 2002 Columbus Day Parade, the organizers promptly
informed him that they were not welcome. After a brief skirmish in
court, the mayor chose to skip the parade and take his guests to an
Italian restaurant in the Bronx instead. Italian-American public figures
weighed in on both sides of the issue, with author Gay Talese affirming his commitment to the First Amendment rights of the show's creators but asking, "[W]ould Al Jolson in blackface singing 'Mammy' be
appropriate for a Martin Luther King parade?"[17] Former organized-
crime prosecutor and mayor Rudolph Giuliani, by contrast, urged
"some Italian-Americans to be less sensitive."[18] (In his 2002 book,
Giuliani shows greater awareness of the problem but concludes that
"the way forward was not to be afraid of the word 'Mafia,' but to use it
and explain what any reasonable person already knows: that the Mafia

is made up of an extremely small percentage of Italians and Italian Americans. It's roughly the same percentage in which every ethnic group commits crimes. Ultimately, 'Mafia' says only that Italians and Italian Americans are human beings. Once we acknowledge that, we take much of the mystique out of it.")[19]

A Chicago-based organization, the American Italian Defense Association (AIDA), moved beyond public debate and political pressure to pursue judicial action against *The Sopranos*. The Individual Dignity Clause of the Illinois Constitution provides, "To promote individual dignity, communications that portray criminality, depravity or lack of virtue in, or that incite violence, hatred, abuse or hostility toward, a person or group of persons by reason of or by reference to religious, racial, ethnic, national or regional affiliation are condemned."[20] According to AIDA, represented by legal scholar Michael Pollelle and attorney Enrico Mirabelli, the television series breaches this clause with respect to Italian Americans. Although the organization sought neither monetary damages nor an injunction against the showing of the program, it requested a declaratory judgment regarding the series' violation of the Illinois Constitution.[21] The trial court dismissed the action on the bases that AIDA had not demonstrated that it represents the interests of Italian Americans and that the Individual Dignity Clause is merely hortatory and does not create a private cause of action.[22] On appeal, a team of attorneys for Time Warner, who must have combed their firm directory for surnames ending in vowels, again convinced the court that AIDA's complaint "does not allege a 'distinct and palpable' injury to a particular Italian American that is traceable to *The Sopranos*. . . . There is absolutely no injury identified by AIDA that could possibly be prevented or redressed by any possible grant of relief."[23] Injuries to the public image of a source community, at least in Illinois, are apparently not justiciable.

Confronted with these charges of negative stereotyping, *The Sopranos*' producer and executive director—whose own grandfather changed the family name from "DeCesare" to "Chase"—responded that his detractors were in the minority among Italian Americans. He further expressed a desire to ask, "Are you an Italian American or are you an American? Because this is an American story."[24] This response to complaints of misuse of a communal image first attempts to divide the source community and marginalize the offended segment and then tries to dissolve the community's relationship to its cultural product altogether. Neither strategy appears likely to silence the debate.

The public image of a cultural group, whether portrayed in film, literature, or other media, is both the fluorescence of its cultural products and a cultural product in itself. The identity tax allows the general public a primary role in the creation of such images, but members of the source community are often active—and sometimes rivalrous—participants. In the absence of a framework for cooperative management of these products, neither side in a fraternal conflict has an incentive to reach agreement on the product's authenticity or associative value, even when it lies at the heart of the source community's public identity.

NORMATIVE USE OF A CULTURAL PRODUCT

After the 9/11 terrorist attacks, American flags spontaneously appeared on cars, homes, store windows, office buildings, and lapels. Flag-themed merchandise quickly followed, as everything from cell phones to Christmas ornaments sported some combination of stars and stripes, while advertisers and politicians wrapped their messages in patriotic bunting. This widespread enthusiasm for the flag as a cultural product echoed its popularity during earlier periods in American history, with one significant difference: in the twenty-first century, such myriad adaptations and expressive uses of the flag do not violate the law.

The early history of the American flag indicates a certain lack of attention to detail or cultural significance. On June 3, 1777, the Continental Congress received a request from a Native American nation for an American flag, together with three strings of wampum intended to cover its cost. Less than two weeks later, on June 14, Congress approved a design description that read, "Resolved that the Flag of the united states be 13 stripes alternate red and white, that the Union be 13 stars in a blue field representing a new constellation."[25] This description, which was unaccompanied by any graphic representation, failed to note the exact placement of the blue field with respect to the stripes, the number of points on the stars, or even the arrangement of the stars. The handiwork of Betsy Ross and others thus incorporated a fair degree of imaginative variation.

Although the flag was occasionally used as a decorative motif during the early years of the Republic, images of George Washington, pictures of the bald eagle, and depictions of a female Liberty and a female Columbia surpassed the flag in popularity until the Civil War. After the outbreak of hostilities, however, Old Glory appeared throughout the North and was enthusiastically adopted as a patriotic symbol and cultural product. In the South, this symbol was an object of physical assault and derision, acts punished by occupying Union troops where possible.[26]

When the war ended, the popularity of the victorious flag continued to increase in the North, where it was regularly transformed for political and commercial purposes. Candidates for office printed their names, slogans, and even pictures on the flag, while the Industrial Revolution and the rise in the mass production of consumer products led to a need for appealing packaging and trademarks, many of which incorporated flag themes. In the absence of any restrictions on the use of the flag, it appeared on umbrellas, scarves, fans, pillboxes, and quilts, as well as coal sacks, patent medicines, the costumes of prize fighters, paper used to wrap fruit and soap, whiskey barrels, and even toilet paper and porcelain urinals.[27] This indiscriminate use of the flag led Union veterans' groups and hereditary patriotic organizations like the Daughters of the American Revolution to launch a flag-protection movement.[28]

The initial efforts in the area of flag protection attacked commercial use of this "sacred" object, adding concerns regarding physical desecration of the flag by political rivals after several reported incidents during the 1896 campaign. The turn-of-the-century "age of anxiety," to borrow T. J. Jackson Lears' phrase, also sparked nativist concerns regarding threats to the flag by "un-American" immigrants, radicals, and trade unions.[29] State flag-desecration laws began to appear, although several convictions for commercial use of the flag were overturned by state courts on grounds that included the defendants' "personal liberty" to pursue their trades and their "existing property rights."[30] The U.S. Supreme Court, however, in the 1907 case of *Halter v. Nebraska*, upheld the constitutionality of a state law preventing the use of the flag in advertising.[31] In an opinion that celebrated the importance of the flag as a national symbol, the Court reasoned that Nebraska's legislative power extended to protecting the public good by prohibiting the commercial use of the flag, in this instance on a beer bottle. The argument that such laws denied property rights in the tangible object carrying the representation of the flag did not persuade the Court, as "such representation—which, in itself, cannot belong, as property, to an individual—has been placed on such thing in violation of the law . . . ."[32]

In 1917 the National Conference of Commissioners on Uniform State Laws urged the states to pass a uniform flag-desecration law, a recommendation later endorsed by the American Bar Association. By 1932, every state had a flag-desecration law—and neither Ralph Lauren nor Tommy Hilfiger, both of whom have used the flag in their clothing designs, would have stood a chance. Over time the enforcement of these laws became lax, and by the mid-1960s both the National Conference of Commissioners on Uniform State Laws and the American Law Institute recommended the elimination of such laws as "obsolete."[33]

With the onset of the Vietnam era, however, state flag-desecration laws were once again both enforced and subject to significant challenge. The primary concern of the flag's latest champions was not opportunistic commercial use but political protest. The defendants' theme was no longer the pursuit of property but freedom of speech. In response to a series of antiwar and civil rights rallies at which flags were defiled, mutilated, or burned, Congress in 1968 passed a federal flag-desecration law narrowly directed at knowingly contemptuous physical attacks on the flag.[34] Meanwhile, more expansive state laws continued to yield indictments not only for flag burning but also for wearing the flag as a patch on the seat of trousers and in other forms, superimposing peace signs and other symbols over the flag, and using the flag in miscellaneous artistic and expressive ways.[35] The Supreme

Court overturned one flag-burning conviction on the narrow grounds that it might have been based on the spoken words of the defendant, and it found that a Massachusetts law that led to a conviction for wearing the flag was unconstitutionally vague.[36]

On the issue of communicative actions involving transformation of the flag, however, the Court appeared reluctant to take a stand. A 1971 tie vote with one justice not participating—and no written opinion—left standing the conviction of an art-gallery owner who displayed protest art incorporating the flag (although the case was later reargued before a federal district court on technical grounds and the conviction was overturned).[37] By contrast, a 1974 per curiam opinion reversed the conviction of an individual who had used black tape to create a peace symbol on a flag and placed it in the window of his home; the Court held that the state had violated the defendant's right to freedom of speech. The narrow factual bases for the court's decision, however—the tape was removable, the flag and the location of its display were both private property, and there was no proof of any risk of breach of the peace—left the scope of permissible uses of the flag unclear.[38]

Not until 1989 did the Supreme Court confront the tension between First Amendment protection of expressive use of the flag, including its mutilation or destruction, and the flag-desecration laws. During the 1984 Republican National Convention in Dallas, a member of the Revolutionary Communist Youth Brigade participated in a protest march and allegedly burned a flag. Gregory Lee Johnson was convicted of violating the Texas Venerated Objects law and sentenced to the maximum penalty of a year in prison and a $2,000 fine. The case reached the U.S. Supreme Court four years later during the 1988 presidential campaign, in which Republican candidate George Herbert Walker Bush repeatedly criticized his Democratic opponent, Michael Dukakis, for vetoing legislation that required public school students to recite the Pledge of Allegiance daily—a requirement that had been declared unconstitutional by the Supreme Court in 1943.[39] With the political stakes running high, the Supreme Court agreed to hear the appeal and in a 5–4 decision declared the Texas law unconstitutional.[40]

Public reaction to the Supreme Court's decision in *Texas v. Johnson* was immediate and dramatic, and politicians debated how best to demonstrate their commitment to the national symbol. In the end, Congress enacted the allegedly content-neutral Flag Protection Act, which prohibited deliberate physical harm to the flag (apart from the disposal of worn or soiled flags) but did not include the "contempt" requirement for prosecution that was part of the earlier federal statute. The new act also contained a provision for expedited Supreme Court review.[41] Flag burning was the obvious means of protesting the law, and consolidated test cases soon appeared before the Court. In another 5–4 decision, the Court once again found a statutory attempt to criminalize flag burning to be a violation of the First Amendment. Although the opinion acknowledged that "[g]overnment may create national symbols, promote them, and encourage their respectful treatment," their value as a cultural expression makes them the property of all who wish to engage in freedom of expression.[42]

Congress created the American flag and gave it to the people, who waited some eighty-five years to adopt it as a cultural product. Its evolution through the material culture and artistry of everyday life and its use in political expression gave rise to a cultural divide regarding the flag's normative use. This debate has been temporarily, if bitterly, settled in favor of unfettered use of the flag; indeed, even the trademark-law provision preventing private registration of the flag or other national, state, or foreign symbols preserves them for general application. As in the case of gay and lesbian participation in certain Saint Patrick's Day parades, however, First Amendment analysis is unable to mediate between or even comprehend the parties' cultural values. Flag burning may be offensive, but its very power to offend makes it protected expression. The opportunistic proliferation of flags and flag merchandise in times of national crisis, which a century ago would have provoked the disapprobation of dowagers and veterans or even criminal prosecution, is today a permitted—even patriotic— expression. Freedom of speech is among the most precious of American liberties and an invaluable limitation on governmental coercion. When applied to internal struggles over the evolution of a culture, however, parties at both ends of the political spectrum may find it an unfortunately blunt instrument for regulating the normative use of cultural products.

Interpretation of a
Cultural Product

Another flag, the Confederate battle flag, or "Southern Cross," is at the center of a debate over not only its normative use but also its core meaning. For many African-American Southerners, the flag evokes a heritage of slavery, segregation, racism, and violence. For many white Southerners, particularly those whose ancestors fought in the Civil War, the flag is a symbol of a common history and of regional pride.

The controversial Confederate flag frequently displayed on pickup-truck bumpers and in certain Southern capitals today was not the only, or even the first, official rebel flag. It was preceded in 1861 by the "Star and Bars," a stripped-down version of the Yankee "Stars and Stripes" with fewer of each. Its strong resemblance to the Union flag disappointed some who had sought a more distinctive symbol, but it generally found favor with Southerners who emphasized their connection to the earlier days and glorious deeds of the young American republic.[43]

By late 1861, however, the flamboyant General P.G.T. Beauregard of Louisiana had introduced a new design based on the diagonal St. Andrew's Cross. Beauregard pragmatically explained that his Southern Cross was more easily distinguishable from the Union flag on the battlefield, but he also took the opportunity to unveil the new flag with high patriotic drama. Central to this flag cult was the invocation of Southern womanhood, the hands that had sewn and thus "consecrated" the new symbol. Although some criticized the overtly Christian symbolism of the new flag and even the fact that the actual stellar constellation known as the Southern Cross was not visible from the Northern Hemisphere, versions of the battle flag quickly spread from regiment to regiment. When the Confederate Congress in 1863 finally adopted its second national flag, a Southern Cross on an all-white field, known as the "Stainless Banner," the Southern Cross itself was already fixed in the Southern popular imagination as a martial emblem for a holy war. From a Northern perspective, the same Confederate emblem was associated with treason and even the devil.[44]

After the Civil War ended, the threatening nature of the rebel flag was slowly obscured by moth-eaten nostalgia for the military glory of the Lost Cause—until many white Southerners united again under a new cause. The banner that had symbolized opposition to abolition in the mid-nineteenth century was raised again to challenge desegregation in the mid-twentieth. Not only did individuals increasingly display the battle flag, but several Southern states raised the flag over their capitol buildings or redesigned their state flags to incorporate the Southern Cross. Dan Carter, a historian of the American South, has testified in federal court that "[b]y the mid-1950's, the Confederate battle flag had become the single most important symbol of white supremacy and defiant opposition to federally mandated laws on nondiscrimination."[45]

In the New South of recent decades, however, the official display of a symbol offensive to many African Americans and liberal whites has provoked ongoing controversy. Both the NAACP and private citizens have mounted legal attacks on state display of the flag since at least 1975, and legal commentators have elaborated similar constitutional challenges. Federal courts, however, have reluctantly refused to remedy the social and cultural harm attributed to display of the Confederate flag. In 1990, the U.S. Court of Appeals for the Eleventh Circuit noted, "It is unfortunate that the State of Alabama chooses to utilize its property in a manner that offends a large portion of its population, but that is a political matter which it is not within our province to decide."[46] The same court chastised another state in 1997, stating, "We regret that the Georgia legislature has chosen, and continues to display, as an official state symbol a battle flag emblem that divides rather than unifies the citizens of Georgia."[47]

In thoughtful reflections on the Confederate flag and other memorials, constitutional law scholar Sanford Levinson opposes display of the flag as an official modern emblem but praises the restraint of the federal courts that have addressed the issue. As he notes, "[O]ne of the issues hovering over this entire debate is the hermeneutics of culture and the presence of sufficient interpretive clarity to say with confidence that the flag-signifier refers to a unique signified (i.e., the system of chattel slavery). If, though, multiple interpretations are genuinely possible, if the flag is truly polysemous, then how precisely can a federal court (or anyone else) justify in effect negating all other interpretive possibilities save the particular one that it chooses to privilege?"[48] Levinson rightly suggests that the context of a symbol may determine meaning with sufficient clarity for even a stubborn semiotician but nonetheless urges that this public debate at least take its natural course.

As it happens, social, political, and economic pressures from parties offended by the flag appear to be succeeding where attempts at legal coercion have failed. While some whites with deep roots in the South express respect for the flag as a reminder of their storied past, and other whites view the flag in terms of quaint regional color, its prevalence as an official state symbol has declined significantly.[49] It no longer flies over the state capitols of Alabama and South Carolina, although the compromise that moved the banner from South Carolina's capitol dome to a Confederate soldiers' monument on the grounds remains controversial. Georgia's flag has been redesigned to minimize the Southern Cross. Only Mississippi's politicians and voters continue to resist alternate proposals for a state flag.[50] Schools and universities nationwide have followed a similar trend away from Confederate symbolism, as many have renamed "Rebel" teams or added prohibitions against the battle flag to school dress codes.[51]

There is no conclusive answer, however, to the question of how to interpret this distinctive cultural product of the American South. It may lie dormant until the next cultural battle, be it a civil war or a civil rights movement, or it may fade into obscurity as the American landscape shifts and changes. Whatever the future of the Southern Cross, its bitterly contested significance may offer a lesson for other cultural products. In most cases, these fraternal contests should be resolved internally, with attention to all points of view within a community and the importance of freedom of speech. The courts should perhaps not be so hasty to absent themselves from all cases, however, particularly those with the potential to cause lasting harm or to inflame old hatreds under the aegis of government authority. If a federal agency can evaluate historical and survey evidence to determine whether the Washington Redskins' trademark in the field of professional football "disparages" Native Americans, a determination subject to judicial review, then federal and state courts could plausibly address similar questions with respect to the symbols of government itself.[52] The meanings of cultural products are often multivalent or subject to interpretation, but the power of these contested symbols is quite definite.

COMMODIFICATION OF
A CULTURAL PRODUCT

Another set of contested uses can arise in the context of the deliberate commodification of a cultural product. Legal scholar Margaret Jane Radin, in her landmark treatment of "contested commodities," discusses the ways in which commodification can adversely affect both individual personhood and community.[53] In the case of images of female sexuality commodified as pornography, women in general and vocal feminists in particular are split on the question of whether this is acceptable expression or whether it degrades and endangers all women. At issue is not merely whether heterosexual pornography causes harm by encouraging men to abuse women, or whether there is frequent physical or psychological harm to women who appear in pornographic works, but whether pornography itself harms all women. From a cultural-products perspective, the issue is one of production, control, and disposition of images of women and how that particular cultural product—a projection of female sexuality—affects the source community as a whole.

Among the combatants are scholar-activists Andrea Dworkin and Catharine MacKinnon, well known for their advocacy of antipornography legislation that extends beyond the limited range of obscenity laws and is designed to offer women greater protection than those laws provide. In the early 1980s, Dworkin and MacKinnon convened hearings in Minneapolis and other cities in order to demonstrate the need for antipornography ordinances.[54] At the hearings, both ordinary women and experts testified regarding specific harms caused by the creation and consumption of pornography. As one woman employee of a government sexual-abuse unit noted, "Porn is already a violent act against women. It is our mothers, our daughters, our sisters, and our wives that are for sale for pocket change at the newsstands in this country."[55] Although the Minneapolis city council passed antipornography laws twice, in 1983 and 1984, they were vetoed by the mayor. Other municipalities enacted similar measures, including an Indianapolis version aimed specifically at violent pornography, only to have them overturned by federal courts on First Amendment grounds.[56]

The forces opposing pornography frequently compare it to African-American slavery. Not only are individual women subject to coercion in the creation of photographs and videos, but the portrayal of women as sexual chattels affects the culture as a whole. One court, in reviewing and ultimately invalidating antipornography legislation, nevertheless observed, "People taught from birth that black people are fit only for slavery rarely rebelled against that creed; beliefs coupled with self interest of the masters established a social structure that inflicted great harm while enduring for centuries."[57] Similarly, persistent images of sexually subordinate women create a societal perception that women are or should be subordinate to men. This belief affects women in all realms—at work, at home, in the public sphere, on the streets.[58] Women who challenge these strictures are dismissed as not authentically feminine or as insubordinate. Drawing on the parallels to slavery, Dworkin asserts, "We will know we are free when pornography no longer exists."[59]

On the other extreme of the pornography debate are ACLU president Nadine Strossen, arguing from the vantage point of freedom of speech, and Judge Richard Posner, occupying classical liberal territory in order to defend individual choice. Strossen, while affirming a commitment to feminism, cites concerns that "procensorship feminists" and their politically conservative allies in the challenge to pornography will silence free expression about sexual issues.[60] A decision by the Canadian Supreme Court incorporating pornography into antiobscenity law, for example, led to the confiscation of gay, lesbian, and feminist material.[61] From this perspective, freedom of speech is necessary to reinforce equality, even while it protects pornography. Strossen further argues that the attack on pornography is a distraction from more important issues affecting women: "The MacDworkinite idea that pornography is violence against women insults the many women who experience actual, brutal, three-dimensional violence in their real lives."[62]

Posner offers a more measured analysis of the relationship between pornography and the social status of women, citing various forms of evidence and ultimately concluding that a causal relation between pornography and incidents of rape or other forms of female subordination has not yet been proven.[63] Indeed, he refers to the harms of pornography as "conjectural and uncertain." Posner, unlike Strossen, nevertheless admits the possibility of a constitutionally valid prohibition on pornography, provided that the definition is limited to "works whose predominant appeal is aphrodisiacal—hence works that rank low in the traditional hierarchy of First Amendment values." Given the limited resources available for law enforcement, and Posner's practical law and economics orientation, however, he argues against expensive and futile efforts "to suppress activities that may be as harmless as witchcraft or heresy."[64]

Among current and former sex-industry workers themselves, opinion on the issue of pornography is similarly divided. Some women who have appeared in pornographic photographs or films relate a personal history of sexual abuse and consider the pornographic works an additional, ongoing violation. This realization may come many years later; one woman writes, "It has taken me twenty years to acknowledge that being used as raw material, being raped, did affect me. In 1967, my hippie ideals told me the real, inner Jane was inviolate. Today, the grown up woman knows it was Jane that was manhandled, raped, used."[65] Other women, by contrast, do not consider themselves harmed or demeaned by their experiences with the pornography industry. In the words of one self-styled feminist porno star, "If the media can have an effect on people's behavior, and I believe it does, why is it assumed that sex movies must always reinforce the most negative imagery of women? That certainly isn't what I'm about. From my very first movie I have always refused to portray rape, coercion, pain-as-pleasure, woman-as-victim, domination, humiliation, and other forms of non-consensual sex."[66] Although these and other individual testimonies shed light on the human beings who appear in two-dimensional pornographic works, and may even nuance the intent of those works, the actual effect of pornography on women as a whole remains a theoretical battleground.

Despite the intensity of the pornography debates, neither side focuses on images of female sexuality as a collaborative creation of all women in society, lesbian, heterosexual, or bisexual, and whether or not associated with the sex industry. Dworkin and MacKinnon acknowledge and abhor the collective impact of commodification beyond sex-industry workers, as well as multiple examples of the victimization of individual women, but are too deep in the trenches to suggest any opportunity for positive communal reconstruction. Strossen and Posner, informed by the traditional legal emphasis on individual rights, lack a vocabulary designed to express either communal creation or communal harm. Instead, Strossen retreats to a practiced defense of individual rights under the First Amendment and Posner to the dictates of law and economics regarding the expenses of law enforcement.

It is generally left to women artists, who often work outside mainstream culture, to reintegrate images of the female body and female self-perceptions.[67] Female sexuality, a cultural product generated by so large an unincorporated group, and a creation with such a long history of contested commodification by both insiders and outsiders, is extremely difficult to return to the influence of the source community. Populist efforts, such as the SuicideGirls website, nevertheless make efforts to recapture images of beauty and sexuality from the perspective of the participants rather than of a commercial industry or its male consumers.[68] Recognition of images of women's sexuality as a cultural product would re-center the debate around communitarian issues rather than around the pornography industry and the hetero-masculine commodification of women.

Release of a Cultural Product into the Public Domain

For another group of cultural products, the focus of community disagreement is whether the public should be allowed access at all. These products arguably retain greater cultural value if they remain private or even secret, their purity, authenticity, and function guarded by a select few. Such artifacts or rituals tend to be of a religious, spiritual, or mystical nature, like the common practice of distributing Christian communion wafers only to church members, although secular examples such as the selection process for Skull and Bones members attach similar value to secrecy. When individual community members disagree about the wisdom of releasing cultural products into the public domain and even undertake to act unilaterally without the prior approval of the community, protracted battles may result.

The academic controversy over the Dead Sea Scrolls provides an example of contested public access to both cultural property and cultural products. In 1947, a young Bedouin shepherd discovered the first of the scrolls, wrapped in linen and sealed in a pot, in a cave in the arid Qumran area near the Dead Sea. Soon the find came to the attention of the scholarly community, and an extensive search for additional scrolls yielded the remnants of approximately eight hundred manuscripts dating from approximately 200 B.C.E. to 68 C.E. These fragments, written in Hebrew and Aramaic by members of a Jewish sect, include the earliest known manuscripts of portions of the Hebrew Bible, or Christian Old Testament. Custody of the scrolls rested first with Jordan and then, after the Six-Day War, with Israel.

From the outset, a small team of international scholars exercised academic control over the Dead Sea Scrolls and enforced a policy that allowed outsiders virtually no access to them. This situation lasted for decades, and scholars excluded from the project became increasingly resentful that this stunning discovery was withheld from them. Among the more vocal of these dissenting scholars was Hershel Shanks, editor of the *Biblical Archaeology Review*, a leading journal published under the auspices of the Biblical Archaeology Society (BAS). Soon the popular media learned of the dispute and weighed in on the side of intellectual freedom and public access. The *New York Times* argued that "the scrolls and what they say about the common roots of Christianity and Rabbinic Judaism belong to civilization, not to a few sequestered professors."[69] The BAS subsequently published a two-volume *Facsimile Edition of the Dead Sea Scrolls* consisting of photographic plates of the scroll fragments from an unnamed source, as well as an official but previously unreleased reconstruction of one scroll. Some years earlier, the Huntington Library in San Marino, California, had come into possession of a set of microfilms of the scroll fragments previously owned by an eccentric philanthropist. After the BAS publication, the Huntington offered scholars free access to its collection, despite the objections of the Israeli Antiquities Authority.

Once the images of the Dead Sea Scrolls had entered the public domain, the locus of the controversy shifted to the claim of one scholar, Elisha Qimron, that the BAS's inclusion of his scroll reconstruction constituted a copyright violation, even though he was not the original author of the two thousand-year-old text. Ultimately, the Supreme Court of Israel agreed with him and upheld a significant award of damages against Shanks. David Nimmer and many other learned scholars of intellectual property law have spent hundreds of pages analyzing the significance of the Dead Sea Scrolls case for copyright law and particularly its implications for the definition of "authorship."[70] The issues surrounding how and why a team of scholars sequestered one of the most significant archaeological discoveries of a generation for over forty years, and how that ivory tower was finally toppled, have remained largely in the background of the intellectual property debates.

From a cultural perspective, however, attention shifts to the struggle within a highly specialized academic enclave over whether to share not only access to objects of study but also the emerging results of decades of study. Both sides of this fraternal contest necessarily imply professional egotism, with jealousy and envy informing the respective players. A more generous reading of the situation, however, suggests legitimate reasons for both secrecy and revelation. The original international team apparently hoped to complete the work of reconstructing the scrolls and publishing them fairly quickly; doing so would have allowed the broader scholarly community to begin interpreting and criticizing the text and its reconstruction in a more timely fashion, albeit with the team's work as the initial interpretive authority. Given the potential significance of the texts for Western civilization—it isn't often that the Bible itself may be rewritten, especially against the backdrop of volatile Mideast politics—a certain caution against overly hasty release or inaccurate textual reconstruction may have appeared prudent. This perspective casts the scholars themselves as a variety of priesthood, a group employing its own arcane knowledge to guard sacred texts against popular misuse or misinterpretation. It is consistent with this attitude that the various team members to whom scroll portions were assigned would, from time to time, share their work with trusted outside colleagues.

As the decades wore on, the team's obsession with secrecy and selective inclusion of others, including their own graduate students, appeared less prudent and more selfish. At the same time, the dawn of the Information Age caused not only scholars but also the general public to be less tolerant of the professional hoarding of knowledge. This cultural shift intensified demands for public release of the scroll fragment themselves, or at least their images, and of particular significant reconstructed portions of the texts. When the new cultural logic found a weakness within the privileged circle of knowledge, Shanks and the BAS were prepared with a medium for the dissemination of its secrets. Although Qimron won his copyright battle, freedom of information won the war. Even the Israeli Antiquities Authority ultimately conceded the point, releasing an authorized, complete edition of the scroll photographs on microfiche.[71] The scholarly community has responded with a myriad of publications and theories on the texts, a form of cultural production that will presumably continue for the foreseeable future.

The Dead Sea Scrolls controversy illustrates the difficulty of developing and maintaining private or secret cultural products, as well as the relative power of insiders who choose to release them into the public domain. Human curiosity, a culture of revelation and inclusion, the natural tendency of intangible goods and information to cross barriers, and the digital immediacy of the internet all combine to influence the outcome of these internal contests. Once a dissenting member has chosen to breach certain boundaries, it may be difficult to restore the equilibrium of the source community with respect to the cultural product.

FRATERNAL CONTESTS OVER the control of cultural products are extremely complex and often resistant to legal resolution, whether they involve limiting membership in the source community, presenting the community to the public, or commodifying culture. The law is appropriately reluctant to involve itself in the internal affairs of a cultural group. As in the case of co-ownership of tangible property, however, an established default rule or dispute-resolution mechanism would facilitate relations now governed largely by inertia. In addition, legal theory has a role to play in highlighting the importance and communal nature of cultural products. Individual rights, including freedom of expression, are indispensable building blocks of a civilization dedicated to personal liberty; nevertheless, the social nature of humankind and our tendency to form mutually reinforcing and creative (if periodically contentious) units should not have to remain unrecognized by the law.

CHAPTER 7

Outsider Appropriation

I made my song a coat
Covered with embroideries
Out of old mythologies
From heel to throat;
But the fools caught it,
Wore it in the world's eyes,
As though they'd wrought it.
                    —W. B. Yeats

HELENA, ARKANSAS, HAS got a right to sing the
blues—at least since a federal court dismissed a class-action lawsuit
against the city. A group of African-American organizations and individuals originally filed suit in 1999, seeking an end to Helena's annual
blues festival. According to the complaint, the city had been involved
in "a racially conspiratorial process which, in effects, kidnaps, steals,
and disrespects, for the purpose of private profit, the musical legacy
of African-American citizens in Phillips County; a portion of the
Arkansas-Mississippi Delta."[1] Much of the dispute appears to have re-
volved around the financial impact of the festival on local merchants, as
well as the alleged de facto allocation of decision-making authority to
white merchants only. The intended plaintiff class, however, extended
to "descendants of African slaves whose sufferance was the genesis of
the blues, who felt and endured that sufferance and who object to that
sufferance being stolen, misused, and prostituted by persons who are
the sponsors of the Helena Blues Festival who are non-African descent
and whose ancestors' conduct towards Africans created the blues."[2]
Although several of the aggrieved parties, including the local chapter
of the NAACP, ultimately withdrew from the case, and Chief Judge

Susan Webber Wright never ruled on the merits, the claims neverthe-less represent an attempt to carry the long-running debate over America's musical heritage into a legal forum.[3] More generally, the case illustrates the differences in perspective, outsider incentives, and insider reactions that characterize cultural appropriation.

Understandings of Cultural Appropriation

Before outsiders can appropriate a cultural product, they must first recognize its existence, source community, and value. African-American musical styles developed from the survival of African music among slaves in the American South and their exposure to European-derived hymns, folk songs, language, rhythms, and instrumentation. By the late nineteenth century, differentiated forms including ragtime, blues, and its close cousin, jazz, had begun to appear.[4] White performers imitated these developments, parodying black musicians in minstrel shows and subsequently becoming bona fide players in a new musical era. Amiri Baraka describes this process as one of discovering a cultural secret, noting that "the first serious white jazz musicians . . . sought not only to understand the phenomenon of Negro music but to appropriate it as a means of expression which they themselves might utilize. The success of this 'appropriation' signaled the existence of an American music, whereas before there was a Negro music."[5]

Integration of black and white musicians began to occur early in the twentieth century, although Louis Armstrong recalled that the legendary cradle of jazz itself, New Orleans, remained segregated. "Speaking of the Red Light District and its Musicians, I was lucky to have heard all of them who played there. The White Boys were also blowing up a storm. There weren't as many White Bands as Negro Bands in the District, but the ones who played there sure was good," he writes. "I did not get to know any of the White Musicians personally, because New Orleans was so Disgustingly Segregated and Prejudiced at the time—it didn't even run across our minds. But I was fortunate to have the opportunity to meet some of them up North in 1922 when I went to Chicago . . . ."[6] Musical contact sometimes evolved into formal relationships. In his controversial autobiography,

Miles Davis recounts his defense of an invitation to a white musician to join his band on the grounds of ability, claiming, "I wouldn't give a damn if he was green with red breath."[7] Despite this collegial interaction among musicians, however, African Americans for decades continued to experience prejudice in hiring by white club owners, Northern and Southern. Even in Harlem, African-American musicians found openings filled by their white counterparts.[8] Davis and others cited white music critics as giving preferential treatment to white musicians.[9] Only in Europe did managers, audiences, and critics frankly prefer African-American performers of the new "American" music.[10]

This early history of African-American music, and in particular the racialized economics of the music business, has led to repeated charges of cultural misappropriation. A century of white musicians ranging from Benny Goodman to Bing Crosby to Elvis Presley to Jerry Lee Lewis to Pat Boone to Vanilla Ice to Eminem has been accused of stealing various forms of black music, in some cases ineptly. The criticism is twofold: first, musicians of non-African descent lack the talent or ability to advance or perhaps even to play African-American music, which derives from unique cultural experiences; second, African-American musical forms are proprietary to their community of origin, and their exploitation by whites in particular is unacceptable. In the context of jazz, cultural critic Gerald Early describes the untenable position of the white musician: "The white player is caught in a curious kind of trap. He is condemned—if he plays something called 'white' jazz—for being unable to swing (the music's *sine qua non*), and therefore of being inauthentic. He is equally inauthentic (and a thief, besides) if he plays something called 'black' jazz. Within these strictures, therefore, it would seem to be impossible to be white and play jazz on any terms."[11] White artists nevertheless continue to build careers around genres from jazz to rap.

The perspectives of individual African-American musicians on cultural appropriation are somewhat obscured by the competing ideals of racial pride and a colorblind musical fraternity. Within the jazz community there exists a heroic legend of resistance to white adulteration of the music, exemplified by the persistent but challenged belief that Dizzy Gillespie, Charlie Parker, Thelonious Monk, and their associates developed bebop in order to exclude less talented white players from after-hours clubs in Harlem.[12] In the modern era, the tenure of Wynton Marsalis as artistic director of Jazz at Lincoln Center has invited charges of racial exclusivity, while the rap movie *8 Mile* challenges similar boundaries in a less genteel environment.[13] At the same time, musicians of all stripes regularly cross color lines in citing their personal mentors and sources of inspiration, as well as in recognizing talent.[14] Jazz lyricist, critic, and historian Gene Lees reports a particular moment when saxophonist Phil Woods questioned his chances of legitimate success as a white musician. Gillespie reportedly told Woods, "You can't steal a gift. Bird [Charlie Parker] gave the world his music, and if you can hear it you can have it."[15] While the vast majority of musicians, black and otherwise, affirm the importance of the African-American source community in creating distinctive new musical forms, many disagree as to the historical role or even the normative presence of white performers.

Within the African-American community as a whole, the charges of white cultural appropriation of cutting-edge black music have long coexisted with some members' reluctance to be associated with that music. Whether a matter of simple taste, class association, or internalized racism, African-American elites have generally been more reluctant than their white counterparts to embrace jazz in the middle of the twentieth century or rap at the cusp of the twenty-first.[16] Saxophonist Benny Golson, for example, recalls that the music faculty at Howard University in the late 1940s required him to play the more legitimate clarinet rather than the saxophone and to study classical rather than jazz composition.[17] Indeed, the plebeian associations of the saxophone have persisted into the present; in Nobel prize–winning novelist Toni Morrison's infamous characterization of Bill Clinton as the nation's first black president, she claimed that he "displays almost every trope of blackness: single-parent household, born poor, working-class, saxophone-playing, McDonald's-and-junk-food-loving boy from Arkansas."[18] Today's white upper middle class, the primary audience for jazz, is more likely to associate the genre with brunch than with an urban underclass.[19] National Security Advisor Condoleezza Rice nevertheless appears in photographs seated at her grand piano rather than holding a tenor sax. From the standpoint of cultural appropriation, some members of the African-American source community may find claims to ownership of certain musical genres more problematic than charges of theft.

Despite the lawsuit against Helena, Arkansas, the law does not generally address claims of cultural ownership or appropriation—but it does offer copyright protection to individual artists. Intellectual property law has not been effective historically in protecting African-American musicians or musical styles, however. As scholars including K. J. Greene and Siva Vaidhyanathan have described, not only unequal bargaining power and established patterns of majority appropriation but also a bias toward communal performance-based creation and oral transmission left African-American contributions unprotected.[20] A copyright system organized around a normative conception of individual authorship and fixed works is ill-suited to creative formation through call-and-response, jam sessions, or rap battles. Comparing creative paradigms of the African and European diasporas, Vaidhyanathan notes, "The 'shape' of West African creativity is a circle, not a line."[21] Charges of cultural appropriation occur when an outsider enters the circle (with or without permission), participates in its creative ferment, and then sets off to create proprietary works or to pursue profits elsewhere.

OUTSIDERS' INCENTIVES

The incentive to use or to copy a cultural product may be as simple as the potential for financial gain or as complex as the reconstruction of identity. In a heterogeneous society, cultural appropriation rarely occurs without at least some consideration of the significance of the original product, if only to ensure its marketability. When a cultural product is copied and sold, used to represent the source community, or borrowed and transformed, its appeal results from both tangible and intangible characteristics. The defining element in this motivational range is the relationship of the copy to the intrinsic values embodied in the original.

In one international example of cultural appropriation, the primary incentive appears to be economic. South Korea's national dish, kimchi, enjoys widespread popularity in Japan and has been produced and marketed by a number of Japanese companies. Korean critics charge that the Japanese skip the traditional, time-consuming fermentation process used to produce the spicy pickled cabbage, instead using artificial flavors and thickeners that create an inferior product. Japanese producers claim that Korea has no more of a monopoly on the term "kimchi" than India has on "curry," a rather conclusory argument from a cultural-products perspective, and that the battle is really over market share. The debate is also informed by a history of hostile Korean-Japanese relations, as well as the negative past treatment of ethnic Koreans living in Japan. Chong Dae Sung, an ethnic-Korean expert on comparative food culture at Shiga Prefectural University in Japan, recalls, "When I was a boy growing up in Japan, the only place we Koreans could eat kimchi was within my family's house because the Japanese looked down on Koreans, saying that we smelled like garlic and red pepper. Today, the situation is totally different."[22] Japanese kimchi producers could have found a ready domestic market only if the stigma once attached to ethnic Koreans had dissipated, at least at the level of cuisine. The producers themselves are not necessarily motivated by cultural exchange, however, but may simply be large corporate entities whose managers are indifferent to the product but adroit at monitoring taste trends and calculating profit margins.

In addition to cultural products' value as commodities, they offer outsiders a medium through which to invoke, describe, or caricature the source community. Such use may occur in marketing, in an educational context such as a museum or classroom, or in entertainment. Models in Hasidic-inspired garb walk between giant menorahs on Jean-Paul Gaultier's runway; schoolchildren file past a dusty glass case of "primitive" weapons or a diorama of a ritual dance; a history of vaudeville includes a film clip of white minstrels in blackface.[23] While some of these appropriations have disappeared in the face of modern social disapprobation or even legislation, the external use of cultural products may still result in the misrepresentation or misuse of source-group identity.[24] Even if an internet startup delivers the groceries,

Mrs. Butterworth and Aunt Jemima are invited to prepare Sunday brunch.[25] In the context of descriptive appropriation, cultural products are a material shorthand for the source communities themselves.

The strong association between source communities and cultural products also renders the tangible embodiments clear targets for iconoclastic attack or expression of disapproval of the source community. Both outsiders and estranged insiders engage in such expression, which may range from alteration to destruction of the cultural products. Roman Catholic religious images, perhaps because of their widespread familiarity in Western culture and perceived antimodernism, are frequent victims of negative appropriation. Examples of such use and the resulting source-community furor include Andres Serrano's *Piss Christ,* a photograph of a crucifix submerged in the artist's urine, which resulted in Senator Alfonse D'Amato's bipartisan crusade against the National Endowment for the Arts; pop singer Sinead O'Connor's destruction of a picture of Pope John Paul II on *Saturday Night Live,* followed the next week by guest host Joe Pesci's display of a reassembled picture; and the Brooklyn Museum's display of a Madonna decorated with elephant dung, which provoked the ire of New York Mayor Rudolph Giuliani.[26] Since oppositional commentary borrows from the multilayered significance of the targeted objects, it may offer simultaneous religious and ethnic criticism. A cover of *Bitch* magazine, for example, depicts a short-haired, frowning Virgin of Guadalupe drinking a cup of coffee and reading a book.[27] While the First Amendment protects external appropriation of cultural products for purposes of protest or negative commentary, the constitutionally recognized value of freedom of speech does not preclude the legal recognition of cultural products any more than it invalidates intellectual property law. Indeed, such expressive use of cultural products would have little meaning in the absence of a link to the source community.

When appropriation of cultural products is appreciative rather than merely economic or descriptive, there is a heightened relationship between the copyist and the source community. The Western physician who explores the benefits of Chinese traditional medicine or the architect who designs a Mediterranean-style villa for her suburban client acknowledges and becomes a student of the cultural product's creators. This cultural apprenticeship may result in mere aesthetic appreciation, or it may prompt the copyist to become an advocate for the source community. In the foreword to a book of photographs, fashion designer Donna Karan writes, "As a designer, I am always asked where my inspiration comes from. The answer lies in the advice my mentor Anne Klein gave me: 'God gave you two eyes. Use them!' . . . Bonnie Young, an invaluable member of our team, travels the world in search of new ideas and expressions, clicking her camera all the while. . . . The inspiration may come from a palette, a texture, a style of beading—or it could be an emotion that Bonnie has captured on a woman's veiled face."[28] The designer's aesthetic appreciation and business acumen are joined by the photographer's homage to her subjects, apparent in her description of the project as "a tribute to the vanishing traditions of tribes whose spirit and creativity have touched my heart."[29] Young's appreciation for the unique beauty and variety of personal adornment that she encountered in her travels led her to record their images, which become not only a form of cultural capital but also a bond between photographer and subject. While this type of appropriation has the potential to become a form of colonialist exploitation, it may simultaneously benefit the source community seeking to preserve or define its identity.

Copying that transforms cultural products, whether in an adaptive or an expressive fashion, presents a more complex association between the copyist and the source community. Such appropriation simultaneously acknowledges the value and significance of the cultural product and asserts the copyist's right to use it in a nontraditional or even nonnormative fashion. The Australian merchant who modified sacred Aboriginal paintings to decorate his carpets, causing great offense to the artists' culture, engaged in transformative appropriation, but so does a Southern cook who spreads Australian Vegemite on her homemade buttermilk biscuits.[30] Similarly, both Serrano's *Piss Christ* and a greeting card depicting former San Francisco City Supervisor Harvey Milk adorned with the golden halo of Orthodox Christian iconography simultaneously reference and transform the borrowed cultural products in order to express an outside point of view. Transformative appropriation, even if complimentary, imposes the will and perspective of the outsider on the altered product.

Adoptive appropriation, in which the copyist internalizes the cultural product as her own, attempts to blur the distinction between the copy and the original. While this incentive to copy demonstrates high regard for the embodied product, it also threatens to erode the source group's boundaries or to make its cultural products generic. The copyist who adopts rather than merely appropriates a cultural product may do so either by seeking to emulate or join the source community or by attempting to subsume the product into her own culture. In the 1960s, for example, "white Indians" patterned their lifestyles on perceptions of Native American environmentalism and spirituality, jettisoning mainstream American culture in favor of beads, braids, and a hybrid nature religion. Today, white suburban teenagers imitate the language, dress, music, and mannerisms of their African-American or Latino urban counterparts. On an earlier national scale, all-American ballpark franks no longer call to mind their German forebears. The modern search for authenticity at the fringes and in the ethnic enclaves of American culture informs this extreme manifestation of cultural appropriation.

Under certain circumstances, source communities may engage in mutual appropriation of each other's cultural products, an exchange that results in a hybrid form. The original cultural products may continue to exist unchanged, or they may be subsumed into the new creation. Tex-Mex cuisine, a hybrid of Native American and Spanish ingredients and cooking techniques that has come to symbolize the American Southwest, exemplifies this process. Similarly, fusion cuisine is celebrated at trendy, cosmopolitan restaurants in both New York and Tokyo. In the case of mutual appropriation, a hybrid cultural product may link two communities or even represent a new cultural metropole, a tertium quid constructed on the middle ground between two older forms.

Economic, descriptive, appreciative, transformative, adoptive, or mutual, the incentive to engage in cultural appropriation reflects the copyist's reaction to a multicultural society that affords liberal access to cultural products. Each copyist's selection, unhindered by community control or legal limits, affects not only the intangible property of the source community but also the fabric of society as a whole. While source communities often have little control over the pattern of cultural appropriation, they nevertheless express strong and sometimes conflicting reactions to the outside use of their cultural products.

INSIDERS' REACTIONS

When outsiders use cultural products, source-community reactions vary according to the significance of the product and the nature of the external use, as well as from member to member within the community. History also plays a role, as each source community takes into account previous treatment or appropriation of its cultural products and its relationship with the nonmember users. Overlap may exist between external use and contested internal use, especially in cases in which insiders either join outsiders in nonconforming uses or deliberately misuse cultural products in order to dissociate themselves from the community. Whether source communities claim a sovereign right to exclude outsiders or merely attempt to familiarize outsiders with the social norms pertaining to cultural products, the law provides little direct assistance.

Source-community responses to cultural appropriation have themselves moved into the realm of popular culture. In a scene from *The Sopranos*, two men enter a Starbucks-style coffee shop looking for information about an alleged car thief. The following heavily accented (and rather colorful) exchange results:

CLERK: I'm sorry sir, but these stores are everywhere.
PUSSY: Tell me about it.
PAULIE: The fucking Italian people. How did we miss out on this?
PUSSY: What?
PAULIE: Fucking espresso, cappuccino. We invented the shit and all these other cocksuckers are getting rich off it.
PUSSY: Yeah, isn't it amazing?
PAULIE: And it's not just the money. It's a pride thing. All our food, pizza, calzone, buffalo mozzarell', olive oil. These fucks have noth-

ing. They ate "pootsie" before we gave them the gift of our cuisine. But this, this is the worst. This espresso shit.
Pussy: Take it easy.[31]

In a later scene, one of the men returns to find his partner staring at a
display of merchandise in the coffee shop.

Pussy: Paulie, you listening to me?
Paulie: Yeah.
Pussy: Oh, again with the rape of the culture? . . .
(Pussy walks away. Paulie takes a 9-cup stovetop espresso pot, sticks it
under his jacket, turns to leave.)[32]

In these vignettes, one character objects to commodification of a
cultural product in the form of an espresso bar. Not only does he
resent the flow of pecuniary rewards to outsiders rather than to members of the source community, but he also refers to outside access to
Italian cultural products as "the gift of our cuisine," a matter of pride.
Apparently it is acceptable for nonmembers to experience and enjoy
Italian food but not to control or commodify this "gift"—actions that
the younger, less concerned or more fatalistic character dismissively
calls "the rape of the culture." Although neither character raises direct
questions regarding the quality or authenticity of the product, apart
from an early expression of disbelief upon learning that the coffee
of the day is New Zealand Peaberry, their disgust with the setting is
evident. There is disagreement between the two source-community
members as to the significance of the corporate transgression but no
challenge to the theft of the coffeepot as a minor act of revenge.

Were Big Coffee to respond to charges of cultural appropriation,
it might note that *Coffea arabica* is native to northern Africa and is now
a significant South American export as well, despite the fact that its
preparation in the form of espresso and cappuccino and the presence
of a coffee shop on every city block are characteristically Italian. The
further development of complex beverages such as grande-nonfat-
double-decaf-with-whip-mocha, the corporate nectar of the modern
American bourgeoisie, is not an export of the Italian peninsula—and
may not fall under the aegis of "culture" at all. Nevertheless, Starbucks

and its imitators have capitalized on the current popularity of northern Italian culture with products such as the Starbucks Italian Heritage coffee sampler, containing small packages of its Espresso Roast, Caffè Verona, and Italian Roast in a box resembling a colonnade. In Starbucks' online history of coffee, however, Italy appears only in the form of a brief reference to Venice as a center of trade.[33] The company's well-publicized Commitment to Origins program is an attempt to exercise corporate responsibility toward coffee growers in less developed countries, but it does not address the more subtle and less urgently existential question of cultural appropriation.[34]

In the absence of legal rules or shared norms regarding cultural appropriation, permissive external access to cultural products may result in loss of source-community control. If the outsiders' version comes to dominate consumer culture, an eventual disjunction may also occur in the popular mind between the community and the embodied product, now generically American. While espresso and cappuccino continue to appear on Italian and Italian-American tables and to invoke Italian culture among outsiders, the mainstreaming of other, more fragile cultural products leads the source community to abandon them. For example, in 1993 the record label Def American Recordings staged a mock funeral for the hip-hop term "def," or excellent, and dropped the word from its name after it appeared in Webster's dictionary. The Reverend Al Sharpton, known for his political and social activism on behalf of the African-American community, presided over the ceremony.[35] While the funeral and subsequent party celebrating the new American Recordings were amusing publicity stunts, the loss of the evocative countercultural power of "def" is a real consequence of outside appropriation. Economic entitlement, racial/ethnic/national pride, linguistic authority, quality, and not least authenticity all play a role in the internal-external tug-of-war over cultural products, but their combined weight seldom affects the steady pull of external appropriation.

WHETHER CONTESTED USE of cultural products is internal to the source community or involves external appropriation, without a legal structure we have no framework for discussion of meaning and normative use, dispute resolution, or even recognition of conflicting values. A system that formally acknowledged the relationship between source communities and their cultural products could provide these benefits, either through extension of the limited-ownership concept expressed in intellectual property law or through trademark-style recognition of a constructed legal authenticity. Before considering the structure of a solution, however, it is necessary to explore further the potential negative and positive effects of cultural appropriation.

CHAPTER 8

Misappropriation and the Destruction of Value(s)

This is my solemn warning to all who hear the prophecies in this book: if anyone adds anything to them, God will add to him every plague mentioned in the book; if anyone cuts anything out of the prophecies in this book, God will cut off his share of the tree of life and of the holy city, which are described in the book.

—Revelation 22: 18–19

ON JANUARY 21, 1984, Michael Heller, a staff photographer for the Santa Fe *New Mexican*, flew at low altitude over the Pueblo of Santo Domingo and photographed a ceremonial dance. The *New Mexican* published the resulting photos on at least two occasions, the second time with a caption inaccurately describing the event as a "pow-wow." In response, the Pueblo filed suit in federal district court, alleging trespass, violation of the Pueblo's ban on photography, and invasion of privacy.[1] Comparison of the Pueblo's legal complaint with the statements of its members and supporters, however, reveals that the available causes of action could not directly address the Pueblo's central concerns regarding the interruption, defilement, and commodification of a religious ritual.

Experiences like that of the Pueblo of Santo Domingo represent the worst-case scenario for cultural appropriation, a situation in which external use or copying of a cultural product may harm or destroy the intangible aspects of the original. The cultural value or message embedded in the product may be diluted or eliminated; in the extreme, public identification of the source community through the cultural product may disappear altogether as the item becomes generic. Within its community of origin, the cultural product may cease to be efficacious or to instantiate collective values. Economic value, too, may decline as unauthorized copies flood the market, eliminating exclusivity and casting doubt on quality and authenticity. Unlike the internal battle over the Dead Sea Scrolls described in Chapter Six, misappropriation and public dissemination of a cultural product by an outsider deny the intrinsic relationship between community members and their performance or craft. A cultural product reduced to the state of a mere commodity by the destruction of its intangible value is unlikely to be restored to the source community, much like a misappropriated trade secret or a genie that cannot be put back into the bottle.[2]

INTERNAL LOSSES

While a degree of cultural appropriation may provide mutual benefit to source communities and society at large, some cultural products and their source communities suffer under conditions of misappropriation. In the words of Pueblo member Peggy Bird, "As the airplane flew over I wondered if they were taking pictures of the dance. . . . The airplane disturbed my oneness with the dance and I feel that it violated and upset the Pueblo's balance of life by its disturbance of the dance that day."[3] The dancer describes not only her own distress at being disturbed by a plane repeatedly flying overhead at low altitude and taking photographs, an action that could disrupt any outdoor activity from a family picnic to a professional athletic event, but also the harm to the Pueblo as a whole.

Ceremonial occasions and the traditional activities that accompany them serve to bind together members of the community. Describing the evolutionary origin of art forms, Ellen Dissanayake notes that "properties of rhythms and modes characterize . . . ritual ceremonies—the songs, dances, and other means by which people have perennially become part of a group and have articulated (and felt) its meaningful systems and stories."[4] A deliberate interruption of that rhythm, like the actions of the aerial photographer, can destroy the opportunity to interact and strengthen ties via the medium of a particular cultural product.

Not only can invasive misappropriation cause harm to the community from a functionalist perspective, but it can diminish the cultural product from a cultural-symbolic or expressive perspective as well.[5] The Pueblo's attorney, Scott Borg, noted that the tribal officials believed that interference "tends to negate the effectiveness of the dances," adversely affecting the metaphysical well-being of tribal members and outsiders alike.[6] At least five local religious leaders from outside the Pueblo offered support, expressing disapproval of the disruption of a spiritual occasion and asserting the rights of every religious group to conduct its rituals without interference.[7] Without such protected freedom, both the source community and the cultural product are at risk. Depending on the nature of the tradition, and the type and pervasiveness of misappropriation over time, the community may even abandon the cultural product altogether and thus lose a medium for expression of its beliefs and values. The group may ask itself, "Why bother to unite in dance (or song, prayer, procession, etc.) if we will only be interrupted and put on display?" or, perhaps, "What's so special about wearing (or eating, crafting, displaying, etc.) that if everyone else does too?" Misappropriation can thus impoverish the cultural development of the source community itself.

Intellectual-property-law scholar Roberta Rosenthal Kwall has spoken and written eloquently of the emotional and spiritual component of creativity in the context of copyrightable works, a dimension shared by communities in their creation of cultural products. As Kwall notes, "Authorship entails an intellectual, emotional, and physical effort, which requires protection from economic encroachment as well as damage to the human spirit."[8] For a Native American tribe that has sought to preserve its traditions in the face of centuries-long attempts to coerce assimilation, the lack of protection for cultural products strikes at the heart of communal self-constitution and ritual expression.

External Misrepresentation

In addition to the internal injuries to the source community, cases of cultural misappropriation may lead outsiders to engage in inaccurate, disparaging, or otherwise harmful characterizations of the community or its cultural products. The *New Mexican's* caption describing the Pueblo's ceremonial dance as a "pow-wow" was, according to the complaint, "denigrating and highly offensive, and [cast] the dances and Santo Domingo in a false light. In fact, pow-wows are such a gravely different activity from Santo Domingo's ceremonial dances that the government of the Pueblo has in the past banned participation in pow-wows by tribal members."[9] Modern pow-wows are Native American dance festivals and sometimes competitions generally attended by representatives of multiple tribes, spectators, craftspeople, and refreshment vendors. Although the dancers offer traditional performances and wear elaborately designed tribal costumes, the dances at a pow-wow are removed from their individual ceremonial contexts. These gatherings are a recognized facet of modern Native American culture and play a role in the ongoing formation of a self-determined pan-Indian social and political identity.

Because the cultural function and significance of a pow-wow are far removed from those of the ceremonial dance at the Pueblo of Santo Domingo, the newspaper's confusion of a religious occasion with a secular public display implied disrespect for the ceremonial dance and diminished the significance of the occasion in the public eye. A century earlier, outsiders' observation and misconstrual of another Native American dance had far more egregious results: misrepresentation of the Ghost Dance at Wounded Knee as a military uprising provoked the now-infamous massacre of Lakota men, women, and children. While the harm to the Pueblo of Santo Domingo from the misappropriation and mischaracterization of its cultural product is on a different scale, such behavior can still adversely affect the source community.

DEPRECIATIVE COMMODIFICATION

Not only does misappropriation put the source community at risk of harmful or offensive stereotyping, but it also threatens to devalue cultural products through inappropriate, acontextual exposure or familiarity. Pueblo member and singer Raymond Garcia noted, "It is important for us to take a stand on this issue; otherwise, our religious ceremonies will be looked on as nothing more than commercial entertainment for the white man. This must never happen."[10] The fear that outsiders would engage in unrestricted commodification of images of the ceremonial dance or the dance itself reflects a world in which Tonto accompanies the Lone Ranger, Ralph Lauren ads feature silver-and-turquoise jewelry, Atlanta celebrates its Braves with a tomahawk chop, Jeep Cherokees rule the highways, and Pocahontas is an animated Disney heroine. Academia, politics, and philanthropy have also been avid consumers of Native American cultural products, from the "Indian" disguises of patriots at the Boston Tea Party to the adoption of Sacagawea as a feminist folk heroine to the promotion of Boy Scouts and Camp Fire Girls.[11] Historians and anthropologists of previous generations in search of knowledge (or scholarly recognition) often collected stories, songs, and artifacts without regard for the disruption that their intrusions into the life of the community caused. In much the way that Karl Marx described the capitalist alienation of labor from workers, Native American cultural products have been repeatedly commodified and divorced from their source communities— while the communities themselves were nearly eliminated.

Under these circumstances, communal concern regarding additional encroachments is quite pragmatic. Some products are likely to retain their internal cultural value despite external appropriation; others may lose significance altogether through a process of depreciative commodification. While cultural exchange is not only valuable but inevitable, subaltern source communities and cultural products of religious or spiritual significance are particularly susceptible to damage through misappropriation.

Legal Paradigms

Even when source communities engage in active protection of sacred or otherwise vulnerable cultural properties, it may be difficult to prevent or remedy misappropriation. Visitors to the Pueblo of Santo Domingo, for example, are prohibited from taking photographs or other visual reproductions unless given express permission by the Tribal Council.[12] An aerial photographer, however, is quite beyond the reach of ordinary enforcement methods, necessitating a post hoc invocation of the extra-tribal legal system. Although the Pueblo's legal counsel skillfully set forth the available arguments for the federal district court, current law remains a rather blunt instrument with which to protect a ceremonial dance. Satellite photos of the same occasion, for instance, might be less likely than low-altitude aerial photography to constitute trespass, meet the standards for invasion of privacy, or fall within the jurisdiction of the Pueblo's rules regarding photography.

A more precise cause of action would recognize the ceremonial dance as a protected cultural product, and it would allow the Pueblo to argue that both the photographer and the newspaper damaged that product through unauthorized appropriation. The intangible cultural elements of that particular dance, unenumerated but apparent to both insiders and sympathetic outside observers, were diminished in the community's lived experience and eliminated entirely in the public eye through designation as a "pow-wow." Given the potentially destructive nature of even one instance of this sort of copying, as well as an acute awareness of postcontact Native American history, the concern that a sovereign nation's cultural products could be treated as commercial entertainment appears almost understated. Although the press must remain free to report newsworthy events, the value of intrusive feature reportage to the newspaper-buying public might be evaluated in the context of not only generic actions for trespass and invasion of privacy, but also the harms of cultural misappropriation.

The case of *E. I. du Pont de Nemours & Company v. Christopher,* concerning misappropriation of trade secrets, suggests another potential approach to analyzing *Pueblo of Santo Domingo v. The New Mexican, Inc.*[13] The defendants' actions in the two cases are unusually parallel. During du Pont's construction of a facility near Beaumont, Texas, employees noticed an airplane circling overhead. Further investigation showed that an undisclosed third party had hired defendants Rolfe and Gary Christopher to take aerial photographs of the unfinished facility, revealing du Pont's secret process for producing methanol.[14] The legal basis upon which the du Pont case proceeded was quite different from that available to the Pueblo, however. The Fifth Circuit, affirming the trial court's denial of the defendants' motions for dismissal or alternatively for summary judgment, ruled that the aerial photography constituted "improper means" of discovering a trade secret under the Restatement of Torts, as adopted by state law.[15] This decision rested upon findings that industrial espionage falls below acceptable standards of commercial morality and that a trade-secret holder need take only "reasonable" precautions to protect its property.[16]

If similar rules were to protect cultural products, a court could conclude that the photographer and the newspaper had breached standards of journalistic ethics by obtaining images of the ceremony through improper means. The affidavit of novelist Tony Hillerman, then a professor of journalism and former department chair at the University of New Mexico, asserts, "If in fact, a *New Mexican* photographer did fly at low altitude over Santo Domingo Pueblo taking pictures of a Pueblo religious ritual, such an action could be justified ethically only if it was taken to meet some important public need for information about the ceremony."[17] If a limited category of cultural products were further analogized to trade secrets, a court could also determine that the Pueblo's strictly enforced and widely publicized ban on photography constituted a reasonable precaution against cultural misappropriation.

Although as a practical matter few cultural products are susceptible of protection in a manner resembling trade secrets, the possible harm from cultural-product infringement is similarly severe. Once completely devalued, in economic or social terms, a cultural product reverts back to the status of an ordinary object or practice, assuming that it continues to exist in any form. Its role as the subject of ongoing community authorship terminates. Like a genericized trademark, or perhaps a patent or copyright abandoned by its owner, the denatured product no longer merits protection. Even when unauthorized appropriation of a cultural product does not result in its destruction, the cumulative harm of many instances of misappropriation may erode the value of the product or the values expressed by its source community. Any legal efforts to protect cultural products must take into account their varying degrees of durability and the potential level of harm to the source community from external appropriation.

Legal Damage

For cultural products that source communities identify as sacred, secret, or otherwise particularly susceptible to damage by misappropriation, appeal to the legal system can itself cause additional harm. The law has its own procedural rules, logical structure, and culture, and these may be at odds with the norms of the group seeking protection. In case of the Pueblo of Santo Domingo, Florence Hawley Ellis, emeritus professor of anthropology, offered her expert testimony in order to "reliev[e] the people of the Pueblo from having to face interrogation about their religion and their beliefs, which they would find very painful."[18] Indeed, nowhere does the complaint name the dance performed on January 21, 1984, or describe its specific purpose.

Even when laws are drafted specifically to protect cultural heritage, the majority legislature or officials may not be sufficiently familiar with the beliefs and value systems of an individual source community to prevent conflict. In Australia, the complex and controversial saga of the Hindmarsh Island Bridge sparked a national debate over state and federal legislation regarding Aboriginal heritage. The struggle began in the late 1980s, when marina developers Tom and Wendy Chapman formulated plans to build a bridge across the Murray River in order to connect the mainland with Hindmarsh Island and eliminate ferry service. Construction began in 1993 but quickly ceased in the face of Aboriginal protests.[19]

When the South Australian state government announced in early 1994 that construction would continue, a legal representative of the Lower Murray Aboriginal Heritage Committee contacted the federal minister for Aboriginal and Torres Strait Islander affairs, Robert Tickner. The letter to the minister indicated that the Ngarrindjeri people, threatened with imminent desecration of a sacred site, had "reluctantly divulged some secret/sacred information about the Hindmarsh Island, the Lakes and Coorong area including the sea, in an attempt to more clearly show the effect of the bridge upon their cultural integrity and tradition. They have given me instructions to disclose this information to you to assist your assessment of the importance of this matter for Aboriginal people and in particular the Ngarrindjeri people."[20] The letter went on to explain that the topography of the proposed bridge site had a specific set of cultural meanings pertaining to the creation and renewal of life that should not be altered, nor should there be a permanent physical link between the island and the mainland. The potential harm to the Ngarrindjeri people was described in terms of "cultural trauma," and the proposed bridge, as "obscene and sacrilegious."[21] Although the letter did not disclose the particular restrictions on secret/sacred knowledge, it was later revealed that the restriction was on what came to be known as "women's business," which could not be disclosed to men.[22]

In response to the letter, Tickner issued an emergency order under the federal Aboriginal and Torres Strait Islander Protection Act of 1984, temporarily halting construction of the bridge. In addition, he commissioned legal scholar Cheryl Anne Saunders, working with an anthropologist, to prepare a report on the significance of the proposed bridge site in Aboriginal culture. When Saunders submitted her report in July 1994, it included a sealed envelope marked confidential and to be read by women only. After reviewing the body of the report and consulting with a female staff member authorized to read the confidential appendices, Tickner issued a twenty-five-year ban on construction in the area.[23]

The Chapmans, whose company had gone into receivership and was ultimately forced to sell the marina for a fraction of its value, challenged Tickner's ban in court. By February 1995, Federal Court Justice Maurice O'Loughlin had concluded that the Saunders Report was flawed and that, in any case, Tickner's decision not to read the confidential material constituted a failure to properly "consider" the report as required by law.[24] Shortly after this decision, another male federal minister publicly announced that his office had come into possession of copies of the secret appendices, which he had deliberately copied and read; he was forced to resign shortly thereafter.[25] While Tickner appealed the quashing of his ban on construction of the bridge, a group of Aboriginal women (as well as men) who became known as the "dissident women" publicly claimed that the secret "women's business" did not exist.[26] A Royal Commission began investigation of the alleged fabrication, but many of the "proponent women," who supported the claims of sacredness, refused to once again entrust their secrets to a government body.[27] In December 1995, the court dismissed Tickner's appeal, and the Royal Commission announced its conclusion that the cultural claims had been fabricated.[28]

Construction of the now-infamous Hindmarsh Island Bridge proceeded, and the bridge opened in March 2001. Ferry service to the island ceased, leaving the proponent women, who refused to cross the bridge, unable to reach the island.[29] Meanwhile, the Chapmans, seeking millions of dollars in damages, sued the Commonwealth of Australia, Tickner, Saunders, and others. In August 2001, Justice John von Doussa dismissed the suit and effectively rejected the findings of the Royal Commission, stating, "I am not satisfied that the restricted women's knowledge was fabricated or that it was not part of genuine Aboriginal tradition."[30] Although the damage to the sacred site would not be reversed, the proponent women celebrated the decision and publicly called for a government apology.[31]

The Chapmans, who had become in conservative circles a symbol of beleaguered white Australians, appealed the decision.[32] In September 2002, however, the two hundred-year-old remains of a Ngarrindjeri woman and her daughter were unearthed near the Goolwa wharf, in the shadow of the Hindmarsh Bridge. These remains served as physical proof that the proponent women's claims, which included the presence of a burial ground in the area, were in fact true.[33] After this discovery, the Chapmans dropped their appeal, leaving them potentially liable for millions of dollars in legal fees.[34]

The local Alexandrina Council responded to the new evidence with a unanimous motion apologizing for the pain and suffering inflicted on the Ngarrindjeri people since European settlement.[35] Under the terms of an agreement signed by the local government and Ngarrindjeri representatives, future development involving traditional lands will be subject to collaborative oversight. This pact is known as the Kungun Ngarrindjeri Yunnan Agreement, translated as "Listen to the Ngarrindjeri People Talking."[36]

Despite the embraces and good intentions for the future, a fundamental set of cultural, legal, and political difficulties remains. Secrecy, sacredness, and exclusivity are fundamental characteristics of the most carefully protected cultural products of many source communities. Western legal systems, however, rely on presentation of evidence and the weighing of testimony by impartial finders of fact. It is difficult for a court to "listen to the Ngarrindjeri people talking" if their beliefs and traditions discourage or prevent them from doing so. The keepers of knowledge within the source community are thus required to choose between revealing their secrets in the hope of receiving government protection and allowing the desecration of a cultural product, whether a ceremonial dance or the normative use of sacred site. Courts, moreover, are correctly reluctant to intervene in disputes that might breach the church/state barrier by involving religious interpretation. For cases in which there is substantial disagreement within the source community, whether or not divided along lines of gender or privilege, judicial involvement becomes still more problematic.

The intervention of anthropologists or others trained to prepare sufficient information to satisfy a legal inquiry while leaving intact the source-community members' commitment to protecting their beliefs from outside scrutiny may facilitate compromise on a case-by-case basis. When millions of American or Australian dollars, development of prime real estate, or other indicia of Western progress are at stake, however, neither courts nor politicians may be willing to defer to claims that cannot be "proven" by reference to a distant, uncorrupted cultural past.[37] By reifying culture or by indirectly encouraging stereotypes of indigenous peoples (like women, slaves, and other non-privileged groups) as "irrational and secretive, yet cunning and interfering," legal intervention may inadvertently cause additional harm.[38]

The public, relatively transparent nature of dispute-resolution proceedings is part of the bedrock of a liberal democracy. Secret tribunals and the exercise of coercive power cannot survive modern constitutional muster; nevertheless, most disputes never reach our judicial system, and the vast majority of those that do are settled out of court for reasons of expense and expediency. This privatization of justice has been the subject of much criticism, and it holds serious implications for equal access to law.[39] Extrajudicial forms of dispute resolution sometimes function well, however, against a background of well-defined law and previously published judicial opinions. In the case of secret or sacred cultural products, the establishment of normative rules regarding appropriation and alternative fora might facilitate protection—especially when judicial involvement risks additional harm. The benefits in these cases may outweigh loss of any pedagogical function of public law in the area of cultural appropriation. In the case of the Pueblo of Santo Domingo, the source community did seek judicial intervention but settled approximately a year after the events occurred, thus avoiding further invasion of their communal life and beliefs.[40]

THE MISAPPROPRIATION OF certain cultural products, often those that the source community considers sacred, secret, or exclusive to members of the community, has the potential to cause significant harm at several levels. Were judicial action generally available, it would not necessarily act as a panacea, given the embedded norms and practices of the legal system. The lack of a legal framework to address cultural misappropriation, whether by analogy to trade secrets, to invasion of privacy, or to some other cause of action, nevertheless leaves communities without guidance or protection. Even if the goal is simply to promote alternative dispute resolution, American law should not remain largely silent regarding cultural misappropriation.

CHAPTER 9

Permissive Appropriation

Think free speech, not free beer.
—Richard M. Stallman

EACH JANUARY *The Watchtower*, an official magazine of the Jehovah's Witnesses, prints a chart detailing the accomplishments of members in spreading information about their beliefs.[1] Witnesses in more than 230 countries collectively spend over a billion hours annually preaching, in addition to devoting time to the dissemination of literature and the baptism of new members.[2] Indeed, you may personally recall politely but firmly shutting the door on an eager believer who was attempting to share the good news. Nevertheless, personal outreach is an intrinsic part of being a Jehovah's Witness, and the normative behavior of each church member includes the communication of information about the community's teachings. The goal of this communication is to persuade listeners to adopt, or appropriate, the same beliefs. Unlike the ceremonial dance at the Pueblo of Santo Domingo discussed in the previous chapter, the Bible and related Jehovah's Witness literature and beliefs exist in the realm of the sacred but are neither secret nor exclusive—indeed, their widespread distribution is itself a positive value.

While some cultural products are by nature incompatible with any form of appropriation, others thrive on regulated external access. In some cases, the positive symbiosis between cultural products and outside use occurs serendipitously. Scholarly interest may preserve a regional dialect, the tourist market may support traditional handicrafts, and "green" consumers may seek out and learn traditional techniques of organic farming. In other cases, the intangible goods develop with an eye to public presentation of community identity, as in the example of a parade or street festival. The most deliberate form of permissive appropriation involves the source community's designation of external access according to group norms as a positive value, as in missionary religions or the open-source software movement. Common to all forms of permissive appropriation is the understanding that, from the source community's perspective, the license to appropriate is not unlimited, and outsiders should respect the intangible cultural aspects of the borrowed products.

FREE FOR ALL, NOT FREE-FOR-ALL

"A vigorous tribe of partisans native to the Internet," frequently known as hackers or geeks, claims the free or open-source software movement as one of its most significant cultural products.[3] As a model of production, open source harnesses the voluntary contributions of thousands of individuals to create arguably better results far more quickly than conventional methods that use technical and legal devices to shield each author's work from others. The informal, collaborative method of software development and the resulting programs such as the Linux operating system are available to anyone who wishes to use or modify them, provided that the source code remains accessible. While open-source software products may be subject to limited commodification—for example to facilitate consumer access and convenience—the source code itself by definition remains subject to free redistribution, thus facilitating perpetual improvement and development of the product.

Cooperative production is, of course, not unique to the internet era. Free or open-source software is frequently analogized to efforts such as an Amish barn raising, the compilation of the original, nineteenth-century Oxford English Dictionary from letters sent by distant etymologists, or even the instinctually orchestrated industry of a beehive.[4] Cultural products, folklore, and traditional knowledge, as apparent from preceding chapters, are fundamentally the result of group authorship. The exponential growth of the open-source production model in the modern corporate world, however, indicates a preliminary shift in perception among the onetime proponents of management flowcharts, assembly lines, and proprietary research. Institutions from IBM to NASA now make use of open-source methods for certain projects. The collaborative technological culture that gave rise to the internet, the ease of online interaction, the perceived need to operate outside restrictive intellectual-property provisions, and new attitudes regarding information management have combined to make this florescence of open source possible.[5]

Computer programmers embrace free or open-source production for different reasons, ranging from hostility to commercial endeavors (embodied by the popular mantra "Microsoft sucks"), and by extension skepticism toward intellectual property law, to the belief that open collaboration simply produces better results. In a working paper for MIT's Sloan School of Management, Karim Lakhani and Robert Wolf published the results of their survey of the motivations of those who contribute to open-source projects.[6] Contrary to earlier theorizing, they found that intrinsic motivations such as intellectual stimulation and enjoyment of the creative process outweighed extrinsic motivations like career advancement. Other important factors included user need, a desire to improve programming skills, belief in the principle of open source, and a sense of obligation to give back to the open-source community.[7]

Some ideological tension exists within the free/open-source community, as apparent in the debate between proponents of digital prophet Richard Stallman's original "free software" terminology, which is intended to emphasize principles of freedom and an antiproprietary stance, and users of the more recent but more common "open source" designation. Stallman, discussing the 1998 decision by some members of the community to adopt the term "open source," claims, "Some who favored this term aimed to avoid the confusion of 'free' with 'gratis'—a valid goal. Others, however, aimed to set aside the spirit of principle that had motivated the free software movement and the GNU [operating-system] project, and to appeal instead to executives and business users, many of whom hold an ideology that places profit above freedom, above community, above principle. Thus, the rhetoric of 'Open Source' focuses on the potential to make high quality, powerful software, but shuns the ideas of freedom, community, and principle."[8] Stallman does not entirely reject the corporate world, however, as his Free Software Foundation solicits and accepts corporate patronage.[9]

The Open Source Initiative (OSI), under the direction of its chronicler and evangelist Eric Raymond, offers a different interpretation of the move to open source terminology. Prompted by Netscape's decision to release the source code of its browser, the group recognized a window of opportunity to teach the corporate world about the merits of an open development process. "We realized it was time to dump the confrontational attitude that has been associated with 'free software' in the past and sell the idea strictly on the same pragmatic, business-case grounds that motivated Netscape. . . . Richard Stallman flirted with adopting the term, then changed his mind."[10] OSI adherents do not necessarily reject the value structure associated with "free software," but they choose to privilege technological over ideological merits. Even among the users of "open source," there is disparity between those with technological and those with teleological aims. Linus Torvalds, the founder of the open-source Linux operating system, often touted as David to Microsoft's Goliath, reflects this distinction, stating, "I'm interested in Linux because of the technology, and Linux wasn't started as any kind of rebellion against the 'evil Microsoft empire.' Quite the reverse, in fact: from a technology angle, Microsoft really has been one of the least interesting companies. . . . Really, I'm not out to destroy Microsoft. That will just be a completely unintentional side effect."[11]

Despite these differences in terminology, perspective, and objectives, participants in the free/open-source software culture regularly refer to citizenship in the movement and to civic behavior associated with it. Whether dogmatic or pragmatic, members agree that their interests are better served by collective effort and free redistribution of source code than by emulation of the Romantic model of authorship. Under this extreme rubric of permissive appropriation, copying does not destroy cultural value; it is a cultural value.

The open-source software community, notwithstanding its informal origins, incorporates clear normative standards; the availability of free software is not aimed at precipitating a technological free-for-all.

Strict social expectations or customary laws govern open-source development, and explicit rules dictate the dissemination of open-source software and derivative works.[12] Successful open-source projects tend to coalesce around a guiding founder, like Torvalds for Linux, and there exists social pressure not to "fork" or divide a project into incompatible parts. As with other cultural products, however, disputes may occur among community members or in response to outside appropriation.

Licensing and even intellectual property law play a significant role in enforcing open-source community standards. Stallman adopted the term "copyleft" to describe principles for distribution of software that ensure continuing access to its source code and that of any modifications, often implemented under the GNU General Public License (GPL).[13] OSI provides links to the GNU GPL and other approved open-source licenses and encourages their use, effectively creating an open-source legal process.[14] In addition, the OSI certification mark and program attempt to ensure that labeled products conform to stated cultural norms or standards.[15] Unlike a collective mark indicating membership in a trade organization, OSI's certification mark is available to any product that meets the organization's requirements and embodies the intangible values of the open-source movement.[16] OSI's decision to utilize a certification mark rather than a collective mark comports with open-source culture's emphasis on informal, permissive appropriation. For other cultural products, an "authenticity mark" could take the form of either a collective mark or a certification mark, depending on the preference of the cultural group.

While source-community norms governing permissive appropriation generally prohibit external commodification of the cultural product itself, users may still benefit economically from the cultural product. In the open-source arena, Red Hat and other companies package and sell the Linux operating system. The purchaser in this case does not buy the actual product, which is available free of charge, but instead pays for training, education, documentation, customer support, and consulting services—that is, "for the convenience of retail packaging and for the support that comes along with it."[17] Raymond compares this business model to giving away the recipe and opening a restaurant.[18] The sellers ideally make a profit, their employees not only write code in their spare time but also make a living, and the buyers receive the necessary technological assistance to engage in permissive appropriation of the source code.

Additional commodification of open source occurs in the context of multinational corporations and governments, which have adopted not only open-source methodology but also Linux and other open-source software. China, Japan, and South Korea have announced plans to collaborate on an open-source alternative to Microsoft, and developing countries like Vietnam have been encouraged by the United Nations Development Program to explore open source as a way of bridging the divide between technology-importing and technology-exporting countries.[19]

Within the source community the limited commercialization of its cultural product remains somewhat controversial, especially among those who believe that proprietary software is unethical or antisocial. Commodification of the individual's value-added, rather than the community's cultural product, and the widespread use of OSI-approved licenses nevertheless represent a compromise between strict, anticommercial limitations on permissive appropriation and unauthorized, subversive misappropriation.

Both free or open-source software programs and the principles and methods of open source are cultural products that thrive on permissive appropriation. While some bugs remain in the model, as apparent from incidents like the SCO Group's copyright challenge to a portion of the Linux code, every problem is an invitation to multiple contributors to seek a solution.[20] The infrastructure of the digital age is ideally suited to open source, and the success of this cultural product can be measured by the speed with which the phrase, the concept, and the software products themselves have gone viral and become part of our daily lives.

IMPLIED PERMISSION

The pilates method of exercise is another cultural product that has spread successfully through permissive appropriation, despite the efforts of a small number of practitioners to transform at least its name into protected intellectual property. Much like Kwanzaa, discussed in Chapter Four, pilates was originally the brainchild of one individual who sought to promote it among members of the public, albeit while charging for his services and publications. Decades after the death of its founder, pilates is a worldwide fitness phenomenon—and trademark litigation has been required to ascertain and preserve the nature of this product.

Josef Hubertus Pilates was born in Germany in 1880. After suffering from asthma and other diseases during childhood, he devoted himself to developing physical strength through bodybuilding, gymnastics, and other athletic activities. At the outset of World War I, Pilates was living in England and was subject to internment as an enemy alien. While in the camp he trained fellow inmates in the system of exercises that he had developed. After the war, he returned to Germany and continued his fitness-training programs. In 1926, Pilates immigrated to America, where he and his wife, Clara, set up an exercise studio in New York City. Word of Pilates' method, which he called "contrology," spread through the professional dance community, and many dancers came to the studio for training or rehabilitation.[21]

At the same time, Pilates continued to promote his method and philosophy to a wider audience, publishing *Your Health: A Corrective System of Exercising That Revolutionizes the Entire Field of Physical Education* in 1934 and *Return to Life through Contrology* in 1945.[22] In his writing he adopted a fervent tone, invoking the welfare of the human race and claiming, "Truth will prevail and that is why I know that my teachings will reach the masses and finally be adopted as universal."[23] According to a former student and master teacher, Romana Kryzanowska, Pilates wanted "the Pilates method everywhere to be for the world so that everyone could benefit from it."[24] Many of Pilates' students went on to become instructors themselves, teaching not only at his own satellite Pilates Studio at the Henri Bendel department store in New York City but also in other facilities around the country. Although Pilates patented several pieces of exercise equipment, neither he nor his wife attempted to limit the use of their name by other instructors. Pilates died in 1967 without leaving a will or otherwise providing for the future of his now-eponymous method of exercise.[25]

After Pilates' death, control of his studio passed through several hands. Clara Pilates continued to run it for several years, followed by Kryzanowska, who taught at the original studio and its subsequent location until it finally closed in 1989. During this period, service marks incorporating or consisting of the Pilates name were registered, lapsed, and were registered again. In 1992, Sean Gallagher, the co-founder of a separate pilates-based business, purchased the existing "pilates" and "pilates studio" service marks. In addition, Gallagher registered a "pilates" trademark for exercise equipment. Unlike his predecessors, Gallagher vigorously policed the marks, sending hundreds of cease-and-desist letters to competing instructors, studios, and equipment manufacturers and also initiating several lawsuits claiming infringement.[26] Two of these cases, *Pilates, Inc. v. Current Concepts, Inc.* and *Pilates, Inc. v. Georgetown Bodyworks Deep Muscle Massage Centers, Inc.*, resulted in the cancellation of the marks as generic, or referring to the exercise method in general rather than to Gallagher's operation in particular.[27]

Although Gallagher and others warned that the courts' decisions would leave the public subject to an adulterated, nonstandard method of exercise, many members of the pilates community celebrated the outcome of the litigation. Not only were studios and instructors outside Gallagher's Pilates Guild relieved for business reasons, but pilates devotees inside and outside the network also celebrated a normative philosophical victory. Pilates (the method) had become the free cultural product that Pilates (the man) had intended, according to his own words and actions, the testimony of his students, and the reasoning of the courts.

The opponents of permissive appropriation of pilates were correct in the sense that unregulated copying often leads to adaptation and reinterpretation. Like other cultural products, pilates can be expected to change and evolve over time; hybrids such as "yogalates" and variations that cater to cardiovascular fitness, weight loss, and pregnancy have already appeared. Just as Josef Pilates incorporated his own fitness training and study of yoga into the method, so too subsequent instructors can be expected to refine pilates training through their own experiences and insights.

Balancing the pressure to innovate, however, are source-community norms that seek to preserve and ensure the integrity of the pilates system. In the absence of any proprietary ownership of the term "pilates" or the method itself, or of an authoritative body analogous to Kwanzaa's Organization Us or to the Rolf Institute of Structural Integration, the authenticity wars have begun. A number of organizations, including Gallagher's Pilates Studio, offer training in "authentic pilates," a phrase that some claim as an unregistered trademark.[28] A brief invocation of Josef Pilates, whether in the form of a quotation or a short biography, is standard practice in pilates manuals and on websites. Studios often display or make available the reissued versions of Pilates' publications. In addition, individual teachers appear to gain authenticity points by tracing their own apprenticeships back through one of several well-known protégés of Josef to the master himself, much the way a German academic might invoke his or her *Doktorvater*. While these appeals to authenticity do not guarantee commercial products that would meet with the founder's approval, they do reflect social pressure to remain faithful to the original exercise method.

The establishment of pilates as a cultural product subject to permissive appropriation was not the direct result of a judicial decision, but rather a by-product of conventional intellectual property litigation. If the marks in question had been registered and maintained at an earlier date or if the widespread popularity of the method had not clearly rendered generic the term "pilates," Pilates' desire for widespread adoption of his work might have been hampered by the posthumous capture and reduction to property of his name. The court in the *Current Concepts* case wisely emphasized Josef Pilates' own desires and actions in declaring the term generic with respect to an exercise method and equipment.[29] If the law had recognized cultural products and established an optional mechanism for permissive appropriation, the court's inquiry could have been limited to Pilates' intent—and the complexities and issue distortion of a trademark battle could have been avoided. A source community's intentions with respect to its cultural products are not always as easy to identify as in the case of pilates, but current intellectual property law does not offer an adequate surrogate legal framework.

LIMITED PERMISSION

In the case of sacred or secret cultural products, limited permissive appropriation can be used to combat the problem of misappropriation discussed in Chapter Eight. Maori tribal leaders in New Zealand adopted this approach to director Peter Jackson's request to use a sacred site in the course of filming J.R.R. Tolkien's *Lord of the Rings* trilogy. Middle Earth locations from the Shire to Mordor are set throughout New Zealand; for one of these, Mount Doom, the filmmakers selected Mount Ruapehu in Tongariro National Park on central North Island. This volcano, however, is sacred to the local Maori, who do not look at its peak and consider drawing or photographing it offensive. As a compromise, Jackson agreed to film the mountain from a nearby ski area and to use digital effects to make it unrecognizable. The resulting fiery, lava-covered slopes conceal the real appearance of Ruapehu while meeting the creative needs of the project.[30] Although this type of cultural appropriation can be successful only against a background of legal or social pressure to respect the limited grant of permission, it has the potential to protect both social and economic values and to avoid harm to the source community or its cultural products.

IF MISAPPROPRIATION REPRESENTS the worst-case scenario for cultural appropriation, then permissive appropriation is the best case. Rather than struggle to exercise exclusive ownership and control over all of their cultural products, some source communities choose to offer them to the general public. Whether free or limited, this permissive appropriation becomes a guided conduit for cultural products and informs the relationships between the source community and outsiders as well as within the source community. Indeed, for some communities and their creations, the promotion of widespread appropriation or copying becomes a positive value in itself. Paradoxically, the grant of access to outsiders may result in greater observance of cultural norms, as the recipients are more likely to be informed of and to respect source-group standards than are mere thieves. Permissive appropriation in the absence of a legal structure exposes cultural products to potential abuse; however, it also offers a distinct and creative model of cultural-product management. With increased legal attention to cultural products, permissive appropriation according to formal or informal community guidelines could play a significant role in the realm of cultural exchange.

CHAPTER 10

Reverse Appropriation of Intellectual Properties and Celebrity Personae

Technology is the campfire of the global village.

—Marshall McLuhan

ACTOR LEONARD NIMOY, known to millions as a member of the original *Star Trek* cast, has written two professional memoirs. The 1975 version, *I Am Not Spock*, addresses the "competition" between actor and famous character and discusses the philosophical and professional difficulties caused by popular conflation of the two.[1] Fans were unsympathetic, to say the least; Nimoy reports receiving letters that said, "We made you and we can break you!"[2] Twenty years later Nimoy published *I Am Spock*, a longer and more cordial analysis of a longer and still more successful association between himself and his alter ego, punctuated with pages of dialogue between the two.[3] The actor continues to create the character, not only when paid to do so for television or the movies but also during personal appearances, in print, and even as a frequent voice in his head. He adds, "And if I'm not listening to Spock's voice, then I'm listening to the voices of those who know the Vulcan and consider him an old friend."[4]

Nimoy, however, is not the only medium for the ongoing expression of Spock, nor is he the sole author of his own celebrity persona. Trekkies demand—and receive—public protestations of the actor's loyalty to his character, and during public appearances they look for elements of the character in the actor. In addition, many celebrated his decision to appear as Spock in an episode of *Star Trek: The Next Generation*, an action that Nimoy describes as having addressed a "family issue" that divided adherents of the original series from those of its successor.[5] In this connection, Nimoy notes that "fan lore" defines the name "Spock" as "uniter" in the character's native Vulcan language.[6] Some fans elevate Nimoy to a still higher plane, characterizing him as a chosen conduit for human acceptance of extraterrestrial intelligence.[7]

Spock is an even more pliable figure than Nimoy in the hands of his devotees, especially those who write "fan fiction" featuring him. Nimoy adopts an amused tone toward these works, mentioning in particular the fantasies expressed by female fans, as opposed to homo-erotic stories involving Spock and Captain Kirk or action/adventure tales chronicling the exploits of the Enterprise and her crew, including Spock.[8] Nimoy acknowledges being flattered by literary and personal attention from fans but adds, "At the same time, I know it's not me, but Spock they want."[9]

The examples of cultural appropriation in earlier chapters involved the proprietary adoption of source-community culture by outsiders, usually in a legal vacuum. In the case of reverse appropriation, it is communities that engage in the creative adoption of individually owned properties. This collective secondary creation—Nimoy's ongoing development of Spock according to popular demand, fans' influence over both the celebrity persona of the actor and the alternative adventures of the character, even the wearing of pointed ears or other costume elements at a *Star Trek* convention—exists against a backdrop of intellectual property law. Paramount Pictures holds copyrights and trademarks related to *Star Trek*, and Nimoy has rights of publicity, or limited rights to control the use of his image, under various state laws. In his second memoir, Nimoy was careful to acknowledge the corporate intellectual properties among his raw material and to note his authorization to use them.[10] Similarly, many works of fan fiction include disclaimers that deny any intention to infringe on or compete with protected source materials.

Intellectual property rights are not absolute; creative fans enjoy some general protection under fair-use provisions and First

Amendment free speech protections.[11] In addition, the permissive cultural norms of the early internet era regarding intellectual property, while offering no legal support to fans, have made draconian enforcement by corporate holders of intellectual property rights unpopular. Some intellectual property owners, moreover, perceive benefit in permitting the public to transform copyrighted or trademarked works freely. Nevertheless, as long as other rights holders place a high value on maintaining control of their works, secondary creative works will continue to exist largely at sufferance, under the shadow of potential legal action by rights holders. Although legal commentators have argued for clearer and more permissive standards with respect to consumer use of intellectual property, noting that all art draws in some way on previous elements of human creation, the status of secondary creative works remains ambiguous.[12]

From the perspective of cultural appropriation, the restrictions of intellectual property law and rights of publicity can appear both one-sided and asocial. While Nimoy drew on his Orthodox Jewish upbringing for the V-shaped hand symbol that forms the Vulcan salute, it is not clear that a synagogue or youth group could sell postcards or paint a mural adapting Spock's (or Nimoy's) image without permission.[13] On a broader scale, the creators of Star Trek drew on the modern folklore that forms the science fiction/fantasy genre and on modern liberal and aesthetic values in order to create an alternative reality and devise a fictional mission to serve as a vehicle for their storytelling. Intellectual property law, to the degree that rights holders choose to avail themselves of it, limits the extent to which these new elements, characters, and stories become part of the public domain and thus available as raw material for future creative endeavors. Although the public is invited to purchase and consume Star Trek and other commercial creations, to internalize or identify with them and become fans, and even to join together in social groups that share a common bond of appreciation for a television show, sports team, or entertainer, this use is typically expected to be passive and not active or transformative. Whether fan clubs gather in person or through the medium of the internet, their expressions of communal creativity are circumscribed by copyright, trademark, and rights of publicity.

Reverse appropriation of individual creations by cultural groups nevertheless occurs on a regular basis.

Reverse Appropriation of Celebrity Personae

The angry fans who responded to Nimoy's first memoir with the claim that they had the power to make or break him were, in one sense, correct. It is apparent without the aid of complex metaphysical analysis that Nimoy the human being and Nimoy the trained professional actor exist independently from the social or psychic investment of an audience; Nimoy the celebrity, however, is dependent upon the collective awareness and goodwill of a segment of society. Science fiction and particularly *Star Trek* fans who celebrate Nimoy/Spock are necessary to the life of the projected celebrity persona, and they have a combined effect on the development of that persona. Certain behaviors, like signing autographs or appearing in character at a *Star Trek* convention, are expected; others, like an apparent attempt to distance actor from character, are rejected. When fans recognize themselves as a cultural group, whether preexisting or newly formed, they may claim a relationship akin to authorship or ownership of a celebrity, naming (or rejecting) him or her as one of their own. Under these circumstances a type of reverse cultural appropriation occurs, and the group asserts a heightened privilege to define, imitate, or edit the image of its celebrity member. This is not to suggest that fans could in any sense own an individual, an assertion that would be anathema under our legal system, but merely that the creation and maintenance of a public persona is often a collective effort.

The interaction between an individual and the public that results in the projection of a celebrity persona is often mutual and voluntary, as when an entertainer, sports figure, politician, activist, or pundit provides the public with the diversion or leadership that it seeks in return for fame and perhaps fortune. One path to celebrity is from within a defined community. Jennifer Lopez, for example, began her career with an emphasis on her Puerto Rican heritage via the Bronx, and even as an international superstar and model for French luxury-goods company Louis Vuitton she still claimed to be "Jenny from the Block."

Other celebrities come to prominence primarily as cultural adoptees. Like many New Yorkers, Babe Ruth was born and began his career elsewhere, but he is best remembered as a Yankee (except perhaps by Boston Red Sox fans). Similarly, neither Barbra nor Judy is a gay man, but both divas have iconic status within the gay community. Still other celebrities are born national or even international, gaining stardom through the vehicle of a hit movie or television show and afterward claimed by a newly formed cadre of fans. In each case publicists and other assistants may facilitate the relationship between an individual and her core constituency, working to define a public image and grooming the celebrity to fit her idealized persona.

Individual notoriety or infamy is less likely to be the product of deliberate mutual creation, unless the subject seeks to project a counter-cultural image. Tales of legendary outlaws like Robin Hood and Jesse James, for example, become part of popular culture and achieve the status of folklore without necessarily reflecting historical reality. More recently, a modern criminal defendant like John Gotti can be assimilated to the prevalent fictional Mafia archetype, raising questions of whether life imitates art. Exaggerated conflicts between hip-hop artists or the heroes and villains of professional wrestling are more entertainment-driven, offering fans the opportunity to embrace favorite antiheroes. While a true celebrity malfeasant may not seek publicity or may deny actual wrongdoing, the public nevertheless imagines and perpetuates an image consistent with the individual's reported statements and acts.

In other situations, a social group may attempt to claim or adopt a celebrity against the express wishes of the individual or in a contested context. Mixed-race golf phenomenon Tiger Woods persistently identifies himself as "Cablinasian," despite pressure to emphasize the African-American portion of his heritage.[14] Although he does not deny his lineage or the troubled social history of the previously all-white game, neither does he make explicit his intrinsic link to other figures who have exploded stereotypes or broken racial barriers. In addition, he has avoided taking a strong stand on related issues like the exclusion of women from major golf courses internationally.[15] Given the complex perceptions and history of race in America, Woods cannot (and perhaps would not chose to) erase color from his public persona. He continues, however, to resist simplified classifications or reverse appropriation by individual communities, civil rights activists, and even fans. Historic figures have less say over their own appropriation; it is unclear whether Abraham Lincoln would choose to be a member of the present-day Republican "party of Lincoln," despite his historical affiliation.

This brief taxonomy of celebrity appropriation, in which a segment of the public embraces a well-known figure as its own, illustrates the importance of individual figures to communal identity formation. Whether voluntary or involuntary, the contribution of celebrity personae to social networks can inspire acts of secondary creativity, from impersonation to emulation to adaptation of the celebrity's image or works, that reinforce the association between individual and community. While celebrity status requires at least the passive participation of the public, creative appropriation or even an expectation that a celebrity conform to a particular image can highlight potentially divergent interests between an individual and a group of fans.

Rights of publicity under various state laws protect an individual's investment in his or her persona, but they fail to recognize or conceptualize any cultural-ownership interest of the audience groups who have contributed to the creation of that persona.[16] Efforts in cyberspace have sporadically challenged this standard; for example, brucespringsteen.com remains a fan site, despite The Boss's attempt to have the domain name transferred to him.[17] The trademark jurisprudence that informs domain-name disputes and other internet usage pertaining to celebrities does not specifically take into account the collective interests of fans, however, but instead relies on individualized concepts such as good faith and fair use. As a result, the overwhelming tendency in domain-name disputes has been to favor the trademark owner over ostensible fans and cybersquatters alike.[18] The legal system has yet to take into account the communal creativity that results in the establishment and sometimes the reverse appropriation of celebrity personae.

Reverse Appropriation of Intellectual Properties

Intellectual properties, like celebrity personae, rely on public contribution in ways not always recognized by the law. While trademarks that are not inherently distinctive must acquire "secondary meaning" in order to enjoy protection, most copyrights, patents, and trademarks are protected *ab initio* regardless of whether they are recognized by their intended markets. Nevertheless, as Rosemary Coombe has described in her landmark study of the appropriation of intellectual properties, the life of an invention or work of authorship depends on public response to these signifiers.[19] The most successful intellectual properties in economic and cultural terms are those in which the public has made the greatest investment. Such creative works become cultural icons, even if still owned by individuals or corporations; Elvis, Mickey Mouse, and McDonald's are as American as Mom, baseball, and apple pie. As in the case of celebrity personae, private ownership of record may conflict with informal public claims of ownership, especially when an intellectual property has particular significance for a defined community. A community may define itself in terms of an intellectual property, like *Star Trek* fans, or in opposition to an intellectual property.[20] In either case, reverse appropriation of the preexisting work can have legal consequences.

Since 1936, Margaret Mitchell's *Gone with the Wind* has become an American icon, defining the antebellum South and its Lost Cause for millions of readers and moviegoers. One of them, twelve-year-old Alice Randall, took exception to this portrayal. Lacking a satisfactory explanation for the relative absence of mixed-race characters or for the limited agency of African Americans in the text, Randall grew up to rewrite the book—and then some. Her work, *The Wind Done Gone*, takes the form of the diary of Scarlett O'Hara's unacknowledged mixed-race half-sister, whose life story offers a different perspective on the events of the original novel and its historical setting. From the title to signature phrases to provocatively renamed characters, Randall's work unapologetically borrows from the original.[21] Indeed, *The Wind Done Gone* is far less coherent without prior knowledge of *Gone with the Wind*.

This reinterpretation roused the ire of the Mitchell estate, which sued to block publication of the "sequel." As legal academics and editorial writers waved the banner of free speech and decried the prospect of intellectual property rights strangling creative expression, attorneys for the author and publisher argued that *The Wind Done Gone* was not a sequel but rather a legally protected parody. The first round went to the copyright owners. A federal district court in Atlanta, the home of both Mitchell and her fictional heroine, issued a preliminary injunction against publication of the book.[22] The U.S. Court of Appeals for the Eleventh Circuit, however, vacated the order and cleared the path to publication.[23] Although the parties ultimately reached a settlement, Randall's sojourn on the best-seller lists owed much to the legal controversy surrounding her iconoclastic work.

Because the lawsuit occurred during a national debate over copyright-term extension, much of the public discussion of *The Wind Done Gone* centered not on whether it was a parody, but on the normative scope of the original author's copyright versus the secondary author's right to engage in free speech.[24] This focus on individual rights, while inherent in our legal system, is misleading. Randall defended her work not as a mere personal statement but as "an antidote to a text that has hurt generations of African-Americans."[25] In other words, her use of elements of *Gone with the Wind* was an act of cultural appropriation and transformation on behalf of an entire community. Those who attempted to read race, racism, or political correctness out of the argument, focusing instead on constitutional issues of ownership and expression, failed to acknowledge that Randall did not act alone. Without the civil rights movement and subsequent generations of American historians, *The Wind Done Gone* would be culturally incoherent.

As French philosopher Jean Baudrillard has noted, it is iconoclasts rather than iconolaters who understand the true value of images.[26] Mitchell's novel is not significant because it reproduces a historically accurate version of the American South, but because so many people have internalized and even developed a nostalgia for the version that she created. Indeed, Mitchell's main character is in some ways a marginal Southerner, the daughter of an Irish-Catholic immigrant who won his plantation in a card game, a woman who disdains social proprieties that restrict her desires. *Gone with the Wind*, rather than Southern history in general, is a necessary target for Randall. If she were to succeed in destroying Mitchell's vision, including the negative stereotypes of African Americans, it would become apparent that the story did not reflect an independent reality. Randall's inherent goal is to join other community members in sweeping away harmful misrepresentations. Her technique in this regard is not unique; while authors have recast universal plots and characters for millennia, the postmodern "death of the author," in Roland Barthes' phrase, seems to have prompted a rash of culturally motivated secondary works.[27] *Lo's Diary*, a retelling of *Lolita* that drew the ire of Vladimir Nabokov's son, takes the perspective of a young girl who is neither merely object nor victim; *Ahab's Wife* offers female insight into the nineteenth-century New England world of Herman Melville's *Moby-Dick*.

Parody in Randall's and her fellow authors' hands is a weapon of the cultural realm, like enfranchisement in the political arena or desegregation in the educational context. The law governing creative expression forced Randall's legal team to adopt the language of individual authorship rights, just as schools are populated with individual students and jobs are defended by individual employees. Such individual actions, whatever their legal posture, are made possible by collective intent and result in communal effect. Randall's novel is in essence neither theft nor fair use but part of a cultural turn. In this particular example, reverse cultural appropriation seeks to destroy portions of an intellectual property rather than to adopt it.

CULTURAL GROUPS ARE frequently the source of creative work that is subject to mainstream appropriation and transformation. The same communities, however, may also engage in the appropriation of creative works of individual authorship, whether intellectual properties or celebrity personae, or even form in response to such works. While cultural appropriation occurs largely outside the legal realm, reverse cultural appropriation is treated as potential infringement by laws that seldom recognize the contribution of the public to either celebrity personae or iconic intellectual properties. The remaining chapters evaluate possible reasons for these disparate legal stances and consider an avenue of reconciliation.

CHAPTER 11

The Civic Role of Cultural Products

To steal a book is an elegant offense.

—Chinese epigram

Steal This Book

—Title of a work by Abbie Hoffman

ACROSS AMERICA, INTELLECTUAL property professors
are having a dystopian moment. It started positively enough when the
Internet Revolution, sparked by advances in technology, produced a
tremendous outpouring of creative artistry and commerce. Because
the new technologies encouraged ordinary folks to engage in cutting
and pasting, sampling, downloading, and otherwise copying preexisting works, however, this madcap digital quilting bee made some large,
powerful content owners quite nervous. As a result, efforts to enforce
the protections granted through copyright, trademark, and patent law
increased, both by fighting technology with technology and by wag-
ing legal battles. Congress, federal courts, law professors, and editorial
writers all debated how best to adapt intellectual property law to the
new Information Age. Along the way, some policymakers arguably
forgot that the law is supposed to promote creativity, not merely to
build fences around existing creations. The law thus placed too much
control in the hands of content owners and of giant corporations,
who now control and police the very infrastructure that made our
creative revolution possible in the first place.

Today, public intellectuals gather to lament the shrinking public
domain, those freely available ideas and creations that should serve as

grist for our (soon to be silenced) mills. Joining legal scholars such as
Jessica Litman, James Boyle, Pamela Samuelson, Yochai Benkler, Mark
Lemley, Eugene Volokh, David Lange, and many others, Lawrence
Lessig warns that unless the children of the Internet Revolution take
action to secure its freedoms for a new generation, the "future of
ideas" is a bleak one.[1] In his words, "The promise of many-to-many
communication that defined the early Internet will be replaced by a
reality of many, many ways to buy things and many, many ways to
select among what is offered. What gets offered will be just what fits
within the current model of the concentrated systems of distribution:
cable television on speed, addicting a much more manageable, malleable, and sellable public."[2] Although concerned parties differ as to
the extent of the danger, virtual portraits of Aldous Huxley and George
Orwell nevertheless grace the halls of the academy.

WHY DOESN'T THE LAW ABHOR THE CULTURAL PROTECTION VACUUM?

This overprotection of intellectual property makes the systemic
lack of protection for cultural products all the more curious. The artistic expressions of source communities circulate freely; indeed, unless
they are sequestered as secret or sacred, they are nearly always discovered and swept into the public domain. Given the increased public
awareness of the value of intangible goods, why does this differential
treatment of intellectual property and cultural products persist?

One solution to this puzzle might rest with the historical conceptualization of intellectual property law according to the paradigm of
Romantic genius rather than communal creation.[3] Not only is the vesting of authorship in an individual simply more efficient than the
acknowledgment of multiple contributions, especially those of an unincorporated cultural group, but it also satisfies a particular conception of
human creativity.[4] Individual authorship emphasizes an initial moment
of inspiration, while cultural production is perceived as emerging and
developing organically over time. As a result of their extended agency
and temporal scope, society may take cultural products for granted and
remain unaware of the potential need for protection.

The relative fluidity of culture also provides an excuse for the failure to protect cultural products. Since "culture" is an ever-shifting construct and societies have borrowed from one another from time immemorial, the argument goes, the vesting of legal rights in a source community would artificially halt cultural development on a national scale and produce frivolous lawsuits.[5] "Authenticity," if defined by slavish adherence to the styles or practices of a particular time and place, is an anachronism unworthy of legal protection; the law of a heterogeneous, mobile polity should not reify and privilege cultural boundaries as they might have existed in 1492.[6] Indeed, the market in local and tribal handicrafts already exerts substantial pressure on source communities to cling to a storied past and produce commercial versions of their artifacts. From this point of view, the protection of cultural products and their source communities would be an exercise in misguided political correctness.

A more activist political response to the legal vacuum might point out that cultural appropriation is often a prerogative of majority groups, colonial powers, and affluent individuals.[7] Destructive misappropriation, in particular, is most likely to occur when the source community has relatively little political power or is otherwise outside of mainstream culture. Under these circumstances, lawmakers have little incentive to address the issue.

The strength of liberal political theory suggests an additional explanation for the lack of protection of cultural products. Civil and political rights in modern Western cultures are the domain of autonomous individuals rather than heads of household or other communal groups, as was often the case less than a century ago—a shift that has allowed greater equality and personal self-determination as well as a more fluid social structure. In the interests of preserving individual rights as a precondition of democratic discourse, liberal theorists may overlook the significance of cultural groups. Jürgen Habermas, for example, challenges the communitarian arguments of Michael Walzer and Charles Taylor that the law is nonneutral, that the current system of individual rights is unable to ensure the survival of certain minority groups, and that the law must therefore intervene to provide protection.[8] Unlike fellow liberals John Rawls and Ronald Dworkin, Habermas does not rest his argument on the assertion of an ethically neutral legal order, but relies on a proceduralist conception of rights intended to safeguard both public and private autonomy.[9] Political liberalism, then, tends to view the recognition of cultural groups, as opposed to individuals who may belong to those groups, as both unnecessary and potentially dangerous to democratic unity. In a thoughtful discussion of multiculturalism, Will Kymlicka acknowledges the concern that the recognition of ethnic and national differences could undermine democracy but argues that only self-government rights pose a threat to social unity.[10] Nevertheless, liberal theorists might logically tend to overlook or resist communitarian efforts to locate property rights in cultural groups rather than exclusively in individuals. The protection of cultural products is not incompatible with liberal theory, but neither is such protection its natural consequence.

Freedom of expression and intellectual property exist in tension with one another, a factor that may also contribute to the extralegal status of cultural products.[11] When intellectual property law protects a particular creation, the rights holder owns a limited monopoly over it. Since a significant aspect of property ownership is the right to exclude others, those who wish to use a protected creation to express themselves may face legal constraints. Sampling someone else's music to create a new recording, borrowing and transforming a ubiquitous advertising slogan, or writing fan fiction all run the risk of infringement. While doctrines such as fair use and parody theoretically protect some forms of expression, the threat of legal action is often enough to deter or silence a speaker.[12] By remaining outside the scope of intellectual property protection, cultural products neither challenge the First Amendment nor limit the availability of their own expressive use.

Perhaps the most pragmatic explanation for the lack of cultural-product protection is that it would be quite difficult. This suggestion may be deceptively simple, however. Laws against speeding, drug use, and littering are next-to-impossible to enforce, yet they remain in force because society disapproves of these activities. If unlimited cultural appropriation were recognized as similarly harmful, the law would at least attempt to assign rights and set guidelines for behavior. Nevertheless, the complexity of the task is a logical deterrent to legislative activity.

While these negative theories have clear explanatory force and assist in maintaining the current legal vacuum, it may also be the case that unfettered appropriation of intangible cultural products plays a positive role in society. Sociological interpretations as diverse as Max Weber's Protestant ethic and Pierre Bourdieu's description of cultural capital affirm the socially constitutive function of markets and acquisition of resources.[13] In a heterogeneous society that seeks to harmonize and reproduce itself, the material cultures and rituals of diverse source communities can be domesticated through market exchange. An ethnoreligious devotional procession honoring the patron saint of a foreign city lacks resonance with a constructed "American" life, but the opportunity to eat—or, better yet, to sell and profit from—*zeppole* or sausage and peppers at the publicly advertised Festival of San Gennaro is a civic act. From this perspective, legal protection is not simply absent but is outweighed by other civic virtues.

FROM AMERICANS TO AMERICA

Many different processes can contribute to the forging of individuals and peoples into a nation with a common myth of origin and shared values.[14] These processes may involve deliberate or dramatic action, such as a struggle for freedom from outside domination or the creation of a constitution. Collective response to a crisis, such as a natural disaster or a terrorist attack, also promotes national solidarity. On an ongoing basis, public education may be a medium for inculcating national values. Even regular economic interaction and interdependence offer incremental steps toward unity, a function exploited by the creation of the European Economic Community as a mechanism for regional stability and a precursor of the European Union. Consumerism facilitates the performance of national identity, as tastes in entertainment, fashion, cuisine, decor, and other indicia of culture come to be shared or experienced in common. From a cultural-products perspective, those that are made available in the marketplace and then widely adopted, whether through voluntary contribution or appropriation, become part of the fabric of the nation.

In the United States and other countries defined by immigration, the political apparatus of the state precedes the formation of a subjective nation. While some nationally celebrated holidays, for example, are the product of underlying majority religious tradition, others are created by law. The normative composition and definition of the nation, moreover, is a subject of ongoing debate and evolution. In each generation, historic events and organic processes, including interactions among cultural groups, combine to influence the tenor of the nation. Public debate further defines the parameters of nationhood: questions regarding the participation of homosexual, Muslim, and apocalyptic communities challenge the limits of citizenship in our era, much as the presence of abolitionist, Jewish, and Amish communities did in the past.

From melting pot to salad bowl, assimilation to multiculturalism, public intellectuals have sought metaphors and theories to describe the desired transformation of Americans into America. Historian David Hollinger, arguing for a new conception of "postethnic America," refocuses attention from rigid cultural categorization to individual agency. According to his definition, "A postethnic perspective favors voluntary over involuntary affiliation, balances appreciation for communities of descent with a determination to make room for new communities, and promotes solidarities of wide scope that incorporate people with different ethnic and racial backgrounds."[15]

The availability of multiple options facilitates this modern shift from destiny to choice, from being to becoming part of one or more culture groups, all of which are in some sense American.[16] Indeed, the range of cultural affiliations continues to widen beyond ethnoracial classifications, as apparent in Hollinger's call for attention to religiously defined cultures and sociologist Nathan Glazer's description of the inclusion of women and homosexuals in the multicultural canon.[17] Even changing fashions within the academy that might appear to diminish the realm of culture, such as the disappearance of "class" as a frequently invoked category, do not preclude individual self-identification with a still-extant group.[18] The experience of culture beyond the ivory tower is broader still, as individuals form associations on the basis of shared profession, avocation, age, geographical region, political commitment, disability, and multiple combinations of these and other cultural markers. Although as yet not all Americans have equal freedom to choose or to reject association with an ethnic or racial group, all have the opportunity to select additional cultural affiliations.[19] Postethnic America is still aspirational, but it offers a useful model of modern (or postmodern) nationhood.

CIVIC BENEFITS OF
CULTURAL APPROPRIATION

Material culture provides access to a myriad of embodied cultural products and thus facilitates the voluntary selection of cultural affiliation that Hollinger envisions. Source communities are (figuratively) taxed to secure the contribution of artifacts, rituals, practices, and styles. Outside individuals may then enter the bazaar, examine the merchandise, and adopt what suits them. Such exchange, whether voluntary or involuntary on the part of the source community, creates a series of potential civic benefits.

As anthropologists and sociologists have noted in studies of individuals and their relationships to and through material objects, each source community can employ cultural products to communicate its identity and values, albeit simplified for public consumption.[20] Such community self-expression may take the form of either direct communication with the public or indirect symbolic statements. Religious tracts or party campaign buttons convey a direct message; a Japanese bento lunchbox or a teenager's extreme hairstyle and multiple body piercings embody cultural values or aesthetics without verbal explanation.[21] In both cases, the public is invited to recognize the existence of a cultural group through its distinctive cultural products and to associate it with a particular embodied expression of viewpoint or identity. This recognition may remain closer to an "orientalist" stereotype than to a nuanced, comprehensive understanding of the source community, but it is at least formulated with a modicum of contribution from the source community rather than cut from the whole cloth of mainstream ignorance.[22] By sharing their cultural products, many source communities are able to have an impact on the popular culture.

Another civic benefit of cultural appropriation is that otherwise xenophobic outsiders may develop the preeminent postmodern virtue of toleration or even respect for the source communities.[23] As Walzer has described, the concept of toleration at the state level encompasses a variety of approaches, from indifference to cultural engagement.[24] In the context of cultural products, the promotion of toleration depends more on outside appropriation over time than on mere acknowledgment or Rawlsian recognition of reasonable differences.[25]

In many cases, the passage from intolerance to toleration of a cultural group may be charted in the wake of appropriation. During the late nineteenth and early twentieth centuries, social reformers sought to assimilate Native Americans, Latinos, and new immigrants by encouraging them to abandon their respective "inferior" cultures and cuisines.[26] These reformers measured success according to the distance an individual had traveled from his or her non-Anglo culture of origin, as illustrated by *Life* magazine's approval of baseball star Joe DiMaggio: "Although he learned Italian first, Joe, now 24, speaks English without an accent, and is otherwise well adapted to most U.S. mores. Instead of olive oil or smelly bear grease he keeps his hair slick with water. He never reeks of garlic and prefers chicken chow mein to spaghetti."[27] Americans, it seems, were willing to adopt the baseball hero, but not his language or cuisine. Efforts at culinary (though not linguistic) assimilation declined between 1920 and 1940, and wartime meat shortages further cemented the acceptance of previously "foreign" cuisines.[28] Today, Mueller's elbow macaroni shares shelf space with gourmet "pasta," pizza graces school lunch trays, nutritionists extol the virtues of the Mediterranean diet, and the historical denigration of Italian Americans as "spaghetti benders" is a quaint anachronism. Even the great DiMaggio's role as a symbol of successful assimilation may have given way to an affirmation of ethnic roots, as suggested by his postretirement return to the public eye as a spokesperson for Mr. Coffee.[29] Acceptance of the source community has apparently followed acceptance of its cultural products.

An unlikely example of this toleration effect appears in an interview with white rap artist Eminem, known for his virulently homophobic lyrics. The performer defended his use of a derogatory label for homosexuals, but when asked whether he would use a similarly negative slur against African Americans on a recording, he responded, "That word is not even in my vocabulary. . . . Those are two completely different things. . . . And I do black music, so out of respect, why would I put that word in my vocabulary?"[30] While Eminem achieved celebrity through uncompensated appropriation of an urban, African-American cultural product, he at least recognizes publicly the importance of the source community.

Even fashion trends that turn to the street in search of authenticity claim to do so out of respect. Like hip-hop before it, cholo style originated in an urban, ethnic context. The Mexican-American gangster image, which evolved in East Los Angeles, incorporates gothic letters, bandanas, Roman Catholic religious imagery, tank tops, and cropped trousers. In the course of cholo style's move from the streets to pop stars to upscale department stores, it has drawn attention to its community of origin. According to the owner of one clothing line, "That's our way of giving props—respect—to the West Coast."[31] If the law were to impose prohibitions on cultural appropriation, it might also limit the range of source-community influence on public discourse and over individual nonmembers.

In its strongest form, the argument that cultural products promote toleration suggests that community groups most in need of protection also stand to gain the most by allowing cultural appropriation. A source community with little social standing or political influence, or even one toward which the majority culture is hostile, might advance its cause by feeding, clothing, instructing, or entertaining the general public with distinctive cultural products. If this result can be achieved without undue harm to the source community or its cultural products, then both community identity and the discursive foundation of a liberal democracy are strengthened.

An additional civic benefit of cultural appropriation is a complex mutual assimilation or homogenization that might best be described as a form of cultural syncretism, or the Reese's peanut-butter-cup effect. Assimilation to American life has traditionally involved the loss of non-Anglo cultural characteristics in order to conform to a mainstream norm, which is perceived as the absence of ethnic culture. White, Anglo-Saxon, Protestant, educated, healthy, straight males from reasonably affluent Mid-Atlantic or Midwestern backgrounds allegedly have "no" accents, eat "normal" food, wear "regular" clothes, play "popular" music, engage in the "usual" pastimes, share "common"

opinions, and have "ordinary" tastes. Newly minted or socially disen-
franchised Americans once aspired to embody this paragon of citizenship, or so some would claim.

Today, the basic force of American culture flows in the same
channel; John Q. Citizen, however, is as likely to absorb new cultural
influences as he is to set a uniform standard. The live audience for the
State of the Union address is still largely a sea of white men in dark
suits, but "everybody" now eats Thai food, listens to the Gypsy Kings,
and incorporates urban slang into daily conversation. The gay community offers a particularly vivid example of mutual transformation.
Since the mid-1980s, homosexual men and women have metamor-
phosed from an alien threat to American "family values" into a source
of urbane wit and style, while at the same time embracing traditional
images of domesticity. Middle America applauds the five gay super-
heroes who each week rescue a different hapless heterosexual from his
sloppy, unkempt ways on *Queer Eye for the Straight Guy*, and promo-
tional material for the *Ellen DeGeneres Show* touts the lesbian come-
dian's "approachability and relatability" as well as her " 'everywoman'
approach to everyday situations."[32] Meanwhile, gay Americans turn to
the venerable *New York Times* Sunday Styles section to read notices of
gay and lesbian commitment ceremonies alongside the marriage an-
nouncements of heterosexual women and men, or at least those who
have escaped the reported epidemic of straight-male commitment
phobia. Formal marital status and the associated legal benefits may be
generally denied to same-sex couples, but the mimetic nature of rituals surrounding such unions indicates that something more than
inheritance rights or state recognition is at stake. While many hetero-
sexuals have internalized a stereotypical gay aesthetic, many homosexuals now imitate and celebrate a family structure based on traditional
marriage bonds.

This serendipitous chocolate-meets-peanut-butter model of civic
evolution through the exchange of cultural products can have concrete effects on formal expressions of national identity. In *Lawrence v.
Texas,* the Supreme Court declared unconstitutional a Texas law prohibiting certain homosexual conduct and overruled its own 1986
precedent, noting, "When sexuality finds overt expression in intimate

conduct with another person, the conduct can be but one element in a personal bond that is more enduring."[33] Rather than allowing Texas to continue to label homosexual individuals as criminals and thus impaired citizens, the Court interpolated a necessary link between sexual activity and personal relationships, perhaps including modern companionate marriage.

Justice Antonin Scalia, in a scathing dissent, accused his brethren of cooing about homosexual relationships and paving the way for a constitutional defense of same-sex marriage.[34] Although Justice Scalia couched his argument in terms of the Court's proper role, he was apparently livid about what he perceives as a misappropriation of matrimony. In the language of cultural products, a fraternal dispute is taking place over the correct source-community response to the appropriation of a ritual that instantiates certain core values—and the forces that favor inclusive use of the contested cultural product have won this round, with definite civic effect. Same-sex marriage has blossomed overnight into a grass-roots movement, sparking intense political debate and widespread civil disobedience with respect to restrictive, traditional marriage laws. Whether this trend will continue and result in national recognition of same-sex marriage, or even whether the gay and lesbian community as a whole would have previously endorsed this goal, remains an unanswered question. Whatever the legal result of this burgeoning civil rights contest, it has permanently altered the American cultural landscape. One might ask whether the cultural syncretism that has produced a breed of suspiciously well-dressed and coifed heterosexual men, dubbed "metrosexuals," will provoke a similar examination of national (or at least masculine) identity.

Among the occasional civic benefits of cultural appropriation is the preservation of certain cultural products themselves. While misappropriation may destroy fragile communal creations, and unrestrained commodification may denature others in the eyes of both the source group and the public, some cultural products continue to exist primarily through the medium of appropriation. The audience for jazz remains more robust in Europe than in the United States and includes more whites than African Americans. The quilts of Gee's Bend would long since have been replaced by inexpensive coverlets from Wal-Mart or Target were it not for the interest of collectors in the women's labor-intensive communal art form. Even indigenous languages around the world are at risk of disappearing in the face of encroaching modernity, save for the efforts of linguists dedicated to their study. Assuming that abundance and variety are positive values, the role of appropriation in saving certain cultural products from extinction enriches the life of the nation.

Viewed from the perspective of utility rather than simple quantity, those cultural products that circulate among outsiders provide raw material for further creation. While few young Indian-American women wear saris on a daily basis, and even fewer Japanese-American or even Japanese women wear kimonos regularly, the exposure of Western designers to elaborate Asian textiles and shapes inspires the creation of new fashions.[35] Similarly, the flavors of South America, Africa, Asia, and Europe appear on cutting-edge restaurant tables as fusion cuisine. Far from lost, the public domain mourned by many intellectual property professors receives a continual infusion of cultural products, and a source of creative ferment is refreshed. To the extent that creation itself is a Judeo-Christian religious value expressed in the Hebrew Bible or Old Testament and thence throughout Western culture, as Roberta Rosenthal Kwall and David Noble have insightfully suggested, any such enhancement of creative potential provides a clear civic benefit.[36]

The absence of legal protection against unrestrained cultural appropriation, then, may not be merely the result of historical oversight or a Foucaultian exercise of power via knowledge of a subaltern other.[37] Cultural products, moreover, are not merely the neglected half-siblings of intellectual property, lacking the requisite spark of genius that would inspire legislative action. Instead, cultural appropriation has the potential to deliver civic benefits to the nation as a whole, as well as to the source communities within it. While the harms of misappropriation are present realities in need of evaluation and corrective measures, the positive contributions of cultural appropriation are important constitutive elements of an expansive and malleable American society.

CHAPTER 12

An Emerging Legal Framework

Life is not a having and a getting, but a being and
a becoming.   —Matthew Arnold

SHAKESPEARE FAMOUSLY LIKENED the world to a
stage, and its inhabitants to players on it. Had he been a modern visual
artist, however, he might have imagined instead an interactive art
installation and a steady stream of visitors—or at least remembered to
thank the set and costume designers. Society does not continually
reinvent itself on an empty platform but is instead enmeshed in systems of property rights, market exchange, and material culture, tangible and intangible. The cultural contribution of voluntary immigrants,
involuntary immigrants, and indigenous peoples to the American
national project not only asserts the presence of those cultural groups,
often well before their members are considered full citizens in a civil
or political sense, but also serves as a catalyst for the construction of an
"authentic" American culture.

This quest for authenticity in an era of impeccable, immediate
copies reveals a peculiar anxiety of our age, to once again invoke T. J.
Jackson Lears.[1] The invention of the printing press bypassed monastic
scriptoria and ecclesiastical control over the reproduction of texts,
prefiguring the Protestant Revolution. The Industrial Revolution
removed production of everyday objects from craftsmen and created
mass markets, prompting a yen for nature that produced both the Boy
Scouts and the Arts and Crafts movement.[2] Our own Internet Revolution gives us ever-increasing access to commodified culture and digital clones of creative works, yet we remain suspicious of the value of
these too-perfect, acontextualized forgeries even as we consume

them. The market recognizes our ambivalence and promises us goods that are "authentic," "original," "genuine," and even "retro." Meanwhile, starlets with unlimited access to couture creations tap into the *zeitgeist* by wearing "vintage" gowns on the red carpet, and world-class chefs offer "home cooking" in the form of gourmet mashed potatoes, meatloaf, and macaroni and cheese. A taste for the "cultural" joins this emphasis on the venerable, as we associate the products of communities outside the mainstream with more genuine, organic lifeways. We do not collectively aspire to belong to working-class, foreign, or transgendered communities, but we congratulate ourselves on our easy familiarity with trucker hats, sushi, and RuPaul.

No less an observer than Alexis de Tocqueville has noted that American society is defined by a central tension between individual and community, independence and interdependence.[3] In the arena of cultural appropriation, existing legal structures have focused on individual rights and on the nation as a whole at the expense of the subcommunities that constitute the American polity. It might be said that American law embraces the principles of *liberté* and *égalité* but neglects *fraternité*. Only through private means or the awkward invocation of analogous legal principles have source communities been able to protect their cultural products against misappropriation. At the same time, proponents and practitioners of cultural appropriation have overlooked its civic benefits and focused instead on individual autonomy and negative rationales for the exclusion of cultural products from legal notice. Perhaps it is time the law move to correct these omissions by striking a balance between protection and appropriation of cultural products in American life.

BEYOND THE LIMITS OF INTELLECTUAL PROPERTY

Extending limited intellectual property protection to intangible cultural products would involve several stages. To begin, the law must reconceive the concept of "authorship" or creation to reflect the reality of unincorporated group collaboration, malleable Foucaultian notions of authorship, and the value of cultural products.[4] This process would harmonize with both utilitarian and ethical theories of intellectual property protection. Cultural products would fall under the utilitarian constitutional classification of "Science and useful Arts," which Congress is empowered to promote by securing exclusive rights to their "Authors and Inventors," the source communities.[5] Similarly, "moral rights" would as easily apply to a source community as to an individual genius; claims of authenticity, in particular, could easily be assimilated to a limited moral right of attribution. Under either theory, source communities would receive a bundle of property rights similar to those of their individual counterparts, albeit with more robust exceptions for fair use designed to promote the civic benefits of limited appropriation.

Next, the law must alter its temporal restrictions on intellectual property protection. The maximum term of protection could reflect the life span of a source community, in place of the life of the author or a simple term of years, or could be divided into shorter terms renewable on a periodic basis. While many source communities endure almost infinitely, some disband or expire. Any cultural products left behind by the American Whig party are long abandoned; likewise, Minnesota Vikings fans need not seek permission to don horned helmets. The novelty and originality requirements of patent and copyright law, respectively, are meaningless in the case of continually evolving cultural products. Instead, the law might adopt a trademark-like emphasis on current use, drawn from the Commerce Clause, or a trade secret–like requirement that the source community continue to derive benefit from the cultural product. In order to preserve the flow of creations and inventions into the public domain, especially in light of the longevity of source communities, the exclusiveness of ownership should be established in rough inverse proportion to the duration of protection, taking into account the relative cultural significance of particular artifacts or rituals.

In addition, the legal system must revise its common law emphasis on the reduction of cultural products to concrete form as a requirement for protection. While individual or defined groups of authors and inventors generally anticipate embodiment or reduction of their work to tangible form prior to its legal recognition, cultural groups may have longstanding preferences and practices regarding intangibility and orality. Since material form is a useful but not strictly necessary precursor to intellectual property protection, as apparent from the protection of aural and olfactory trademarks and the absence in civil law of any requirement of tangibility in copyright, source-group election in favor of intangibility should not affect the availability of protection for cultural products.

These modifications to the class of beneficiaries, as well as to the temporal and material limitations of intellectual property law, would serve to establish the broad outlines of a category of cultural-product protection. This is not necessarily to suggest that current intellectual property law statutes be modified to include cultural products, a process that might result in overprotection of cultural products at the expense of beneficial cultural exchange, particularly in light of current international minimum standards for the established categories of intellectual property protection. Instead, the current system of intellectual property law provides a functional template that can be modified to address the concerns of source communities regarding intellectual property protection and societal concerns regarding cultural development and the public domain. Such protection would complement the UNESCO Convention for the Safeguarding of the Intangible Cultural Heritage, which calls upon nations to engage in protective and educational activities such as documentation and education.[6]

DEGREES OF
CULTURAL-PRODUCT PROTECTION

Protection of cultural products ideally should involve not merely the expansion of intellectual property law, but also an institutionalized mechanism to facilitate cultural exchange. One method of promoting a balance between source-community interests and the civic role of intangible cultural products might be for intellectual property law to develop multiple levels of protection corresponding to the nature of the protected good. Such differentiation among protected works within the separate intellectual property categories of copyright, trademark, and patent occurs in only a few cases, and it is generally disfavored or forbidden by international treaty. Cultural products as yet enjoy no such worldwide recognition, despite growing global concern. A *sui generis* legal regime of cultural-product protection could therefore be more narrowly tailored to different types of cultural production on a national basis. As indicated in the table, the type of protection afforded each cultural product would depend on its source-community classification as a private good or public good (in the sense of a product voluntarily released outside the community, rather than a noncompetitive good) and on whether or not the source community has voluntarily commodified the product. As in defining the scope of property itself, the law may choose to exclude elements such as human life and aspects of human sexuality from the rubric of cultural-product ownership altogether.

Cultural-Product Protection

	Private	Public
Noncommodified	Enhanced trade secret –style protection	©/Patent-style protection
Commodified	©/Patent-style protection	®-style/"Authenticity-mark" protection

Private, Noncommodified Cultural Products

Sacred, secret, or exclusive products that would otherwise risk destruction through cultural appropriation, such as the ceremonial dance of the Pueblo of Santo Domingo described in Chapter Eight, could receive a high level of protection in a manner similar to that of trade secrets. The source community would bear reasonable responsibility for excluding the general public from the cultural product or placing strict limitations on access, and outside appropriation in violation of these community restrictions would be strictly forbidden. A sacred song entrusted to a particular individual, a set of scriptures intended only for initiates, or the use of a particular plant ingested in the context of a religious ritual could each be protected in this manner. Unlike trade secrets, however, disclosure of the private, noncommodified product by a single dissenting or careless insider should not result in loss of protection and thus harm the entire community.

Private, Commodified Cultural Products

Cultural products intended for use and market exchange primarily among members of the source community, or private, commodified products, could receive a slightly lesser degree of protection analogous to patent or copyright. This category might include an object used in the practice of religion, like a menorah, rosary, or prayer rug. In such cases, it is important that the form of the cultural product and perhaps even the process of its creation follow community specifications. The source community could exercise the usual rights to exclude, to transfer, and to use or possess its embodied cultural products, subject to limited outside appropriation analogous to the fair use of copyrighted material or experimental use of a patented invention. Outsiders might legitimately possess, display, or critique these objects, or even copy or use them in an expressive fashion to invoke or criticize the source community. This limited appropriation, however, would not extend to outside commodification of the cultural products, which must retain a degree of purity or objective authenticity in order to instantiate the values of the source community.

Public, Noncommodified Cultural Products

As in the example of open-source code discussed in Chapter Nine, some source communities choose to make their cultural products public without commodifying them. While the principal open-source standards organization, OSI, has worked within existing trademark law to create a certification mark, and the use of licenses to protect the free distribution of open-source software is commonplace, hackers and similarly situated source communities could have significantly more control over their cultural products if a regime similar to copyright or patent law were to protect those products. The open-source software community's situation is unusual in that few outsiders have the technical capacity to appropriate and commodify its cultural products. If that circumstance were to change, or if other source communities wished to share their cultural products on the condition that they remain uncorrupted and virtually free of charge, stronger protection could assist in both enforcing the creators' wishes and ensuring the continued vitality of their cultural products. Source communities would not have absolute control under such a regime, which would be subject to broad limitations analogous to fair use, but would retain an affiliation with their products.

Public, Commodified Cultural Products

The largest category of cultural products, those both deliberately commodified and made available to the public, should theoretically enjoy the least protection against outside appropriation. These intangible goods are likely to be more durable than their protected, private counterparts, and their appropriation is least likely to seriously damage the source communities. The pervasive civic benefits bestowed on a heterogeneous polity through cultural group contributions in the form of distinctive cuisine, popular music, habits of dress, and elements of language, moreover, are too extensive to support legal elimination of cultural appropriation.

Nevertheless, the law should not continue to deny source-community interest in these creations. The Australian Aboriginal didgeridoo, for example, is a sacred instrument traditionally made from a tree hollowed out by insects and painted with designs that vary according to region and intended ceremonial use. Knockoffs for the tourist trade are made of artificial materials and incorporate non-Aboriginal designs, to the distress of the source community. While the Australian government makes no attempt to halt the trade in didgeridoo copies, it has instituted a program for the labeling of authentic Aboriginal art destined for the market, including musical instruments.[7]

A general program for the creation, registration, and placement of "authenticity marks" on commodified, tangible cultural products that originate from within the source community would preserve the relationship between community and product and create an affiliative ownership without halting the fertile exchange inherent in much cultural appropriation. This balance could be facilitated through specially designed laws or programs, as in the case of protection of indigenous handicrafts in the United States and Australia, or through source-community adaptation of existing trademark provisions.[8] Periodic renewal of the grant of an authenticity mark according to evolving community standards could avoid reifying the communal culture.

Even fraternal disputes over authenticity could be addressed through a trademark-style system of authentication. The possibility of multiple or competing grants of product recognition analogous to kosher certifications would permit the public expression of multiple points of view from within the source community. As with each suggested degree of cultural-product protection, existing federal administrative agencies would provide a suitable forum for source communities seeking the assistance of law.

BOTH OUR DIVERSE nation and our postmodern consciousness have taught us to appreciate commodified cultural products. Intellectual property law should reinforce this lesson not by allowing unlimited appropriation of these intangible goods, but instead by protecting them. While the above schema represents only one attempt to balance the interests of communal creation and the public domain and to systematize a complex pattern of exchange steeped in history and habit, culture and pride, it is a balance central to the past and the future of American national culture.

THE ROLE OF LAW IN CULTURAL PERSPECTIVE

The problem of unincorporated group authorship invokes issues of cultural evolution versus authenticity, constructed communal identity versus free expression, ownership versus appropriation, privacy versus collaboration. Resolution of these tensions now occurs on an ad hoc basis, if at all. Absent a jurisprudence of cultural protection or even the shared understandings that undergird customary law, each source community and its intangible cultural products are largely subject to the values of the general public. Although the social cohesion of a heterogeneous nation rests in part on cultural groups' payment of an identity tax in the form of these cultural products, the social contract that should in turn protect cultural groups resembles instead an exaction of tribute. Intellectual property law may provide the mechanism to balance the scales, to temper cultural contribution with cultural protection.

The suggestion that law cease to ignore cultural products, whatever the benefits of unregulated cultural appropriation, should not be interpreted as tantamount to an encouragement of more lawsuits or other means of formal dispute resolution. Contrary to popular belief, not all lawyers aspire to run late-night commercials informing unsuspecting members of the public that they may have been harmed and should pursue (potentially lucrative) justice. Except in cases of demonstrable harm to a source community, courts should not be at the forefront of the everyday business of regulating culture.

Admittedly, the association of even limited, associative property rights with cultural products bears the risk of distorting relations within source communities and altering cultural products, as their value as both signifiers and economic resources increases. In cases of misappropriation, outside intervention may already have harmed communal artistry, and the law is less likely to do additional damage. For examples of cultural appropriation more generally, the proposed creation of authenticity marks attempts to avoid trapping culture in the corridors of legal formalism by establishing ownership rights only in the marks themselves rather than in the cultural products they legitimate. Still, even this *via media* is not free of risk.

The function of law is nevertheless not only to decide cases, but also to establish values and reasonable expectations around which citizens can order their interactions. If the law states that cultural products are valued creations of their source communities, should be treated with respect according to the norms of those source communities, and yet should in most cases be accessible in the public domain for civic reasons, then well-intentioned members of society are afforded guidelines for civil interaction. Similarly, internal community disputes regarding cultural products may not be resolved through the application of statutes, but the law can at least provide a vocabulary and framework for discussion that acknowledges the significance of the matters at hand. This role of law as pedagogue, rather than exclusively as judge and jury, is a feature of Western jurisprudence dating back at least to Aquinas, who attributes many of his insights on this matter to Aristotle. Humanity "has a natural aptitude for virtue, but the perfection of virtue must be acquired by man by means of some kind of training," whether through social interaction or the mechanisms of law.[9] For a heterogeneous polity in which differing community norms may exist in relative ignorance of one another, law is called upon to facilitate the development of a national culture, not least in the matter of cultural appropriation.

According to Oscar Wilde, "'Know thyself' was written over the portal of the antique world. Over the portal of the new world, 'Be thyself' shall be written."[10] An authentic American society in the subjective philosophical sense consists not only of autonomous individuals or of separate communities defined by consanguinity or a multitude of affinities, but also of a would-be nation continually striving to create itself. Much of this interaction takes place in the world of material culture, property, and now virtual property, as we exchange, borrow, create, and construct a common—or at least aspirational—identity. Legal recognition of cultural products is a totemic element of this project.

WHEN I FIRST concluded a series of arguments for the limited regulation of cultural appropriation, I was sitting in a West Coast café named for an Italian city. Outside the window, the sun shone on a university campus where the student body no longer includes a majority of any single cultural group. Around me were patrons of every race and multiple nationalities, several displaying symbols or head coverings of different religious groups and many with T-shirts proclaiming additional cultural affiliations. The multilingual buzz of conversation competed with the periodic hiss of the industrial-strength espresso machine downstairs, expertly operated by a Latino and a woman of northern European descent. At the time I blithely concluded, if this scene were to any extent a dividend of the appropriation of one of my ancestral cultural products, "Let them drink coffee!"

Since that time, the postmodern era in America has ended—or rather, we are all postmodernists now. The watershed moment of our generation is, of course, 9/11. While the liberal project of toleration and the postmodern emphasis on diverse perspective still pervade our national consciousness, perhaps with more urgency than before, we aspire to reclaim a unity of purpose that would fulfill the promises of our national myth. Whether through the adoption of a prophetic pragmatism, a revival of nineteenth-century idealism, or some other emergent projection of unity in diversity, America seeks not only to absorb the authenticities of its constituent communities but also to achieve its own internal authenticity.[11] As Lionel Trilling reminds us in the context of artistic culture, the quest for authenticity is an inherently powerful and even violent project, requiring an extreme exercise of personal will to overcome the sentiment of nonbeing.[12] If we are to succeed, our collective performance of America will both appropriate and preserve its constituent cultures and their contributions to the project of nationhood. And, as companions in this quest, we will not only break bread or matzoh or pita or naan or tortillas or *injera* together, but also share that cup of coffee.

APPENDIX: DEFINING PROPERTY

In order to ask who owns culture, and particularly cultural products, nonlawyers (or lawyers for whom introductory property classes are but a distant memory) may find a systematic explanation of property ownership useful. The objects and entitlements of ownership vary across legal systems, as does the degree of private access to public property and vice versa. For our purposes, we will focus on the Anglo-American, or common law, system and the way in which it reflects the structure and values of our society.

The roots of property law lie in centuries past, when ownership of land or "real property" determined social status; legal rights and even hereditary titles were (and are) linked to particular geographic areas or estates. Land, as a result of its social significance and permanence, is therefore the paradigmatic form of property in our legal system. With the Industrial Revolution and the increase in vast personal fortunes not tied to real estate, "personal property" in the form of moveable goods or liquid assets increased in importance as an indicator of success or status. Wealthy individuals nevertheless continue to purchase trophy properties, and *Town and Country* magazine is more likely to profile a prominent family's home than its stock portfolio. "Intellectual property," or ownership of ideas that can be expressed or embodied in some tangible form, is a relative newcomer to the realm of property. Among its distinctive features is the element of human creativity in its formation; unlike real property, intellectual property cannot simply be claimed or annexed. At the height of the dot.com boom, the creation and ownership of intellectual property was an extremely fashionable method of accumulating wealth, and the law moved quickly to define and increase the protection of intellectual property assets. Today, while some internet barons still rival the descendants of robber barons in wealth and social status, the pursuit of intellectual property is considered in more sober terms. Nevertheless, intellectual property has joined real property and personal property at the core of the property-law canon.

PROPERTY OWNERSHIP

Laws of science govern things; the law of property governs relationships among people with respect to things. While many American law school textbooks and first-year property classes avoid defining "property," and scholars ruminate inconclusively on its meaning, the relational aspects of property law are implicit in its study.[1]

To illustrate, consider the frequent description of property as a "bundle of sticks" that may be divided among various persons. Each stick represents a legal right, grouped generally into the rights to exclude, to transfer, and to use or possess. These groups of rights may be further subdivided—for example, into methods of transfer—and may also be divided temporally or spatially. The rights to exclude other persons from property and to transfer property to other persons describe self-evidently social behaviors; it is impossible to exercise rights to exclude or to transfer without involving parties other than the original property owner.

The right to use or to possess property may be theoretically asocial, as it is possible to imagine an owner using her property without involving outside parties. In practice, however, even the most libertarian regime limits an owner's use of property when such use may adversely affect others or society at large. This minimum restriction on the right to use property is described by the common law maxim, "*Sic utere tuo ut alienum non laedas*," an admonition to use one's property so that it does not harm anyone else's.[2] Modern society places detailed, complex restrictions—ranging from zoning ordinances to environmental regulations to tenants' rights—on the possession and use of ostensibly private property, further controlling the impact of property use on third parties and the community as a whole.

Each stick in the bundle of rights that describes property ownership is defined, directly or indirectly, in terms of the relationship between the owner and others. Even property that formally meets the criterion of possessive individualism set forth at the beginning of the venerable *Black's Law Dictionary* entry, "That which is peculiar or proper to any person; that which belongs exclusively to one," is nevertheless enmeshed in a web of communal rights and responsibilities.[3] Property is, in essence, a social system.

CO-OWNERSHIP OF PROPERTY

When there is more than one recognized owner of a single piece of property, the social dynamic of property ownership is not merely external but internal as well. To define this internal dynamic among co-owners, the common law developed standard forms of concurrent ownership.[4] Types of concurrent ownership are distinguished from one another primarily on the basis of the presence or absence of rights of survivorship, equal ownership interests in the estate, and certain other factors present at the creation of the concurrent estate. Additional modern forms of concurrent ownership, including condominiums and other common-interest communities, rely on private, often detailed contractual arrangements. As property law scholar Carol Rose has noted, however, the potential uses and benefits of "limited common property" regimes in Western legal systems are in need of further examination.[5]

The standard common law forms of concurrent ownership of real property express the principle that each owner holds an undivided fractional interest in the entire property.[6] In other words, none of the co-owners can lay exclusive claim to a particular section of the property—the South Forty, the northwest quadrant, or the guest cottage—but each co-owner has the simultaneous right to occupy and use the whole, subject to the rights of fellow owners. While this legal construction apparently contradicts the scientific principle that no two objects can occupy the same space at the same time, it accurately reflects the informal norms of many familiar types of concurrent ownership or occupation of property, including the family residence and its inclusion of both owner and nonowner inhabitants. As property law scholar Robert Ellickson has pointed out, 91 percent of American households include multiple members and thus exemplify the limited-access commons.[7] In theory, all co-owners have the legal right to use the entire property (save perhaps the teenager's bedroom); in practice, the law identifies the co-owners and assumes this limited group to be capable of working out a mutually acceptable system of shared usage. Indeed, economist Ronald Coase famously argued that in the absence of transactions costs, individuals will bargain around existing legal rights to achieve the greatest value of production or utility.[8]

Only if co-owners prove unable to agree on the management of the property does the law provide mechanisms for dispute resolution. This resolution may take the form of either an equitable distribution of profits and expenses or the more final dissolution of the community of owners and distribution of the property or its monetary value among them.[9] The law thus proves reluctant to manage or direct the internal affairs of a group of co-owners, but instead merely sets the outer boundaries of their individual and collective ownership rights and leaves them to construct their own rules. In this manner, real property law both respects the diverse social dynamics of group ownership and protects the rights of individual co-owners.

Real property, whether owned by an individual or a group, thus functions in the common law as both a building block of normative community social structures and a potential laboratory for private social-group experimentation.

NOTES

PREFACE AND ACKNOWLEDGMENTS

1. United Nations Educational, Scientific, and Cultural Organization, "Convention for the Safeguarding of the Intangible Cultural Heritage," October 17, 2003, http://portal.unesco.org/en/ev.php-URL_ID=17716&URL_DO=DO_TOPIC&URL_SECTION=201.html, September 23, 2004.
2. Terry Eagleton, *The Idea of Culture* (Oxford: Blackwell, 2000), 1.
3. See Claudia Strauss and Naomi Quinn, *A Cognitive Theory of Cultural Meaning* (Cambridge: Cambridge University Press, 1997), 3–10; Adam Kuper, *Culture: The Anthropologists' Account* (Cambridge, Mass.: Harvard University Press, 1999), 1–20.
4. For an example of a philosophy of culture developed by a legal academic, see J. M. Balkin, *Cultural Software: A Theory of Ideology* (New Haven, Conn.: Yale University Press, 1998). The culture of the rule of law itself is also a distinct subject of study. See, e.g., Paul W. Kahn, *The Cultural Study of Law: Reconstructing Legal Scholarship* (Chicago: University of Chicago Press, 1999); Austin Sarat and Thomas R. Kearns, eds., *Law in the Domains of Culture* (Ann Arbor: University of Michigan Press, 2000).
5. Jürgen Habermas, *The Complete Theory of Communicative Action*, vol. 2: *Lifeworld and System: A Critique of Functionalist Reason*, trans. Thomas McCarthy (Boston: Beacon Press, 1987).
6. Lawrence Lessig, *The Future of Ideas: The Fate of the Commons in a Connected World* (New York: Random House, 2001); cf. Rosemary J. Coombe, "Fear, Hope, and Longing for the Future of Authorship and a Revitalized Public Domain in Global Regimes of Intellectual Property," *DePaul Law Review* 52 (Summer 2003): 1171–1191.
7. Thomas Hobbes, *Leviathan*, ed. C. B. MacPherson (1651; New York: Penguin Books, 1985), 186.
8. Silke von Lewinski, ed., *Indigenous Heritage and Intellectual Property: Genetic Resources, Traditional Knowledge and Folklore* (The Hague: Kluwer Law International, 2004); Michael F. Brown, *Who Owns Native Culture?* (Cambridge, Mass.: Harvard University Press, 2003).
9. The author and editors are aware that "America" can refer not only to the United States but also to North, Central, and South America more generally. In keeping with common legal usage, however, this work uses "America" and "Americans" to refer to the United States and its citizens.

10. Susan Scafidi, "Intellectual Property and Cultural Products," *Boston University Law Review* 81 (2001): 793–842.

CHAPTER 1   THE COMMODIFICATION OF CULTURE

1. Benedict Anderson, *Imagined Communities: Reflections on the Origin and Spread of Nationalism*, rev. ed. (1983; New York: Verso, 1991).
2. Linda Hamilton Krieger, "The Content of Our Categories: A Cognitive Bias Approach to Discrimination and Equal Employment Opportunity," *Stanford Law Review* 47 (1995): 1198.
3. See Thomas Hine, *I Want That! How We All Became Shoppers: A Cultural History* (New York: HarperCollins, 2002).
4. Clifford Geertz, *The Interpretation of Cultures* (New York: Basic Books, 1973), 49.
5. For a description of the bohemian migration to Greenwich Village in the early decades of the twentieth century, see Christine Stansell, *American Moderns: Bohemian New York and the Creation of a New Century* (New York: Henry Holt, 2000), 40–45.
6. Pierre Bourdieu, *Distinction: A Social Critique of the Judgement of Taste*, trans. Richard Nice (Cambridge, Mass.: Harvard University Press, 1984), 12.
7. James Romm, *Herodotus* (New Haven, Conn.: Yale University Press, 1998), 100.
8. Bruce Ziff and Pratima V. Rao, "Introduction to Cultural Appropriation: A Framework for Analysis," in *Borrowed Power: Essays on Cultural Appropriation*, ed. Bruce Ziff and Pratima V. Rao (New Brunswick, N.J.: Rutgers University Press, 1997), 1.
9. Jürgen Habermas, *The Complete Theory of Communicative Action*, vol. 2: *Lifeworld and System: A Critique of Functionalist Reason*, trans. Thomas McCarthy (Boston: Beacon Press, 1987), 322 (emphasis omitted).
10. Max Horkheimer and Theodor W. Adorno, *Dialectic of Enlightenment*, trans. John Cumming (1944; New York: Continuum, 2001), 154.
11. U.S. Const., art. 1, § 8, cl. 8.

CHAPTER 2   OWNERSHIP OF INTANGIBLE PROPERTY

1. For example, the Copyright Act provides, "Ownership of a copyright, or of any of the exclusive rights under a copyright, is distinct from ownership of any material object in which the work is embodied. Transfer of ownership of any material object . . . does not of itself convey any rights in the copyrighted work embodied in the object; nor, in the absence of an agreement, does transfer of ownership of a copyright or of any exclusive rights under a copyright convey property rights in any material object." 17 U.S.C. § 202 (2000).
2. The Federal Patent Act, for example, provides, "Subject to the provisions of this title, patents shall have the attributes of personal property." 35 U.S.C. § 261 (2000). Note, however, that the characterization of trademarks as property rather than simple source indicators for commercial goods and services is historically somewhat controversial, although it is becoming less so as trademarks increase in importance as business assets. The prohibition

against assignments of trademarks in gross (without any underlying corporate assets) in U.S. law, but not in the multinational Agreement on Trade-Related Aspects of Intellectual Property Rights (TRIPS), indicates such a transition. Lanham Act, § 10, 15 U.S.C. § 1060 (2000); TRIPS, April 15, 1994, art. 21, in *The Results of the Uruguay Round of Multilateral Trade Organizations: The Legal Texts* (Geneva: GATT Secretariat, 1994).

3. See Lawrence Lessig, *Code and Other Laws of Cyberspace* (New York: Basic Books, 1999), 122–141, on the potential roles of trespass laws and electronic fences in cyberspace.

4. Barbara J. Tucker, *Samuel Slater and the Origins of the American Textile Industry, 1790–1860* (Ithaca, N.Y.: Cornell University Press, 1984); Robert F. Dalzell, Jr., *Enterprising Elite: The Boston Associates and the World They Made* (Cambridge, Mass.: Harvard University Press, 1987).

5. Felix Cohen, "Dialogue on Private Property," *Rutgers Law Review* 9 (1954): 374.

6. Michael A. Heller, "The Boundaries of Private Property," *Yale Law Journal* 108 (1999): 1174.

7. Harold Demsetz, "The Private Production of Public Goods," *Journal of Law and Economics* 13 (1970): 295.

8. *A&M Records, Inc. v. Napster, Inc.,* 114 F. Supp. 2d 896, 896 (N.D. Cal. 2000), *aff'd in part, rev'd in part,* 239 F.3d 1004 (9th Cir. 2001).

9. Ibid., 911.

10. If such broadcasts were near-simultaneous and thus "hot news," however, state-law misappropriation claims would apply. See *Nat'l Basketball Ass'n v. Motorola, Inc.,* 105 F.3d 841, 843 (2d Cir. 1997); *Pittsburgh Athletic Co. v. KQV Broadcasting,* 24 F. Supp. 490, 494 (W.D. Pa. 1938).

11. Jodi Wilgoren, "Cubs Sue Neighborhood Bars on Rooftop Use," *New York Times,* December 18, 2002.

12. *Nat'l Basketball Ass'n,* 105 F.3d at 843, 846–847. By contrast, simultaneously recorded broadcasts of live events, including sporting events, are copyrightable. See *Nat'l Basketball Ass'n,* 105 F.3d at 847; Copyright Act, 17 U.S.C. § 101 (2000).

13. Because intellectual property is an umbrella category, encompassing patent, copyright, trademark, and trade-secret and unfair-competition law, any attempt to formulate unified jurisprudential theories is admittedly overgeneralized. For our purposes, this section focuses primarily on the justifications for creation of copyrights and patents.

14. U.S. Const., art. 1, § 8, cl. 8.

15. Marci A. Hamilton, *Copyright and the Constitution*, Occasional Papers in Intellectual Property 5 (New York: Cardozo School of Law, 1999), 12.

16. U.S. Const., art. 1, § 8, cl. 3.

17. Peter Jaszi and Martha Woodmansee, "Introduction," in *The Construction of Authorship: Textual Appropriation in Law and Literature,* ed. Martha Woodmansee and Peter Jaszi (Durham, N.C.: Duke University Press, 1994), 3. For additional description and criticism of the development of copyright and the role of Romantic authorship, see Mark Rose, *Authors and Owners: The Invention of Copyright* (Cambridge, Mass.: Harvard University Press, 1993); Keith Aoki, "(Intellectual) Property and Sovereignty: Notes Toward a Cultural Geography of Authorship," *Stanford Law Review* 48 (1996): 1293–1355.

18. Michel Foucault, "What Is an Author?" in *Language, Counter-Memory, Practice,* trans. Donald F. Bouchard and Sherry Simon (1969; Ithaca, N.Y.: Cornell University Press, 1977), 124–131. Scholars reflecting Foucault's critique include Peter Jaszi, "On the Author Effect: Contemporary Copyright and Collective Creativity," *Cardozo Arts & Entertainment Law Journal* 10 (1992): 294–295; James Boyle, *Shamans, Software, & Spleens: Law and the Construction of the Information Society* (Cambridge, Mass.: Harvard University Press, 1996), x–xiii.

19. Henry Hansmann and Maria Santilli, "Authors' and Artists' Moral Rights: A Comparative Legal and Economic Analysis," *Journal of Legal Studies* 26 (1997): 95–96. Different legal systems offer various degrees and combinations of moral rights protection.

20. See John Locke, *Two Treatises of Government,* ed. Peter Laslett (1698; Cambridge: Cambridge University Press, 1967).

21. Martha Woodmansee, "On the Author Effect: Recovering Collectivity," in *The Construction of Authorship: Textual Appropriation in Law and Literature,* ed. Martha Woodmansee and Peter Jaszi (Durham, N.C.: Duke University Press, 1994), 16.

22. Wendy J. Gordon, "A Property Right in Self-Expression: Equality and Individualism in the Natural Law of Intellectual Property," *Yale Law Journal* 102 (1993): 1535.

23. Hansmann and Santilli, "Authors' and Artists' Moral Rights," 95–143; Kenneth Port, "The Congressional Expansion of American Trademark Law: A Civil Law System in the Making," *Wake Forest Law Review* 35 (2000): 827–913; Heinz Bardehle, "A New Approach to Worldwide Harmonization of Patent Law," *Journal of the Patent and Trademark Office Society* 81 (1999): 303–310.

24. Hansmann and Santilli, "Authors' and Artists' Moral Rights," 96–97; Visual Artists' Rights Act of 1990, Pub. L. 101-650, 104 *Stat.* 5128, codified as amended at 17 U.S.C. §§ 101, 102, 106A, 107, and 601 (2000).

25. TRIPS, art. 9(1).

26. Federal Patent Act, 35 U.S.C. §§ 101, 111, 112 (2000); Copyright Act, 17 U.S.C. §§ 102(a), 411–412 (2000); Lanham Act, § 1, 15 U.S.C. § 1051 (2000); Uniform Trade Secrets Act, § 1(4)(i).

27. See Rochelle Cooper Dreyfuss, "Collaborative Research: Conflicts of Authorship, Ownership, and Accountabilty," *Vanderbilt Law Review* 53 (2000): 1164; Jaszi, "On the Author Effect," 315; Laura G. Lape, "A Narrow View of Creative Cooperation: The Current State of the Joint Work Doctrine," *Albany Law Review* 61 (1997): 51; Patricia Kimball Fletcher, "Joint Registration of Trademarks and the Economic Value of a Trademark System," *University of Miami Law Review* 36 (1982): 299; Margaret Chon, "New Wine Bursting from Old Bottles: Collaborative Internet Art, Joint Works, and Entrepreneurship," *Oregon Law Review* 75 (1996): 257–258.

28. Avner D. Sofer, "Joint Authorship: An Uncomfortable Fit with Tenancy in Common," *Loyola Los Angeles Entertainment Law Journal* 19 (1998): 8–9.

29. Dreyfuss, "Collaborative Research," 1161–1232; Carey R. Ramos and Joseph P. Verdon, "Joint Ownership of Intellectual Property: Pitfalls, Alternatives, and Contractual Solutions," *Practicing Law Institute: Patents, Copy-*

rights, Trademarks, and Literary Property Course Handbook Series 559 (1999): 17–26.

30. Among the limited provisions for concurrent ownership, copyright law allows *ab initio* co-ownership of joint works, defined as those on which the authors intended to collaborate, and treats all co-owners as tenants in common with independent rights to use the work, subject to a duty of accounting for profits to the other co-owners. Copyright Act, 17 U.S.C. §§ 101, 201 (2000); Melville B. Nimmer and David Nimmer; *Nimmer on Copyright: A Treatise on the Law of Literary, Musical, and Artistic Property, and the Protection of Ideas* (Albany, N.Y.: Matthew Bender, 2004), § 6.09 (updated looseleaf volume). Under certain circumstances, copyright's work-for-hire doctrine considers an employer, rather than the employee or independent contractor who created the work, to be the work's author. Copyright Act, 17 U.S.C. § 201 (2000). Patent law places fewer restrictions on collaborative creation and *ab initio* co-ownership, allowing inventors to file joint patent applications even if they did not work together and even if a joint inventor refuses to join the application or cannot be reached. Federal Patent Act, 35 U.S.C. § 116 (2000). The patent system, however, also provides less guidance as to the structure of co-ownership, as it allows joint owners to profit from their patents without the consent of the other joint owners and without accounting to them; 35 U.S.C. § 262 (2000). Finally, the Lanham Act allows concurrent registration of trademarks under limited conditions, provided that such use will not likely confuse or deceive the public. Lanham Act, § 2(d),15 U.S.C. § 1052(d) (2000); Lanham Act, § 5, 15 U.S.C. § 1055 (2000).

31. Indian Arts and Crafts Act of 1990, Pub. L. 101-664, *Stat.* 4462 (1990), amending 25 U.S.C. § 305 and 18 U.S.C. §§ 1158–1159 (2000). Legal scholars' discussions of intellectual property and indigenous rights include Angela R. Riley, "Recovering Collectivity: Group Rights to Intellectual Property in Indigenous Communities," *Cardozo Arts & Entertainment Law Journal* 18 (2000): 175–225; Christine Haight Farley, "Protecting Folklore of Indigenous Peoples: Is Intellectual Property the Answer?" *Connecticut Law Review* 30 (1997): 1–57; Richard A. Guest, "Intellectual Property Rights in Native American Tribes," *American Indian Law Review* 20 (1996): 111–139; Rosemary J. Coombe, "The Properties of Culture and the Possession of Identity: Postcolonial Legal Struggle and the Legal Imagination," in *Borrowed Power: Essays on Cultural Appropriation*, ed. Bruce Ziff and Pratima V. Rao (New Brunswick, N.J.: Rutgers University Press, 1997), 74–96; Silke von Lewinski, ed., *Indigenous Heritage and Intellectual Property: Genetic Resources, Traditional Knowledge and Folklore* (The Hague: Kluwer Law International, 2004).

CHAPTER 3   CULTURAL PRODUCTS AS ACCIDENTAL PROPERTY

1. Oliver Sacks, *Seeing Voices: A Journey into the World of the Deaf* (Berkeley: University of California Press, 1989), 16–18, 23, 139–140.
2. Ibid., 142–143.
3. Ibid., 147–148.

4. National Wheelchair Basketball Association, "History of Wheelchair Basketball," www.nwba.org, September 23, 2004.

5. National Wheelchair Basketball Association, "NWBA Mission Statement," www.nwba.org, September 23, 2004.

6. National Wheelchair Basketball Association, "Constitution and Interpretations of the National Wheelchair Basketball Association" (2002–2003) (on file with author). The bylaws have since been edited and the list of purposes simplified.

7. Ibid.

8. Holland Cotter, "Quilts That Hew to Discipline Even as They Dazzle," *New York Times*, July 9, 1999.

9. Jacqueline L. Tobin and Raymond G. Dobard, *Hidden in Plain View: The Secret Story of Quilts and the Underground Railroad* (New York: Doubleday, 1999).

10. See, e.g., Donald B. Kraybill and Steven M. Nolt, *Amish Enterprise* (Baltimore: Johns Hopkins University Press, 1995), 45–47, 63.

11. Patricia Leigh Brown, "Design Notebook: From the Bottomlands, Soulful Stitches," *New York Times*, November 21, 2002.

12. Roberta Hershenson, "Stitches in Time: College Exhibition Features Historic Quilts," *New York Times*, July 12, 1992.

13. John Beardsley et al., *The Quilts of Gee's Bend* (Atlanta: Tinwood Books, 2002).

14. Michael Kimmelman, "Jazzy Geometry, Cool Quilters," *New York Times*, November 29, 2002.

15. The information on the history of the tango in this and the foregoing paragraphs is drawn primarily from Simon Collier et al., *¡Tango! The Dance, the Song, the Story* (London: Thames & Hudson, 1995).

16. Lois Draegin, "Tango Traces a Society," *New York Times*, June 23, 1985; Jennifer Dunning, "When Folkways Point the Way to Innovation," *New York Times*, June 1, 1997.

17. Copyright Act, 17 U.S.C. § 102 (2002); Federal Patent Act, 35 U.S.C. §§ 112–114 (2002); TRIPS, April 15, 1994, art. 15(1), in *The Results of the Uruguay Round of Multilateral Trade Organizations: The Legal Texts* (Geneva: GATT Secretariat, 1994).

18. UNESCO and WIPO, "Model Provisions for National Laws on the Protection of Expressions of Folklore against Illicit Exploitation and Other Prejudicial Actions," 1982, http://www.wipo.int/tk/en/documents/pdf/1982-folklore-model-provisions.pdf, September 23, 2004. Additional studies on this subject include Silke von Lewinski, ed., *Indigenous Heritage and Intellectual Property: Genetic Resources, Traditional Knowledge and Folklore* (The Hague: Kluwer Law International, 2004); Stephen B. Brush and Doreen Stabinsky, *Indigenous People and Intellectual Property Rights* (Washington, D.C.: Island Press, 1996); Darrell A. Posey and Graham Dutfield, *Beyond Intellectual Property: Toward Traditional Resource Rights for Indigenous Peoples and Local Communities* (Ottawa: International Development Resource Center, 1996).

19. Marshall McLuhan, *Understanding Media: The Extensions of Man*, ed. W. Terrence Gordon (1964; Corte Madera, Calif.: Ginko Press, 2003), 19.

20. See Jonathan M. Bloom, *Paper before Print: The History and Impact of Paper in*

the *Islamic World* (New Haven, Conn.: Yale University Press, 2001), 92; James Elkins, *The Domain of Images* (Ithaca, N.Y.: Cornell University Press, 1999), 95–96; Hans Belting, *Likeness and Presence: A History of the Image before the Era of Art* , trans. Edmund Jephcott (Chicago: University of Chicago Press, 1994), 159; Alain Besançon, *The Forbidden Image: An Intellectual History of Iconoclasm*, trans. Jane Marie Todd (Chicago: University of Chicago Press, 2000), 77–81.

21. Nadine Brozan, "Chronicle," *New York Times*, January 25, 1994.
22. Qur'an 96:1. While some English translations use "read" rather than "recite," this is traditionally taken to mean "read aloud." See Bloom, *Paper before Print*, 94–95.
23. Bloom, *Paper before Print*, 94–97. For a discussion of the social and cognitive effects of orality, see Michael E. Hobart and Zachary S. Schiffman, "Orality and the Problem of Memory," in *Information Ages: Literacy, Numeracy, and the Computer Revolution* (Baltimore: Johns Hopkins University Press, 1998), 11–31.
24. Bloom, *Paper before Print*, 95, 98–99.
25. See John Schmid, "Islam's Books Go Unread in the West," *International Herald Tribune*, October 18, 2001. Islamic countries have begun to develop effective intellectual property laws, including copyright, in accordance with international norms. See Abu-Ghazaleh Intellectual Property (TMP Agents), *Intellectual Property Laws of the Arab Countries* (The Hague: Kluwer Law International, 2000).
26. Bloom, *Paper before Print*, 90; Bernard Lewis, *What Went Wrong? Western Impact and Middle Eastern Response* (New York: Oxford University Press, 2002), 142–144.
27. James Fentress and Chris Wickham, *Social Memory* (Oxford: Blackwell, 1992), 59.
28. See Colleen McDannell, *Material Christianity: Religion and Popular Culture in America* (New Haven, Conn.: Yale University Press, 1995), 63–64. Many religions have a complex material culture that operates in the commercial realm, as the popularity of images of the Buddha and other iconography would imply. For a discussion of the "spiritual products" of African-based belief systems such as Voodoo and Santería in America, see Carolyn Morrow Long, *Spiritual Merchants: Religion, Magic and Commerce* (Knoxville: University of Tennessee Press, 2001).

CHAPTER 4   CATEGORIZING CULTURAL PRODUCTS

1. Alex Haley, *Roots: The Saga of an American Family* (New York: Dell, 1976), 332, 348.
2. Brenda E. Stevenson, *Life in Black and White: Family and Community in the Slave South* (New York: Oxford University Press, 1996), 228–229.
3. Harriette Cole, *Jumping the Broom: The African-American Wedding Planner* (New York: Henry Holt, 1993).
4. Kemba J. Dunham, "Sweep of History Helps Propel a Boom in Keepsake Brooms," *Wall Street Journal*, October 15, 1999.
5. Liz Crihfield Dalby, *Kimono: Fashioning Culture* (New Haven, Conn.: Yale University Press, 1993), 4.

6. See Malcolm Barnard, *Fashion as Communication*, 2nd ed. (New York: Routledge, 2002), 187–188.
7. Roland Barthes, *The Fashion System*, trans. Matthew Ward and Richard Howard (1967; Berkeley: University of Califoria Press, 1990), 236.
8. Maulana Karenga, *Kwanzaa: A Celebration of Family, Community, and Culture*, rev. ed. (Los Angeles: University of Sankore Press, 1998); Organization Us, "Kwanzaa: Roots and Branches," http://www.officialkwanzaawebsite.org, September 23, 2004.
9. Ibid.
10. Henri Schindler, *Mardi Gras: New Orleans* (New York: Flammarion, 1997), 10–16.
11. Mikhail Bakhtin, *Rabelais and His World*, trans. Hélène Iswolsky (Bloomington: Indiana University Press, 1984), 5–12.
12. Samuel Kinser, *Carnival, American Style: Mardi Gras at New Orleans and Mobile* (Chicago: University of Chicago Press, 1990), 3.
13. James Gill, *Lords of Misrule: Mardi Gras and the Politics of Race in New Orleans* (Jackson: University Press of Mississippi, 1997), 7.
14. Kinser, *Carnival, American Style*, 318.
15. *Hurley v. Irish American Gay, Lesbian, and Bisexual Group of Boston*, 515 U.S. 557, 570 (1995); Melville B. Nimmer and David Nimmer, *Nimmer on Copyright: A Treatise on the Law of Literary, Musical, and Artistic Property, and the Protection of Ideas* (Albany, N.Y.: Matthew Bender, 2004), § 2.03[B][2] n. 33 (updated looseleaf volume).
16. *Production Contractors, Inc. v. WGN Continental Broadcasting Co.*, 622 F. Supp. 1500 (N.D. Ill. 1985).
17. Silke von Lewinski, ed., *Indigenous Heritage and Intellectual Property: Genetic Resources, Traditional Knowledge and Folklore* (The Hague: Kluwer Law International, 2004).
18. Bill Lambrecht, "Amazon Tribal Leaders Challenge U.S. Patent; They Say American Has No Right to Plant Used in Healing," *St. Louis Post-Dispatch*, March 31, 1999; Brenda Sandburg, "Farmers, Indigenous Folk Fight Patenting of Plants, *National Law Journal*, December 13, 1999; Glenn M. Wiser, "U.S. Patent Office Rejects Patent on Indigenous Medical Plant," *Environmental Compliance & Litigation Strategy* 15, no. 8 (January 2000): 5.
19. Commission on Intellectual Property Rights (U.K.), *Integrating Intellectual Property Rights and Development Policy: Report of the Commission on Intellectual Property Rights* (London, September 2002), 76–78. For an analysis of the controversies surrounding turmeric, basmati rice, and neem, see Shubha Ghosh, "Globalization, Patents, and Traditional Knowledge," *Columbia Journal of Asian Law* 17 (2003): 73–120.
20. Convention on Biological Diversity, June 5, 1992, art. 8(j), http://www.biodiv.org/convention/articles.asp, September 23, 2004.
21. World Trade Organization, "Ministerial Declaration," November 14, 2001, WT/MIN(01)/DEC/1, para. 19, http://www.wto.org/english/thewto_e/minist_e/min01_e/mindecl_e.htm, September 23, 2004.
22. United Nations Educational, Scientific, and Cultural Organization, "Convention for the Safeguarding of the Intangible Cultural Heritage," October 17, 2003, art. 2, http://portal.unesco.org/en/ev.php-URL_ID=17716&URL_DO=DO_TOPIC&URL_SECTION=201.html, September 23, 2004.

23. Organization Us, "Fundamental Questions about Kwanzaa: An Interview," http://www.officialkwanzaawebsite.org, September 23, 2004.
24. See Lyndel V. Prott and Patrick J. O'Keefe, "'Cultural Heritage' or 'Cultural Property'?" *International Journal of Cultural Property* 1 (1992): 307–320.
25. John Henry Merryman, "Two Ways of Thinking about Cultural Property," *American Journal of International Law* 80 (1986): 831.
26. Patty Gerstenblith, "Identity and Cultural Property: The Protection of Cultural Property in the United States," *Boston University Law Review* 75 (1995): 562.
27. Steen Eiler Rasmussen, *Experiencing Architecture* (Cambridge, Mass.: MIT Press, 1959), 139.
28. The primary international treaties intended to protect cultural property are the Hague Convention on the Protection of Cultural Property in the Event of Armed Conflicts, *United Nations Treaty Series* 249 (1954), and the UNESCO Convention on the Means of Prohibiting and Preventing the Illicit Import, Export, and Transfer of Ownership of Cultural Property, *United Nations Treaty Series* 823 (1970).
29. Phil McCombs, "Maya Lin and the Great Call of China; The Fascinating Heritage of the Student Who Designed the Vietnam Memorial," *Washington Post*, January 3, 1982.
30. Maya Ying Lin, "Design Submission to the Vietnam Veterans Memorial Competition," *National Park Service*, http://www.nps.gov/vive/memorial/description.htm, September 23, 2004.
31. Louis Menand, "The Reluctant Memorialist," *New Yorker* (July 8, 2002): 55.
32. *San Francisco Chronicle*, May 26, 1983, quoted in John Henry Merryman, "The Public Interest in Cultural Property," *California Law Review* 77 (1989): 349.
33. For addition discussion of the Elgin marbles controversy, see Christopher Hitchens, *The Elgin Marbles: Should They Be Returned to Greece?* (1987; London: Verso, 1997); Theodore Vrettos, *The Elgin Affair: The Abduction of Antiquity's Greatest Treasures and the Passions It Aroused* (New York: Arcade, 1997); John Henry Merryman, "Thinking About the Elgin Marbles," *Michigan Law Review* 83 (1985): 1881–1923.

CHAPTER 5   CLAIMING COMMUNITY OWNERSHIP
                 VIA AUTHENTICITY

1. Mark Stevenson, "Victims of Piracy in Mexico Dissatisfied with Enforcement of IP Laws," *U.S. Mexico Free Trade Reporter*, July 31, 1995.
2. *Oxford English Dictionary*, online ed., 2004, s.v. "Authentic."
3. Ibid.
4. Jacob Golomb, *In Search of Authenticity: From Kierkegaard to Camus* (New York: Routledge, 1995), 33. For Kierkegaard's famous work on the achievement of authenticity, in the form of a reflection on the Biblical story of Abraham and Isaac, see Søren Kierkegaard, *Fear and Trembling*, in *Fear and Trembling; Repetition*, Kierkegaard's Writings VI, trans. Howard V. Hong and Edna H. Hong (Princeton, N.J.: Princeton University Press, 1983).
5. Martin Heidegger, *Being and Time*, trans. Joan Stambaugh (Albany: State University of New York Press, 1966), 282–287. For a critique of *inter alia*

Heidegger and his response to Kierkegaard, see Theodor W. Adorno, *The Jargon of Authenticity*, trans. Knut Tarnowski and Frederic Will (Evanston, Ill.: Northwestern University Press, 1973).

6. Virginia Postrel, *The Substance of Style: How the Rise of Aesthetic Value Is Remaking Commerce, Culture, and Consciousness* (New York: HarperCollins, 2003).

7. Organization Us, http://www.officialkwanzaawebsite.org.

8. Brian Spooner, "Weavers and Dealers: The Authenticity of an Oriental Carpet," in *The Social Life of Things: Commodities in Cultural Perspective*, ed. Arjun Appadurai (Cambridge: Cambridge University Press, 1986), 200.

9. International agreements governing the protection of geographical indications, much of which takes place under national laws, include TRIPS, April 15, 1994, art. 22–24, in *The Results of the Uruguay Round of Multilateral Trade Organizations: The Legal Texts* (Geneva: GATT Secretariat, 1994); the Lisbon Agreement for the Protection of Appellations of Origin and Their International Registration, October 31, 1958, http://www.wipo.int/lisbon/en/legal_texts/lisbon_agreement.htm, September 23, 2004; and Council of the European Communities, Council Regulation (EEC) No. 2081/92, July 14, 1992, on the Protection of Geographical Indications and Designations of Origin for Agricultural Products and Foodstuffs.

10. Indian Arts and Crafts Act of 1990, Pub. L. 101-664, 104 *Stat.* 4462 (1990), amending 25 U.S.C. § 305 and 18 U.S.C. §§ 1158–59 (2000).

11. For critiques of the Indian Arts and Crafts Act of 1990, see Gail K. Sheffield, *The Arbitrary Indian: The Indian Arts and Crafts Act of 1990* (Norman: University of Oklahoma Press, 1997); Jon Keith Parsley, "Regulation of Counterfeit Indian Arts and Crafts: An Analysis of the Indian Arts and Crafts Act of 1990," *American Indian Law Review* 18 (1993): 487–514; William J. Hapiuk Jr., "Of Kitch and Kachinas: A Critical Analysis of the Indian Arts and Crafts Act of 1990," *Stanford Law Review* 53 (2001): 1009–1075.

12. Indian Arts and Crafts Association, http://www.iaca.com, September 23, 2004.

13. Carole Goldberg, "A Law of Their Own: Native Challenges to American Law," *Law and Social Inquiry* 25 (2000): 263–264.

14. Michael Gross, *Genuine Authentic: The Real Life of Ralph Lauren* (New York: HarperCollins, 2003).

15. B.K.S. Iyengar, *Light on Yoga*, rev. ed. (1966; New York: Schocken Books, 1977), 19; Barbara Stoler Miller, trans., *Yoga: Discipline of Freedom: The Yoga Sutra Attributed to Patanjali* (New York: Bantam Books, 1998).

16. Ian Whicher, *The Integrity of the Yoga Darana: A Reconsideration of Classical Yoga* (Albany: State University of New York Press, 1998), 6–9.

17. Georg Feuerstein, *The Yoga Tradition: Its History, Literature, Philosophy, and Practice* (Prescott, Ariz.: Hohm Press, 1998), 29–31.

18. Marina Budhos, "Culture Shock," *Yoga Journal*, no. 167 (May/June 2002): 92.

19. David Sipress, *New Yorker* (September 17, 2001): 108. Among yoga practitioners Bikram Choudhury has sparked controversy by trademarking his name, copyrighting the structure of his classes, and threatening legal action against other studios. Vanessa Grigoriadis, "Controlled Breathing, in the Extreme," *New York Times*, July 6, 2003.

20. Marina Budhos, "Out of India," *Yoga Journal,* no. 166 (March/April 2002): 90–95, 181–183; Marina Budhos, "Culture Shock," 88–93, 164–167.
21. Kate Betts, "Yoga, Unlike Fashion, Is Deep. Right?" *New York Times,* December 15, 2002.
22. The information on the history of freestyle skateboarding in this and the following paragraphs is drawn primarily from C. R. Stecyk III and Glen E. Friedman, *Dogtown: The Legend of Z-Boys* (New York: Burning Flags Press, 2000); *Dogtown and Z-Boys,* dir. Stacy Peralta, Sony Pictures, 2002; G. Beato, "The Lords of Dogtown," *Spin Magazine* (March 1999).
23. Stecyk and Friedman, *Dogtown,* 100.
24. Neil Strauss, "Where the Wheel Was Reinvented," *New York Times,* April 28, 2002.
25. Kate Betts, "The Whoosh of What You'll Be Wearing," *New York Times,* May 5, 2002.
26. Intellectual-property-law scholar Madhavi Sunder offers such a cautionary tale of cultural protectionism in her analysis of conservative objections to Deepa Mehta's film *Fire.* Madhavi Sunder, "Intellectual Property and Identity Politics: Playing with *Fire,*" *Journal of Gender, Race and Justice* 4 (2002): 75. For additional exploration of the same theme, see Madhavi Sunder, "Piercing the Veil," *Yale Law Journal* 112 (2003): 1399–1472.
27. Berta Esperanza Hernandez-Truyol, "Women's Rights as Human Rights—Rules, Realities, and the Role of Culture: A Formula for Reform," *Brooklyn Journal of International Law* 21 (1996): 657–660.
28. Spooner, "Weavers and Dealers," 228.
29. Ten Thousand Villages, "Welcome," brochure. Additional information is available at http://www.villages.ca.
30. See United States Patent and Trademark Office, http://www.uspto.gov. Note that a number of courts have declared unconstitutional state statutory provisions intended to prevent fraud in the kosher food industry, thus leaving evaluation of such products to the consumer marketplace. *Commack Self-Service Kosher Meats, Inc. v. Weiss,* 294 F.3d 415 (2d Cir. 2002), *cert. denied,* 537 U.S. 1187 (2003); *Ran-Dav's County Kosher, Inc. v. State of New Jersey,* 608 A.2d 1353 (N.J. 1992), *cert. denied sub nom. National Jewish Com'n on Law and Public Affairs (COLPA) v. Ran-Dav's County Kosher, Inc.,* 507 U.S. 952 (1993); *Barghout v. Bureau of Kosher Meat and Food Control,* 66 F.3d 1337 (4th Cir. 1995). For further discussion of the public and private regulation of the kosher food industry, see Shayna M. Sigman, "Kosher without Law: The Role of Nonlegal Sanctions in Overcoming Fraud within the Kosher Industry," *Florida State University Law Review* 31 (2004): 509–601.
31. See United States Patent and Trademark Office, "Press Release: USPTO Establishes Database of Official Insignia of Native American Tribes," August 29, 2001, http://www.uspto.gov/web/offices/com/speeches/01-37.htm, September 23, 2004.

CHAPTER 6   FAMILY FEUDS

1. David N. Dinkins, "Keep Marching for Equality," *New York Times,* March 21, 1991.

2. Anna Quindlen, "Erin Go Brawl," *New York Times*, March 14, 1991.
3. *Hurley v. Irish-American Gay, Lesbian, and Bisexual Group of Boston*, 515 U.S. 557, 560 (1995).
4. *New York County Board of Ancient Order of Hibernians v. Dinkins*, 814 F. Supp. 358, 363 (1993).
5. *Irish-American Gay, Lesbian, and Bisexual Group of Boston v. City of Boston*, 636 N.E.2d 1293, 1295 (Mass. 1994), *rev'd. sub nom. Hurley v. Irish-American Gay, Lesbian, and Bisexual Group of Boston*, 515 U.S. 557 (1995).
6. Ibid.
7. *Hurley*, 515 U.S. at 568, quoting Susan G. Davis, *Parades and Power: Street Theatre in Nineteenth-Century Philadelphia* (Philadelphia: Temple University Press, 1986), 6.
8. Ibid., 569.
9. Ibid., 572–576.
10. Marilyn Halter vividly illustrates the American transformation of Saint Patrick's Day when she notes that many Irish Americans planning a trip to their ancestral homeland around the occasion had been disappointed at the holiday's lack of importance in Ireland. To remedy this problem, the Irish Tourist Board in 1996 committed "a good chunk of money" to fabricate entirely new celebrations, parades, and festivals to mark the occasion. Marilyn Halter, *Shopping for Identity: The Marketing of Ethnicity* (New York: Random House, 2000), 168.
11. Vera Dika, "The Representation of Ethnicity in *The Godfather*," in *Francis Ford Coppola's* The Godfather *Trilogy*, ed. Nick Browne (Cambridge: Cambridge University Press, 2000): 81; Ruth Vasey, *The World According to Hollywood, 1918–1939* (Madison: University of Wisconsin Press, 1997), 142.
12. Vasey, *The World According to Hollywood*, 120.
13. Ibid., 143.
14. Dika, "The Representation of Ethnicity in *The Godfather*"; Roland Barthes, "The Rhetoric of the Image," in *Image, Music, Text*, trans. Stephen Heath (New York: Hill & Wang, 1977), 32–51.
15. Dika, "The Representation of Ethnicity in *The Godfather*," 80; Peter Bart, afterword to *The Godfather* by Mario Puzo (1969; New York: New American Library, 2002).
16. "'Sopranos' Banned from County Property," *New York Times*, December 17, 2000; "Page Six: Back to School," *New York Post*, November 7, 2000.
17. Jennifer Steinhauer with Robert Worth, "His 'Sopranos' Guests Excluded, Mayor Will Skip Columbus Day Parade," *New York Times*, October 12, 2002.
18. Ibid.
19. Rudolph W. Giuliani with Ken Kurson, *Leadership* (New York: Hyperion, 2002), 196–197.
20. Ill. Const., art. 1, § 20.
21. *AIDA v. Time Warner Entertainment Company, L.P.*, 772 N.E.2d 953, 956 (Ill. App. Ct. 2002).
22. Ibid., 957.
23. Ibid., 959.
24. David Chase, interview by Terry Gross, *Fresh Air*, National Public Radio, June 22, 2000. For additional commentary, see Juan Williams, "Mob Images

in Popular Culture and Why Americans Are So Drawn to the Mafia," *Talk of the Nation*, National Public Radio, August 23, 2000.

25. Boleslaw Mastai and Marie-Louise D'Otrange Mastai, *The Stars and the Stripes: The American Flag as Art and History, from the Birth of the Republic to the Present* (New York: Knopf, 1973), 43.

26. Robert Justin Goldstein, *Saving Old Glory: The History of the American Flag Desecration Controversy* (Boulder, Colo.: Westview Press, 1996), 4–7.

27. Mastai and Mastai, *The Stars and the Stripes*, 175–213; Goldstein, *Saving Old Glory*, 9. Since 1905, U.S. law has forbidden the registration of trademarks that consist of or comprise any local or national flag or insignia. Lanham Act, § 2, 15 U.S.C. § 1052(b) (2003).

28. Goldstein, *Saving Old Glory*, 12–18.

29. Ibid., 18–30.

30. Ibid., 47–50.

31. *Halter v. Nebraska*, 205 U.S. 34 (1907).

32. Ibid., 43.

33. Goldstein, *Saving Old Glory*, 2, 45, 100. During the 1990s, when commercial use of the flag was no longer popularly or legally considered desecration, established fashion designer Ralph Lauren and trendy newcomer Tommy Hilfiger waged a marketing battle over association with the symbol. Teri Agins, *The End of Fashion* (New York: HarperCollins, 1999), 80–126.

34. Federal Flag Desecration Law, Pub. L. 90-381, 82 *Stat.* 291 (1968) (codified at 18 U.S.C. § 700) (held unconstitutional).

35. Goldstein, *Saving Old Glory*, 140–141.

36. *Street v. New York*, 394 U.S. 576 (1969); *Smith v. Goguen*, 415 U.S. 566 (1974).

37. *Radich v. New York*, 401 U.S. 531 (1971). For additional discussion and commentary, see Goldstein, *Saving Old Glory*, 112–118.

38. *Spence v. Washington*, 418 U.S. 405 (1974).

39. *West Virginia State Board of Education v. Barnette*, 319 U.S. 624 (1943). For discussion of the Bush-Dukakis race, see Goldstein, *Saving Old Glory*, 200.

40. *Texas v. Johnson*, 491 U.S. 397 (1989).

41. Flag Protection Act of 1989, Pub. L. 101-131, 103 *Stat.* 777 (1989) (codified at 18 U.S.C. § 700) (held unconstitutional).

42. *United States v. Eichman*, 496 U.S. 310, 318 (1990).

43. Robert E. Bonner, *Colors and Blood: Flag Passions of the Confederate South* (Princeton, N.J.: Princeton University Press, 2002), 45.

44. Ibid., 82–87, 96, 105, 108, 125.

45. *Coleman v. Miller*, 117 F.3d 527, 529 (11th Cir. 1997).

46. *National Association for the Advancement of Colored People (NAACP) v. Hunt*, 891 F.2d 1555, 1566 (11th Cir. 1990). For a critical discussion of this case and the constitutionality of official display of the Confederate battle flag, see James Forman Jr., "Driving Dixie Down: Removing the Confederate Flag from Southern State Capitols," *Yale Law Journal* 101 (1991): 505–525.

47. *Coleman*, 117 F.3d at 530.

48. Sanford Levinson, "They Whisper: Reflections on Flags, Monuments, and State Holidays, and the Construction of Social Meaning in a Multicultural Society," *Chicago-Kent Law Review* 70 (1995): 1102. Levinson's extended

reflections on the subject are available in Sanford Levinson, *Written in Stone: Public Monuments in Changing Societies* (Durham, N.C.: Duke University Press, 1998).

49. Eric Boehlert, "Lott Falls, but Democrats Don't Rise" (includes an interview with Charles Bullock, professor of political science), *Salon.com*, December 21, 2002, http://salon.com/politics/feature/2002/12/21/bullock/index_np.html, September 23, 2004.

50. Janita Poe, "S.C. NAACP Sticks to Boycott; Flag Flap Shifts Annual Convention to Georgia," *Atlanta Journal and Constitution*, October 13, 2002.

51. For a discussion of the use of Confederate symbols in schools, see Kathleen Riley, "The Long Shadow of the Confederacy in America's Schools: State-Sponsored Use of Confederate Symbols in the Wake of Brown v. Board," *William and Mary Bill of Rights Journal* 10 (2002): 525–549.

52. *Harjo v. Pro-Football, Inc.*, 50 U.S.P.Q.2d 1705 (T.T.A.B. April 2, 1999), *rev'd.* 284 F.Supp.2d 96 (D.D.C. 2003).

53. Margaret Jane Radin, *Contested Commodities: The Trouble with Trade in Sex, Children, Body Parts, and Other Things* (Cambridge, Mass.: Harvard University Press, 1996).

54. Catharine A. MacKinnon and Andrea Dworkin, *In Harm's Way: The Pornography Civil Rights Hearings* (Cambridge, Mass.: Harvard University Press, 1997).

55. Catharine A. MacKinnon, "Pornography, Civil Rights, and Speech," *Harvard Civil Rights–Civil Liberties Law Review* 20 (1985): 62 (quoting testimony of Cheryl Champion).

56. MacKinnon and Dworkin, *In Harm's Way*, 17; *American Booksellers Association, Inc. v. Hudnut*, 771 F.2d 323 (7th Cir. 1985), *aff'd. without opinion* 475 U.S. 1001 (1986).

57. *American Booksellers Association, Inc.*, 771 F.2d at 329.

58. Ibid.

59. Andrea Dworkin, *Pornography: Men Possessing Women* (New York: Dutton, 1979), 224.

60. Nadine Strossen, *Defending Pornography: Free Speech, Sex, and the Fight for Women's Rights* (New York: New York University Press, 1995), 15.

61. Ibid., 229–244; *Butler v. The Queen*, [1992] S.C.R. 452.

62. Strossen, *Defending Pornography*, 275–276.

63. Richard A. Posner, *Sex and Reason* (Cambridge, Mass.: Harvard University Press, 1992), 365–374.

64. Ibid., 381.

65. Jane Smith, "Making Movies," in *Sex Work: Writings by Women in the Sex Industry*, ed. Frédérique Delacoste and Priscilla Alexander, 2nd ed. (San Francisco: Cleis Press, 1998), 141.

66. Nina Hartley, "Confessions of a Feminist Porno Star," in *Sex Work: Writings by Women in the Sex Industry*, ed. Frédérique Delacoste and Priscilla Alexander, 2nd ed. (San Francisco: Cleis Press, 1998), 144.

67. Amelia Jones, ed., *The Feminism and Visual Culture Reader* (New York: Routledge, 2003), 370. For additional discussion of the use of the body in artistic endeavors, see Linda S. Kauffman, *Bad Girls and Sick Boys: Fantasies in Contemporary Art and Culture* (Berkeley: University of California Press, 1998).

68. SuicideGirls, "SuicideGirls Tour," http://suicidegirls.com/tour/.
69. Editorial, *New York Times*, September 7, 1991.
70. Background information on the Dead Sea Scrolls controversy in this section is drawn primarily from the extensive discussion by David Nimmer, "Copyright in the Dead Sea Scrolls: Authorship and Originality," *Houston Law Review* 38 (2001): 1–217.
71. Ibid., 74.

CHAPTER 7   OUTSIDER APPROPRIATION

1. Class Action/Complaint for Temporary and Permanent Injunctive Relief, Refund of Illegally Exacted Funds and Refund of Counterfeit Proceeds at 8, *National Association for the Advancement of Colored People v. City of Helena* (E.D. Ark. 1999) (No. H-C-99-152).
2. Ibid., 7.
3. Order, *National Association for the Advancement of Colored People v. City of Helena,* April 20, 2000; Judgment, *National Association for the Advancement of Colored People v. City of Helena,* May 25, 2000.
4. Alyn Shipton, *A New History of Jazz* (London: Continuum, 2001), 6; Ted Gioia, *The History of Jazz* (New York: Oxford University Press, 1997), 3–27.
5. Amiri Baraka, "Jazz and the White Critic," in *The Jazz Cadence of American Culture,* ed. Robert G. O'Meally (New York: Columbia University Press, 1998), 138.
6. Louis Armstrong, *Louis Armstrong, in His Own Words: Selected Writings*, ed. Thomas Brothers (New York: Oxford University Press, 1999), 33.
7. Miles Davis with Quincy Troupe, *Miles, the Autobiography* (New York: Simon & Schuster, 1989), 117.
8. Shipton, *A New History of Jazz*, 427.
9. Davis, *Miles, the Autobiography*, 119.
10. Ibid., 129; Gene Lees, *Cats of Any Color: Jazz, Black and White* (1995; New York: Da Capo Press, 2000), 191–194.
11. Gerald Early, "White Noise and White Knights: Some Thoughts on Race, Jazz, and the White Jazz Musician," in *Jazz: A History of America's Music*, by Geoffrey C. Ward (New York: Knopf, 2000), 324.
12. Lees, *Cats of Any Color*, 218.
13. Ibid., 190.
14. Richard M. Sudhalter, *Lost Chords: White Musicians and Their Contribution to Jazz, 1915–1945* (New York: Oxford University Press, 1999), xviii; "Freedom of Expression with a Groove: An Interview with Wynton Marsalis," in *Jazz: A History of America's Music*, by Geoffrey C. Ward (New York: Knopf, 2000), 118–119.
15. Gene Lees, *You Can't Steal a Gift: Dizzy, Clark, Milt, and Nat* (New Haven, Conn.: Yale University Press, 2001), 96.
16. Lees, *Cats of Any Color*, 131; "People, News, Gossip, Scoops," *St. Louis Post-Dispatch,* December 3, 2003 (describing film director Spike Lee's attack on rap music during a lecture at Brown University).
17. Lees, *Cats of Any Color*, 131.
18. "The Talk of the Town," *New Yorker* (October 5, 1998): 32.

19. For a discussion of the largely white composition of the modern jazz audience, see Ron Wynn, "Where's the Black Audience?" *Jazz Times* 33, no. 1 (February 2003): 74–78.
20. K. J. Greene, "Copyright, Culture & Black Music: A Legacy of Unequal Protection," *Hastings Communication & Entertainment Law Journal* 21 (1999): 360; Siva Vaidhyanathan, *Copyrights and Copywrongs: The Rise of Intellectual Property and How It Threatens Creativity* (New York: New York University Press, 2001), 125–126.
21. Vaidhyanathan, *Copyrights and Copywrongs*, 125.
22. Quoted in Calvin Sims, "Cabbage Is Cabbage? Not to Kimchi Lovers; Koreans Take Issue with a Rendition of Their National Dish Made in Japan," *New York Times*, February 5, 2000.
23. Amy M. Spindler, "Patterns," *New York Times*, March 16, 1993 (reporting on a fashion designer's use of "Judaism as an inspiration" in his runway designs). For a discussion of the sociological significance of Hasidic dress, see Fred Davis, *Fashion, Culture, and Identity* (Chicago: University of Chicago Press, 1994), 181.
24. For an example of legislation regarding a form of cultural appropriation, see the Native American Graves Protection and Repatriation Act of 1990 (NAGPRA), 25 U.S.C. §§ 3001–3013, 18 U.S.C. § 1170 (2000), which requires museums to return human remains, grave goods, and sacred objects found on federal lands to Native American tribes. Because NAGPRA addresses cultural property rather than cultural products, it does not affect the creation of displays or dioramas using replicas of the original objects. Further discussion of NAGPRA highlighting the importance of the indigenous role in its implementation may be found in Rennard Strickland, "Implementing the National Policy of Understanding, Preserving, and Safeguarding the Heritage of Indian Peoples and Native Hawaiians: Human Rights, Sacred Objects, and Cultural Patrimony," *Arizona State Law Journal* 24 (1992): 175–191.
25. As Alice Deck notes, "One of the prevailing images of black women in American culture that has persisted since the early days of slavery is that of the quintessential cook and housekeeper. . . . All of this renders the black Mammy, as we see her depicted in American popular culture, as a fetish—an idealized representation of an autonomous black woman." Alice A. Deck, "Now Then—Who Said Biscuits? The Black Woman Cook as Fetish in American Advertising, 1905–1953," in *Kitchen Culture in America: Popular Representations of Foods, Gender, and Race*, ed. Sherrie A. Inness (Philadelphia: University of Pennsylvania Press, 2001), 69–70.
26. Lynette Holloway, "Chronicle," *New York Times*, October 5, 1992 (reporting O'Connor's action); Nadine Brozan, "Chronicle," *New York Times*, October 12, 1992 (quoting Pesci's disapproval). For the federal district court's decision regarding the Brooklyn Museum, see *Brooklyn Institute of Arts and Sciences v. City of New York*, 64 F. Supp. 2d 184 (E.D.N.Y. 1999). Popular interest in the controversial nature of such creations is apparent in newspaper reports of the Brooklyn Museum controversy, including Gustav Niebuhr, "Anger over Work Evokes Anti-Catholic Shadow, and Mary's Power as Icon," *New York Times*, October 3, 1999; Michael Kimmelman, "A

Madonna's Many Meanings in the Art World," *New York Times,* October 5, 1999; David Barstow, "Giuliani Ordered to Restore Funds for Art Museum," *New York Times,* November 2, 1999). It is ultimately unclear whether the artist in this case, Chris Ofili, a Roman Catholic of Nigerian descent, intended the elephant dung as desecration, a symbol of fertility, or both. This particular juxtaposition of image and material does, however, recall actions from ninth-century Byzantium and sixteenth-century Europe, when iconoclasts removed images from churches and deliberately defiled them. For reflections on the controversy over Ofili's work, see Lawrence Rothfield, ed., *Unsettling "Sensation": Arts-Policy Lessons from the Brooklyn Museum of Art Controversy* (New Brunswick, N.J.: Rutgers University Press, 2001).

27. Andi Zeisler, cover painting, *Bitch: Feminist Response to Pop Culture,* no. 13 (2001). For a history of more traditional representations of Our Lady of Guadalupe and her cultural significance, see D. A. Brading, *Mexican Phoenix: Our Lady of Guadalupe: Image and Tradition across Five Centuries* (Cambridge: Cambridge University Press, 2001).

28. Donna Karan, foreword to *Colors of the Vanishing Tribes,* by Bonnie Young (New York: Abbeville Press, 1998). Karan is far from the only designer to engage in such systematic search for "inspiration"; see Guy Trebay, "Imitation Is the Mother of Invention," *New York Times,* July 7, 2002.

29. Young, *Colors of the Vanishing Tribes.* In the area of world music, a similar sentiment (as well as a preservationist impulse) is expressed in Mickey Hart with K. M. Kostyal, *Songcatchers: In Search of the World's Music* (Washington, D.C.: National Geographic, 2003).

30. The case holding that an Australian rug merchant had misappropriated sacred Aboriginal designs is *Milpurrurru v. Indofurn Pty. Ltd.* (1994) 54 F.C.R. 240 (Austl.).

31. *The Sopranos* (HBO televison program), season 1, episode 2, 1999.

32. Ibid.

33. Starbucks Corporation, "History of Coffee," http://www.starbucks.com/ourcoffees/coffee_edu2.asp?category%5Fname=History+of+Coffee, September 23, 2004. The Starbucks chain itself was inspired by a visit that the company chairman, Howard Schultz, made to Italy. "It's a Grande-Latte World: Starbucks CEO Serves Up Tales of Global Frappuccino: Green Tea, or Strawberries?" *Wall Street Journal,* December 15, 2003.

34. Starbucks Corporation, "Commitment to Origins," http://www.starbucks.com/aboutus/origins.asp, September 23, 2004.

35. Bill Higgins, "Def's Excellent Adventure Dies," *Los Angeles Times,* August 30, 1993.

CHAPTER 8   MISAPPROPRIATION AND THE DESTRUCTION
             OF VALUE(S)

1. Complaint for Damages and Injunctive Relief, *Pueblo of Santo Domingo v. The New Mexican, Inc.* (D.N.M. 1984) (No. CIV 84-0192-C).

2. The analogy to a genie released from the bottle is common in unfair-competition law since, once disclosed, a trade secret typically cannot be

returned to the exclusive control of its original owner but will be known to all its competitors. For an example of this usage, see *Phillip Morris Inc. v. Reilly,* 113 F. Supp. 2d 129, 142 (D. Mass. 2000).

3. Affidavit of Peggy L. Bird at 2, *Pueblo of Santo Domingo v. The New Mexican, Inc.*

4. Ellen Dissanayake, *Art and Intimacy: How the Arts Began* (Seattle: University of Washington Press, 2000), 130.

5. For a discussion of academic theories of the role of ritual in society, see Catherine Bell, *Ritual: Perspectives and Dimensions* (New York: Oxford University Press, 1997).

6. "Suit to Make Example of Paper: Pueblo," *New Mexican* [Santa Fe], February 14, 1984.

7. Affidavits of Reverend Tony Anaya, First Avenue Baptist Church of Albuquerque, New Mexico, at 3–5; Dr. Leonard J. Arrington, Church of Jesus Christ of Latter-Day Saints, at 3; Reverend James D. Brown, First Presbyterian Church, at 3; Reverend Dr. Wallace Ford, Christian Church (Disciples of Christ), at 3; and Right Reverend Richard M. Trelease Jr., Episcopal Bishop for the Diocese of the Rio Grande, at 3, *Pueblo of Santo Domingo v. The New Mexican, Inc.*

8. Roberta Rosenthal Kwall, "'Author-Stories': Narrative's Implications for Moral Rights and Copyright's Joint Authorship Doctrine," *Southern California Law Review* 75 (2001): 61–62.

9. Complaint at 9, *Pueblo of Santo Domingo v. The New Mexican, Inc.*

10. Affidavit of Raymond B. Garcia, *Pueblo of Santo Domingo v. The New Mexican, Inc.*

11. For discussion of Anglo interpretation and appropriation of Native American culture, see Philip J. Deloria, *Playing Indian* (New Haven, Conn.: Yale University Press, 1998); Donna J. Kessler, *The Making of Sacagawea: A Euro-American Legend* (Tuscaloosa: University of Alabama Press, 1996); Sherry L. Smith, *Reimagining Indians: Native Americans through Anglo Eyes, 1880–1940* (New York: Oxford University Press, 2000).

12. Complaint at 6, *Pueblo of Santo Domingo v. The New Mexican, Inc.*

13. *E. I. du Pont de Nemours & Company v. Christopher,* 431 F.2d 1012 (5th Cir. 1970), *cert. denied,* 400 U.S. 1024 (1971).

14. Ibid., 1013–1014.

15. Ibid., 1017.

16. Ibid., 1016–1017.

17. Affidavit of Tony Hillerman at 3, *Pueblo of Santo Domingo v. The New Mexican, Inc.*

18. Affidavit of Florence Hawley Ellis at 2, *Pueblo of Santo Domingo v. The New Mexican, Inc.*

19. *Chapman v. Luminis Pty. Ltd.* [No. 5] (2001) F.C.A. 1106 (offering a report of the events leading to the decision).

20. Ibid.

21. Ibid.

22. Ibid.

23. Ibid.

24. *Chapman v. Minister for Aboriginal and Torres Strait Islander Affairs* (1995) 133 A.L.R. 74.

25. Diane Bell, *Ngarrindjeri Wurruwarrin: A World That Is, Was, and Will Be* (North Melbourne, Victoria: Spinifex Press, 1998), 7–8.

26. *Chapman v. Luminis Pty. Ltd.* (offering a report of the events leading to the decision); Bell, *Ngarrindjeri Wurruwarrin*, 8.

27. Ken Gelder and Jane M. Jacobs, *Uncanny Australia: Sacredness and Identity in a Postcolonial Nation* (Carlton South, Victoria: Melbourne University Press, 1998), 128.

28. *Norvill v. Chapman* (1995) 133 A.L.R. 226; *Chapman v. Luminis Pty. Ltd.* (offering a report of the events leading to the decision).

29. "Controversial Bridge Finally Opens for All," *Courier Mail* [Queensland], March 5, 2001.

30. *Chapman v. Luminis Pty. Ltd.*

31. "$20m Bridge Claim Rejected by Court," *Herald Sun [Melbourne]*, August 22, 2001; "Shock Ruling Backs Secret Women's Business," *Sydney Morning Herald*, August 22, 2001.

32. Kate Uren, "$5.5m Claim on Chapmans," *The Advertiser [South Australia]*, October 17, 2001.

33. Penelope Debelle, "Bones Discovery at Bridge Unearths Proof of Land Claim," *Sydney Morning Herald*, December 10, 2002.

34. Colin James, "Chapmans End $25m Battle of the Bridge," *The Advertiser [South Australia]*, November 20, 2002.

35. Thea Williams, "Bone Find Triggers Apology on Bridge," *The Australian [Sydney]*, October 8, 2002.

36. Rachel Hancock, "Two Cultures Unite with a Simple Sorry," *The Advertiser [South Australia]*, October 9, 2002.

37. In the United States, the struggle for recognition by certain Native American tribes turns on historical connection, raising the question of whether the re-formation and public reassertion of cultural identity can constitute the basis of an externally recognized authenticity. For the controversial history of one example, see Kim Isaac Eisler, *Revenge of the Pequots: How a Small Native American Tribe Created the World's Most Profitable Casino* (Lincoln: University of Nebraska Press, 2002).

38. Gelder and Jacobs, *Uncanny Australia*, 120. For an insightful study of the social effects of the legacy of colonialism and its relationship to the performance of "authentic, traditional culture" in Australia, see Elizabeth A. Povinelli, *Cunning of Recognition: Indigenous Alteritites and the Making of Australian Multiculturalism* (Durham, N.C.: Duke University Press, 2002).

39. Perhaps the best-known discussion of the dangers of secrecy in the legal context is Owen M. Fiss, "Against Settlement," *Yale Law Journal* 93 (1984): 1073–1090.

40. Order of Dismissal with Prejudice, *Pueblo of Santo Domingo v. The New Mexican, Inc.*

CHAPTER 9   PERMISSIVE APPROPRIATION

1. Jehovah's Witnesses, "Statistics: 2003 Report of Jehovah's Witnesses Worldwide," *Watchtower: Official Website of Jehovah's Witnesses*, http://www.watchtower.org/statistics/worldwide_report.htm, September 23, 2004.

2. Ibid.

3. Eric S. Raymond, *The Cathedral and the Bazaar: Musings on Linux and Open Source by an Accidental Revolutionary* (Sebastopol, Calif.: O'Reilly and Associates, 1999), 2. See also John Katz, *Geeks: How Two Lost Boys Rode the Internet out of Idaho* (New York: Villard, 2000); Chris DiBona et al., eds., *Open Sources: Voices from the Open Source Revolution* (Sebastopol, Calif.: O'Reilly and Associates, 1999); Open Source Initiative, "Open Source," http://www.opensource.org.

4. Thomas Goetz, "Open Source Everywhere," *Wired* (November 2003): 164.

5. Ibid.

6. Karim R. Lakhani and Robert G. Wolf, "Why Hackers Do What They Do: Understanding Motivation Effort in Free/Open Source Software Projects," Working Paper 4425-03, MIT Sloan School of Management, September 2003.

7. Ibid., 2.

8. Richard M. Stallman, "The GNU Operating System and the Free Software Movement," in DiBona et al., eds., *Open Sources*, 69–70.

9. Free Software Foundation, "GNU Operating System—Free Software Foundation," http://www.gnu.org, September 23, 2004.

10. Open Source Initiative, "History of the OSI," http://www.opensource .org/docs/history.php, September 23, 2004.

11. David Diamond, "The Sharer: Questions for Linus Torvalds," *New York Times Magazine*, September 28, 2003. Torvalds' own history of Linux appears in Linus Torvalds and David Diamond, *Just for Fun: The Story of an Accidental Revolutionary* (New York: HarperBusiness, 2001).

12. Raymond, *The Cathedral and the Bazaar*, 87–135.

13. Stallman, "The GNU Operating System," 59–60.

14. Open Source Initiative, "The Approved Licenses," http://www .opensource.org/licenses/, September 23, 2004.

15. Open Source Initiative, "OSI Certification Mark and Program," http:// www.opensource.org/docs/certification_mark.php, September 23, 2004.

16. For the statute governing registration of certification marks, see Lanham Act § 4, 15 U.S.C. § 1504 (2000).

17. Robert Young and Wendy Goldman Rohm, *Under the Radar: How Red Hat Changed the Software Business—and Took Microsoft by Surprise* (Scottsdale, Ariz.: Coriolis Group, 1999), 10. Additional information on the development of Linux and other operating systems is available in Peter Wayner, *Free for All: How Linux and the Free Software Movement Undercut the High-Tech Titans* (New York: HarperBusiness, 2001); Neal Stephenson, *In the Beginning . . . Was the Command Line* (New York: Avon, 1999).

18. Raymond, *The Cathedral and the Bazaar*, 165.

19. Ben Stocking, "Vietnam's Solution to Software Piracy: 'Eliminate Microsoft,'" *San Jose Mercury News*, October 30, 2003.

20. William M. Bulkeley, "Caldera Accuses IBM in Lawsuit of Sharing Unix Trade Secrets," *Wall Street Journal*, March 7, 2003.

21. Sean P. Gallagher and Romana Kryzanowska, *The Pilates Method of Body Conditioning* (Philadelphia: BainBridgeBooks, 1999), 9.

22. Josef Hubertus Pilates, *Your Health: A Corrective System of Exercising That Revolutionizes the Entire Field of Physical Education* (1934; Incline Village,

Nev.: Presentation Dynamics, 1998); Josef H. Pilates and William John Miller, *Return to Life through Contrology* (1945; Incline Village, Nev.: Presentation Dynamics, 1998).

23. Pilates, *Your Health*, 2.
24. *Pilates, Inc. v. Current Concepts, Inc.*, 120 F. Supp. 2d 286, 299 (S.D.N.Y. 2000).
25. Ibid., 291.
26. Ibid., 291–294.
27. Ibid.; *Pilates, Inc. v. Georgetown Bodyworks Deep Muscle Massage Centers, Inc.*, 157 F. Supp. 2d 75 (D.D.C. 2001).
28. The Pilates Studio, "Welcome to Pilates, Inc. On-Line," http://pilatesstudio.com/, September 23, 2004.
29. *Pilates, Inc. v. Current Concepts, Inc.*, 120 F. Supp. 2d at 299.
30. Robert K. Elder, "The Land of the Rings," *Chicago Tribune*, December 2, 2001.

CHAPTER 10 REVERSE APPROPRIATION OF INTELLECTUAL PROPERTIES AND CELEBRITY PERSONAE

1. Leonard Nimoy, *I Am Not Spock* (Cutchogue, N.Y.: Bucaneer Books, 1975).
2. Leonard Nimoy, *I Am Spock* (New York: Hyperion, 1995), 8.
3. Ibid.
4. Ibid., 332.
5. Ibid., 328.
6. Ibid.
7. Ibid., 14.
8. Ibid., 87. Rosemary J. Coombe discusses *Star Trek* fanzine culture among women in *The Cultural Life of Intellectual Properties* (Durham, N.C.: Duke University Press, 1998), 117–123. For a general treatment of the legal rules affecting fan fiction, see Rebecca Tushnet, "Legal Fictions: Copyright, Fan Fiction, and a New Common Law," *Loyola of Los Angeles Entertainment Law Journal* 17 (1997): 651–686.
9. Nimoy, *I Am Spock*, 88. Fans' creativity extends beyond literary efforts, as described in Heather R. Joseph-Witham, *Star Trek Fans and Costume Art* (Jackson: University Press of Mississippi, 1996).
10. Ibid., iv.
11. For a natural-rights approach to the use of intellectual property that goes beyond fair use and free speech, see Wendy J. Gordon, "A Property Right in Self-Expression: Equality and Individualism in the Natural Law of Intellectual Property," *Yale Law Journal* 102 (1993): 1533–1609.
12. Among the works focusing on consumers of intellectual property is Joseph P. Liu, "Copyright Law's Theory of the Consumer," *Boston College Law Review* 44 (2003): 397–431.
13. Nimoy, *I Am Spock*, 67–69.
14. Michael Sokolove, "The Tiger Files," *New York Times*, July 14, 2002.
15. Jere Longman with Clifton Brown, "Debate on Women at Augusta Catches Woods Off Balance," *New York Times*, October 20, 2002.
16. For discussions of rights of publicity that focus on their cultural value, see

Michael Madow, "Private Ownership of Public Image: Popular Culture and Publicity Rights," *California Law Review* 81 (1993): 127–240; Jane M. Gaines, *Contested Culture: The Image, the Voice, and the Law* (Chapel Hill: University of North Carolina Press, 1991).

17. *Bruce Springsteen v. Jeff Burgar*, WIPO Case D2000-1532 (January 25, 2001), http://arbiter.wipo.int/domains/decisions/html/2000/d2000-1532.html, September 23, 2004.

18. The issue of fan websites is discussed in Jessica Elliott, "Copyright Fair Use and Private Ordering: Are Copyright Holders and the Copyright Law Fanatical for Fansites?" *DePaul LCA Journal of Art and Entertainment Law* 11 (2001) 329–359.

19. Coombe, *The Cultural Life of Intellectual Properties*, 164.

20. For an insightful treatment of the relationship between personal identity and trademarks in the modern world, as well as a cautionary tale regarding corporate control, see Keith Aoki, "How the World Dreams Itself to be American: Reflections on the Relationship Between the Expanding Scope of Trademark Protection and Free Speech Norms," *Loyola of Los Angeles Entertainment Law Journal* 17 (1997): 523–547.

21. Alice Randall, *The Wind Done Gone* (Boston: Houghton Mifflin, 2001).

22. *Suntrust Bank v. Houghton Mifflin Co.,* 136 F. Supp. 2d 1357 (N.D. Ga. 2001).

23. *Suntrust Bank v. Houghton Mifflin Co.,* 268 F.3d 1257 (11th Cir. 2001).

24. Among the learned analyses focusing on individual expression is Yochai Benkler, "Through the Looking Glass: Alice and the Constitutional Foundations of the Public Domain," *Law and Contemporary Problems* 66 (2003): 173–224.

25. Michiko Kakutani, "Within Its Genre, a Takeoff on Tara Gropes for a Place," *New York Times*, May 5, 2001.

26. Jean Baudrillard, *Simulacra and Simulation*, trans. Sheila Faria Glaser (Ann Arbor: University of Michigan Press, 1994), 5.

27. Roland Barthes, "The Death of the Author," in *Image, Music, Text*, trans. Stephen Heath (New York: Hill & Wang, 1977), 142–148.

CHAPTER 11   THE CIVIC ROLE OF
             CULTURAL PRODUCTS

1. Lawrence Lessig, *The Future of Ideas: The Fate of the Commons in a Connected World* (New York: Random House, 2001); Jessica Litman, *Digital Copyright* (Amherst, N.Y.: Prometheus, 2001); James Boyle, *Shamans, Software, & Spleens: Law and the Construction of the Information Society* (Cambridge, Mass.: Harvard University Press, 1996); Pamela Samuelson, "Copyright and Freedom of Expression in Historical Perspective," *Journal of Intellectual Property Law* 10 (2003): 319–344; Yochai Benkler, "Free as the Air to Common Use: First Amendment Constraints on Enclosure of the Public Domain," *New York University Law Review* 74 (1999): 354–446; Mark A. Lemley and Eugene Volokh, "Freedom of Speech and Injunctions in Intellectual Property Cases," *Duke Law Journal* 48 (1998): 147–242; David Lange, "Recognizing the Public Domain," *Law and Contemporary Problems*

44 (Autumn 1991): 147; Kembrew McLeod, *Owning Culture: Authorship, Ownership, and Intellectual Property Law* (New York: Peter Lang, 2001).

2. Lessig, *The Future of Ideas*, 7.

3. Martha Woodmansee, "On the Author Effect: Recovering Collectivity," in *The Construction of Authorship: Textual Appropriation in Law and Literature*, ed. Martha Woodmansee and Peter Jaszi (Durham, N.C.: Duke University Press, 1994), 16.

4. For a discussion of the economic costs and benefits of property regimes in the context of emerging forms of property, see Carol M. Rose, "The Several Futures of Property: Of Cyberspace and Folk Tales, Emission Trades and Ecosystems," *Minnesota Law Review* 83 (1998).

5. For a collection of critical views on cultural borrowing, see Bruce Ziff and Pratima V. Rao, eds., *Borrowed Power: Essays on Cultural Appropriation* (New Brunswick, N.J.: Rutgers University Press, 1997).

6. The philosophical quest for personal authenticity is expressed in terms of transcendent individualism, a subjective, self-referential rather than externally determined standard. See Jacob Golomb, *In Search of Authenticity: From Kierkegaard to Camus* (New York: Routledge, 1995). Walter Benjamin, in his famous essay, "The Work of Art in the Age of Mechanical Reproduction," in *Illuminations*, ed. Hannah Arendt, trans. Harry Zohn (New York: Schocken Books, 1968), 217–251, applied similar standards to the ideals of human creativity. In the context of cultural products, the search for authenticity is ideally an expression of the essential nature of the source community, analogous to a Romantic ideal, rather than a shallow external adherence to historical forms.

7. For various perspectives on colonialism and collecting, see Ruth B. Phillips and Christopher B. Steiner, eds., *Unpacking Culture: Art and Commodity in Colonial and Postcolonial Worlds* (Berkeley: University of California Press, 1999); Susan Pearce, ed., *Museums and the Appropriation of Culture* (London: Athlone Press, 1994).

8. Jürgen Habermas, *The Inclusion of the Other: Studies in Political Theory*, ed. Ciaran Cronin and Pablo De Grieff (Cambridge, Mass.: MIT Press, 1998), 203–236; Charles Taylor, "The Struggle for Recognition," in *Multiculturalism: Examining the Politics of Recognition*, ed. Amy Gutmann, rev. ed. (Princeton, N.J.: Princeton University Press, 1994), 25–73; Michael Walzer, *On Toleration* (New Haven, Conn.: Yale University Press, 1997).

9. Habermas, *The Inclusion of the Other*; John Rawls, *The Law of Peoples* (Cambridge, Mass.: Harvard University Press, 1999); Ronald Dworkin, *Law's Empire* (Cambridge, Mass.: Belknap Press, 1986).

10. Will Kymlicka, *Multicultural Citizenship: A Liberal Theory of Minority Rights* (New York: Oxford University Press, 1995), 173–192.

11. Among many works dealing with the tension between freedom of expression and intellectual property protection is Benkler, "Free as the Air."

12. Copyright Act, 17 U.S.C. § 107 (2004); Lanham Act, § 43, 15 U.S.C. § 1125 (2004). For a discussion of current fair-use jurisprudence in copyright, see David Nimmer, " 'Fairest of Them All' and Other Fairy Tales of Fair Use," *Law and Contemporary Problems* 66 (2003): 263–287.

13. Max Weber, *The Protestant Ethic and the Spirit of Capitalism*, trans. Talcott

Parsons (1904–1905; New York: Routledge, 1992); Pierre Bourdieu, *Distinction: A Social Critique of the Judgement of Taste*, trans. Richard Nice (Cambridge, Mass.: Harvard University Press, 1984).

14. Benedict Anderson, *Imagined Communities: Reflections on the Origin and Spread of Nationalism*, rev. ed. (1983; New York: Verso, 1991).

15. David A. Hollinger, *Postethnic America: Beyond Multiculturalism* (New York: Basic Books, 1995), 3.

16. Marilyn Halter, *Shopping for Identity: The Marketing of Ethnicity* (New York: Random House, 2000), 194. For additional discussion of the composition of the American nation, see Edward Countryman, *Americans: A Collision of Histories* (New York: Hill & Wang, 1996); Ronald Takaki, *A Different Mirror: A History of Multicultural America* (New York: Little, Brown, 1993).

17. Hollinger, *Postethnic America*, 14; Nathan Glazer, *We Are All Multiculturalists Now* (Cambridge, Mass.: Harvard University Press, 1997), 14.

18. See Glazer, *We Are All Multiculturalists Now*, 14–16; Paul Fussell, *Class: A Guide through the American Status System* (New York: Simon & Schuster, 1983), 15; bell hooks, *Where We Stand: Class Matters* (New York: Routledge, 2000), vi.

19. See Glazer, *We Are All Multiculturalists Now*, 147.

20. Arjun Appadurai, "Introduction: Commodities and the Politics of Value," in *The Social Life of Things: Commodities in Cultural Perspective*, ed. Arjun Appadurai (Cambridge: Cambridge University Press, 1986), 3–63; Mihaly Csikszentmihalyi and Eugene Rochberg-Halton, *The Meaning of Things: Domestic Symbols and the Self* (Cambridge: Cambridge University Press, 1981); Mary Douglas and Baron Isherwood, *The World of Goods: Toward an Anthropology of Consumption* (New York: Basic Books, 1979).

21. See Kenji Ekuan, *The Aesthetics of the Japanese Lunchbox*, ed. David B. Stewart (Cambridge, Mass.: MIT Press, 1998); Gavin Badeley, *Goth Chic* (London: Plexus, 2002); Paul Hodkinson, *Goth: Identity, Style and Subculture* (New York: Oxford University Press, 2002).

22. See Edward W. Said, *Orientalism* (New York: Random House, 1978).

23. This benefit may be described through the sociological approach of symbolic interactionism, in which a person is believed to act toward a thing on the basis of its meaning, which derives in turn from social contact with others. These actions and meanings are continually modified through an interpretive process. In the case of appropriation of a cultural product, it may be used by an outsider, with its meaning derived at least partially from contact with the source community, causing the outsider to reevaluate both the embodied product and the community that produced it. For descriptions of symbolic interactionism, see Herbert Blumer, *Symbolic Interactionism: Perspective and Method* (Berkeley: University of California Press, 1969); Joel M. Charon, *Symbolic Interactionism: An Introduction, an Interpretation, an Integration*, 7th ed. (Saddle River, N.J.: Prentice Hall, 2000); George Herbert Mead, *Mind, Self, & Society from the Standpoint of a Social Behaviorist*, vol. 1 of *Works of George Herbert Mead*, ed. Charles W. Morris (1934; Chicago: University of Chicago Press, 1967).

24. Walzer, *On Toleration*.

25. Rawls, *The Law of Peoples*, 16.

26. Donna R. Gabaccia, *We Are What We Eat: Ethnic Food and the Making of Americans* (Cambridge, Mass.: Harvard Univeristy Press, 1998), 122–136.

27. Joseph Durso, "Joe DiMaggio, Yankee Clipper, Dies at 84," *New York Times*, March 9, 1999 (quoting *Life*, 1939).

28. Gabaccia, *We Are What We Eat*, 144–148.

29. Durso, "Joe DiMaggio." For additional discussion of coffee as an Italian cultural product, see Chapter Seven.

30. Anthony DeCurtis, "Eminem Responds: The Rapper Addresses His Critics," *Rolling Stone* (August 3, 2000): 18.

31. Ruth La Ferla, "First Hip-Hop, Now Cholo Style," *New York Times*, November 30, 2003.

32. Warner Brothers Studios, "The Ellen DeGeneres Show: About the Show," *Ellen: The Ellen DeGeneres Show*, http://ellen.warnerbros.com/showinfo/about.html, March 1, 2004.

33. *Lawrence v. Texas*, 539 U.S. 558, 567 (2003).

34. Ibid., 604–605 (Scalia, J., dissenting). The current trend toward and defense of same-sex marriage may have deeper roots than Justice Scalia and others believe; see John Boswell, *Same-Sex Unions in Premodern Europe* (New York: Villard Books, 1994).

35. See Richard Martin and Harold Koda, *Orientalism: Visions of the East in Western Dress* (New York: Metropolitan Museum of Art, 1994); Valerie Steele and John S. Major, *China Chic: East Meets West* (New Haven, Conn.: Yale University Press, 1999).

36. Roberta Rosenthal Kwall, "'Author-Stories': Narrative's Implications for Moral Rights and Copyright's Joint Authorship Doctrine," *Southern California Law Review* 75 (2001): 64; David F. Noble, *The Religion of Technology: The Divinity of Man and the Spirit of Invention* (New York: Knopf, 1997) (offering a critical analysis of the effects of the "religion of technology" in the modern era).

37. See generally Michel Foucault, *Power/Knowledge: Selected Interviews and Other Writings*, ed. and trans. Colin Gordon (New York: Pantheon Books, 1980).

Chapter 12   An Emerging Legal Framework

1. T. J. Jackson Lears, *No Place of Grace: Antimodernism and the Transformation of American Culture, 1880–1920* (New York: Pantheon Books, 1981).

2. Ibid.; for critiques of cultural and artistic tendencies toward the "primitive," see Roger Sandal, *The Culture Cult: Designer Tribalism and Other Essays* (Boulder, Colo.: Westview Press, 2001); E. H. Gombrich, *The Preference for the Primitive* (London: Phaidon Press, 2002).

3. Alexis de Tocqueville, *Democracy in America*, trans. Henry Reeve (1835; New York: Bantam Books, 2000), 519–520, 620–636.

4. Michel Foucault, "What Is an Author?" in *Language, Counter-Memory, Practice*, trans. Donald F. Bouchard and Sherry Simon (1969; Ithaca, N.Y.: Cornell University Press, 1977), 113–138.

5. U.S. Const., art. 1, § 8, cl. 8.

6. United Nations Educational, Scientific, and Cultural Organization,

"Convention for the Safeguarding of the Intangible Cultural Heritage," October 17, 2003, http://portal.unesco.org/en/ev.php-URL_ID=17716& URL_DO=DO_TOPIC&URL_SECTION=201.html, September 30, 2004.

7. Leila Abboud, "The Didgeridoo Is Sacred to Aborigines, Who Hate the Fakes," *Wall Street Journal*, July 9, 2002.

8. Ibid.; Indian Arts and Crafts Act of 1990, Pub. L. 101-664, 104 *Stat.* 4462 (1990).

9. Thomas Aquinas, *Summa Theologica*, trans. Fathers of the English Dominican Province (1267–1273; New York: Benziger Brothers, 1947), Part II.I, question 95.

10. Oscar Wilde, *The Soul of Man under Socialism* (Portland, Maine: T. B. Mosher, 1905), 24.

11. See Cornel West, "Prophetic Pragmatism: Cultural Criticism and Political Engagement," in *The American Evasion of Philosophy* (Madison: University of Wisconsin Press, 1989), 211–235.

12. Lionel Trilling, *Sincerity and Authenticity* (Cambridge, Mass.: Harvard University Press, 1971), 131–132.

APPENDIX   DEFINING PROPERTY

1. See Thomas C. Grey, "The Disintegration of Property, *Nomos* 22 (1980): 69–85; for a criticism of this conceptualization of property, cf. Thomas W. Merrill and Henry E. Smith, "What Happened to Property in Law and Economics?" *Yale Law Journal* 111 (2001): 357–398.

2. *Black's Law Dictionary*, 6th ed. (1990), s.v. "*Sic utere tuo ut alienum non laedas.*"

3. Ibid., s.v. "Property."

4. William B. Stoebuck and Dale A. Whitman, *The Law of Property*, 3rd ed. (St. Paul, Minn.: West, 2000), § 5.1. Modern American law recognizes three of these forms of concurrent ownership in real property: tenancy in common, joint tenancy, and tenancy by the entirety. Neither common law tenancy in coparceny nor tenancy in partnership exists today, and tenancy by the entirety can be created only in a minority of states. An additional form of concurrent ownership, community property, derives from the European civil law rather than common law and is recognized by those Southern and Western states with a significant Spanish legal heritage.

5. Carol M. Rose, "The Several Futures of Property: Of Cyberspace and Folk Tales, Emission Trades and Ecosystems," *Minnesota Law Review* 83 (1998): 180–182.

6. Stoebuck and Whitman, *The Law of Property*, § 5.1–5.5.

7. Robert C. Ellickson, "Property in Land," *Yale Law Journal* 102 (1993): 1394–1395.

8. Ronald H. Coase, "The Problem of Social Cost," *Journal of Law and Economics* 3 (1960): 1–15.

9. Stoebuck and Whitman, *The Law of Property*, § 5.8–5.13.

Index

abolition, opposition to, 80
Aboriginal and Torres Strait Islander
  Protection Act (1984), 111
Aboriginal Australians, 7, 110–113,
  153
academia, and Native American cultural products, 107
accidental property, protection of, 35
ACLU, 83
activities, as cultural products, 43
Adorno, Theodor, 10
African Americans: attitudes toward,
  83, 142; and Confederate flag, 79,
  80; musical heritage of, 90–94, 142;
  prejudice experienced by, 92, 130; as
  source community, 5, 27, 39, 47, 93,
  94; stereotypes and, 133; traditions
  of, 27–28, 38–39, 40
African culture, 41, 94
agency, tests of, 21
agents of creation, and law, 19
Agreement on Trade-Related Aspects
  of Intellectual Property (TRIPS),
  19, 31, 46, 172n. 9
Alabama, and Confederate flag, 80, 81
America: collective performance of,
  157; defined, 163n. 9; nation of
  nations, 5; postethnic, 140–141
American Bar Association (ABA), 76
American Italian Defense Association
  (AIDA), 73

American Law Institute, 76
Americans, defined, 163n. 9
American Sign Language (ASL), 21,
  24. See also sign language
Amish: barn raising, 116; quilts, 26, 27,
  31. See also Pennsylvania Dutch
Ancient Order of Hibernians, 67
Andean musicians, 7
animals, as cultural products, 44
anthropologists, x; intervention of, 113
antimodernism, perceived, 96
antipornography laws, 83. See also
  pornography
appreciation. See cultural appreciation
apprenticeship, cultural, 97
Aquinas, Thomas, 155
architectural forms: as cultural property, 48–49, 96–97; as intellectual
  property, 48
Aristotle, 155
Arkansas-Mississippi Delta, blues festivals in, 90
Armstrong, Louis, 91
art forms: community-generated, 1;
  evolutionary origin of, 104; recognition of, 32
Arts and Crafts movement, 147
artworks, community-based, xii
Astaire, Fred, 71
Australia, Hindmarsh Island Bridge
  controversy in, 110–112

About the Author

Susan Scafidi is a member of the law and history faculties at Southern Methodist University. In addition, Professor Scafidi has taught at the University of Chicago Law School, Saint Louis University School of Law, and most recently the Yale Law School.